Forty years ago I dreamed of teaching Gurukula students with Śrīla Prabhupāda's *Śrīmad-Bhāgavatam* serving as the central text. Toward realizing that goal, I had compiled the *Bhāgavatam* into its essential stories, for I trusted Śrīla Prabhupāda 's words that such study would truly educate and prepare my students on every level for a satisfying and worthwhile life.

But Kṛṣṇa had a more wonderful plan. The opportunity to fulfill Śrīla Prabhupāda's desire – like a fragrant lotus in the form of this *Śrīmad-Bhāgavatam: A Comprehensive Guide for Young Readers* – has been carefully placed into the open hands of Mātājī Aruddhā Devī Dāsī and her team of parents and educators. May the fortunate children who take advantage of their love-laden offering gain a taste for this sweet, potent literature. May those children continue throughout their lives to taste and distribute to others that which they have relished in their childhood and youth. May the *Śrīmad-Bhāgavatam* safeguard their rapid journey to the lotus feet of Śrī Kṛṣṇa. And may Śrīla Prabhupāda bless those who have sought to fulfill his desire by compiling this offering and placing it into his lotus hands.

Gratefully,

– Bhurijana dasa

Śrīmad-Bhāgavatam: A Comprehensive Guide for Young Readers, to our reading and from all reports, is an unsurpassed resource for teachers of *Śrīmad-Bhāgavatam*, both in families and in schools. The variety of materials and amount of work that went into producing the book as a gift to Śrīla Prabhupāda are astonishing.

– Hanumatpreśaka Swami (Prof. H.H. Robinson)

As I travel around United States, I get to personally witness how much devotee families have benefitted from HG Aruddhā Devī Dāsī and her homeschooling methods, which are completely based on Śrīla Prabhupāda's books and his teachings. I am an ardent supporter of her and the models of education which she develops and promotes through her books and various home schooling seminars.

It's very pleasing to note that she and her team has come up with a second project, *Śrīmad-Bhāgavatam: A Comprehensive Guide for Young Readers*. The series' main objective is to provide children with a *Bhāgavatam*-centered education, with lots of activities created by parents and teachers that are geared toward different learning styles, while meeting devotional, cognitive and language objectives of a growing child in Kṛṣṇa consciousness. This innovative and systematic compilation of various activities in book form is a great resource for any homeschooling parents who want their children go deeper in the messages of *Śrīmad-Bhāgavatam*.

– Romapāda Swami

From my reading of Aruddhā Devī Dāsī's book on studying *Śrīmad-Bhāgavatam*, it is evident that she is fulfilling Śrīla Prabhupāda's desire that our children get the best Kṛṣṇa conscious education. As Śrīla Prabhupāda said in a lecture on SB 1.5.13 given in New Vrindaban in 1969: "When one can understand *Śrīmad-Bhāgavatam* in true perspective, then he's to be understood that he has finished his all educational advancement. *Avadhi*. *Avadhi* means 'this is the limit of education.' *Vidyā-bhāgavatāvadhi*."

This book gives the highest knowledge in an interesting way so that children may access the *Bhāgavatam* on many levels, including higher-level thinking and application to their lives, as well as artistic, dramatic and journalistic approaches. I recommend this book for all parents who want to give their children a higher taste for reading Śrīla Prabhupāda's *Śrīmad-Bhāgavatam*.

– Narāyaṇī Devī Dāsī

Śrīmad Bhāgavatam

– A Comprehensive Guide for Young Readers –

Canto 2

Śrīmad Bhāgavatam

– A Comprehensive Guide for Young Readers –

Canto 2

Compiled and edited by
ARUDDHĀ DEVĪ DĀSĪ

Krishna Homeschool

Library of Congress Cataloging-in-Publication Data

Śrīmad-Bhāgavatam: a study guide for children / compiled by Aruddha devi dasi.
Pages: 338
ISBN 978-1-7339272-2-2
1. Puranas. Bhagavatapurana--Textbooks. 2. Hinduism--Textbooks.
I. Aruddha, devi dasi.
BL1140.4.B436S745 2014
294.5'925--dc23
2014005526

Cover illustration: Lord Hayagrīva returning the stolen Vedas to Lord Brahmā.

For more information, contact:

Krishna Homeschool

Contact the author at: aruddha108@yahoo.com

RAIVATA DESIGN
Designing with the Soul

Design by Raivata Dāsa
design@raivata.pro
www.raivata.pro

Contents

This book is a tribute to the spiritual master of the entire world, His Divine Grace A. C. Bhaktivedanta Swami Prabhupāda, who gave us the invaluable gift of *Śrīmad-Bhāgavatam.* Śrīla Prabhupāda spent hours each night translating this vast literature from Sanskrit to English, and writing his erudite purports. He emphasized that anyone who studies *Śrīmad-Bhāgavatam* will be liberated from misery and directly connected to Kṛṣṇa. It was Śrīla Prabhupāda's great desire that our children be educated in *Śrīmad-Bhāgavatam*.

Acknowledgments

This book is a tribute to the spiritual master of the entire world, His Divine Grace A.C. Bhaktivedanta Swami Prabhupāda, who gave us the invaluable gift of *Śrīmad-Bhāgavatam*. Śrīla Prabhupāda spent many hours at night translating this vast literature from Sanskrit to English, and promised that anyone who studies his books will be liberated from the miseries of material life and directly connected to Kṛṣṇa.

My humble obeisances to my spiritual master, His Holiness Gopal Kṛṣṇa Gosvāmī, a dear and dedicated disciple of Śrīla Prabhupāda, who is untiring in his efforts to preach Kṛṣṇa consciousness throughout the world. He always encourages me to share my experiences regarding Kṛṣṇa conscious parenting with devotees.

My gratitude to my husband, Anantarūpa Prabhu, my sons, Rādhika Ramaṇa and Gopal Hari, and my daughters-in-law, Amṛta Keli and Devī Mūrti who were very supportive of my efforts to bring this book to completion. They were patient and tolerant as I spent many months writing, coordinating and reviewing the work of the contributors.

My profound thanks go to all the contributors of this book who spent many hours creating resources for the 10 chapters of the Second Canto. They hail from countries around the world. I would like to offer my heartfelt gratitude to:

Australia

Jāhnavī Jīvana Dāsī for creating word search and crossword puzzles.

Pṛśni Devī Dāsī for English activities.

Soumya Buyya for creating all the illustrations in the book. Her beautiful drawings brought the book to life.

India

Mohan from India for doing the front cover artwork.

Pūrṇeśvari Rādhā Devī Dāsī for critical thinking and analogy activities.

Raivata Prabhu for working on design and layout of the book under tight deadlines.

Oṁkāra Prabhu for troubleshooting problems in the areas of the publication of this book.

New Zealand

Bhāva Sandhi Devī Dāsī for creating beautiful art activities.

Mānada Devī Dāsī for suggesting art illustrations for the book.

United Kingdom

Śucirāṇī Devī Dāsī for chapter activities.

Sudevī Sundarī Devī Dāsī for character descriptions.

Vṛndākiśorī Devī Dāsī and Svarṇa Rādhikā Devī Dāsī for chapter summaries

United States

Amol Bakshi for reviewing, editing, and proofreading the content with care and attention. He could spot minute errors, worked under tight deadlines and was always ready to help at a moment's notice.

Anādi Devī Dāsī for spending many hours writing chapter summaries, higher thinking questions and English activities, with an eye for perfection.

Amṛta Sundarī Devī Dāsī for analogy, critical thinking, and theatrical activities.

Arcanā Bakshi for creating English activities

A special thanks to Nimai Devī Dāsī from England who graciously and kindly edited the book by taking time off from her busy schedule.

Finally, I am deeply grateful to my publisher, Advaita Candra Prabhu, who took up the project with enthusiasm and made into a reality. Many thanks to Raivata and Yamarāja Prabhus for design and layout, making the book polished and attractive to children.

This book is the product of many hands, and it would not exist without the dedication of all these devotees. I am deeply indebted to them for taking time from their busy schedules to create a valuable resource for children everywhere.

Introduction

While conducting seminars on homeschooling and Kṛṣṇa conscious parenting throughout the world during the last seven years, I met many parents who wanted to teach their children *Śrīmad-Bhāgavatam*, but needed more guidance on exactly how to do it. It was then that I started doing workshops, during which we would sit together with their children and I would demonstrate how to guide a discussion in a way that evoked the child's curiosity about the nature of the world, God, the self, and the purpose of life. Together, we would read the translations of a chapter of *Śrīmad-Bhāgavatam* and discuss the stories, main themes, and great personalities. We would talk about the relevance of *Śrīmad-Bhāgavatam* in our own lives – how it provides spiritual solutions to material problems. Both the children and parents were thoroughly absorbed in the discussion.

When I explained at seminars how I taught my boys *Śrīmad-Bhāgavatam* through interactive reading and discussion, hundreds of parents were inspired to follow. However, I also realized that many parents who wanted to study the *Bhāgavatam* with their children were uncertain about how to do it. They needed a formal curriculum for studying *Śrīmad-Bhāgavatam*. I pondered how this would be possible, for it would take a long time to do this. This is when I decided to start a collaborative project, involving devotee parents from around the world. I formed an online Yahoo group in which approximately 15 parents – from Australia, New Zealand, South Africa, the United Kingdom and the United States – worked together to create study resources for each chapter of Canto 1. Every parent would send their creations to others in the group, who would use the material with their own children and offer feedback. I would go through all the materials, offering direction on content, organization, and activity design.

All of the parents brought special skills to the book. Our team included English teachers, musicians, artists and computer professionals. All of them have children of their own, with a strong motivation to give them a *Bhāgavatam*-centered education. The result? An innovative collection of material on every chapter of Canto 1. The creators used the curriculum with their own children as they designed it, seeing the results firsthand.

Of course, having all this material in email attachments is beneficial only to a certain extent – it had to be edited and organized and compiled. So we began the painstaking task of putting together a book for use by parents anywhere, which was published by Torchlight as *Śrīmad Bhāgavatam: A Comprehensive Guide for Young Readers, Canto 1 Part 1*. We then went through a similar process for Canto 1 Part 2 and now the complete Canto 2. This book is primarily geared for children between the ages of 6 and 12, but much of the material can be adapted for children younger than 6, or older than 12.

WHY STUDY ŚRĪMAD-BHĀGAVATAM?

Śrīla Prabhupāda said that from the very beginning, children "should be taught Sanskrit and English, so in the future they can read our books. That will make them MA, Ph.D." Because the knowledge in these books is so advanced, children would be well-educated, happy, satisfied, and even go back home, back to Godhead (Jagadīśa, April 6, 1977).

As is evident in many of his lectures, Śrīla Prabhupāda desired that children in his *gurukula* schools read *Śrīmad-Bhāgavatam*. In 1974, speaking on *Śrīmad-Bhāgavatam* (1.16.22), Śrīla Prabhupāda confirmed that the *Bhāgavatam* would equip one to know any subject. Please read the following quotation carefully: "So in *Śrīmad-Bhāgavatam* you will find everything, whatever is necessity, for the advancement of human civilization, everything is there described. And knowledge also, all departments of knowledge, even astronomy, astrology, politics, sociology, atomic theory, everything is there. *Vidyā-bhāgavatāvadhi*. Therefore, if you study *Śrīmad-Bhāgavatam* very carefully, then you get all knowledge completely. Because *Bhāgavatam* begins from the point of creation: *janmādy asya yataḥ*." (July 12, 1974, Los Angeles)

By giving them this foundation, children become confident of their spiritual identity and also do well academically. Prabhupāda's books inspire critical reasoning and creative thinking, which are the main elements of academic education. *Śrīmad-Bhāgavatam* is pure and perfect and can equip one with the highest knowledge, both material and spiritual.

Parents and teachers who have taught their children *Śrīmad-Bhāgavatam* from their early lives have experienced how easily they pick up English language skills, especially reading, comprehension, and analytical reasoning. *Śrīmad-Bhāgavatam* is full of analogies, allegories, figurative speech, and metaphors. Even a seven-year-old child can understand difficult concepts because the subject matter of *Śrīmad-Bhāgavatam* encourages good thinking skills.

Śrīmad-Bhāgavatam is a wonderful book to teach from because it gives the philosophy of the *Bhagavad-gītā* through stories, and children love stories. These stories are not fictitious; rather, they are the lives of great saintly personalities and the pastimes of Kṛṣṇa and His *avatāras*. By reading these, one directly associates with the great personalities and their teachings. By such association, one begins to develop the character of these same personalities. As children grow older, they learn to appreciate the instructions given by Queen Kuntī, Prahlāda Mahārāja, Dhruva Mahārāja, Kapiladeva and so many others. In fact, many of the devotees described in the *Bhāgavatam*, such as Prahlāda and Dhruva, are children themselves, so our own children have perfect examples and heroes to follow.

The scriptures tell us that Śrī Caitanya Mahāprabhu heard the stories of Dhruva Mahārāja and Prahlāda Mahārāja hundreds of times while growing up, and still he was never bored. The example and instructions of these saints are so valuable that no other moral book can compare with them. Children develop good character, saintly qualities, and pure *bhakti* by reading *Śrīmad-Bhāgavatam*. Indeed, *Śrīmad-Bhāgavatam* is the very essence of Lord Caitanya's *saṅkīrtana* movement.

HOW TO USE THE BOOK

(A) *Discussion*

In my book, *Homeschooling Kṛṣṇa's Chidren*, I emphasize the necessity of giving our children a Kṛṣṇa conscious education, based on Śrīla Prabhupāda's books. I explain my own experience of homeschooling my two boys with a curriculum based on *Śrīmad-Bhāgavatam*. I discuss the methodology of studying *Śrīmad-Bhāgavatam* through interactive reading and discussion – the most important element of the process. We sit in a circle and take turns reading only translations, pausing frequently for discussion. (For children who cannot read, they can listen as their parents read and paraphrase the translations). This method has been followed for thousands of years by the great sages of Vedic India, as we see in the *Bhāgavatam* itself.

Discussion is an important part of reading. For children it breaks up the monotony of reading, and can add both interest and challenge. By using *Śrīmad-Bhāgavatam* as our basic text, children can learn all aspects of language arts, composition, comprehension and vocabulary, along with critical thinking and analytical reasoning. The children often drive the discussion by asking questions, raising doubts, or making observations about what they read. By having the opportunity to express themselves, children will understand the material better, gain self-confidence and learn communication skills. Parents can pick up on their children's cues and ask questions of their own to encourage deeper understanding. Parents can also present their own realizations, play devil's advocate, and relate the stories to practical life, thus making the *Bhāgavatam* study a dynamic learning experience. Reading and discussion lead to good speaking, debate, and logical thinking. The nature of *Śrīmad-Bhāgavatam* is such that it encourages a person to ask questions, think critically, and work creatively because the *Bhāgavatam* is full of analogies, metaphors and figurative speech. For example, the analogy of the car and the driver that Prabhupāda uses to describe the difference between the body and the soul is practical and simple, but it allows a child to appreciate a foundational principle of Kṛṣṇa consciousness. Some analogies may be difficult for a four or five-year-old, but as he or she grows older, these analogies will become the basis for strong reasoning skills.

Before reading a chapter (translations) with their children, parents should read the chapter on their own and go through the discussion (higher-thinking) questions provided in this book. The discussion questions are meant to give parents some ideas of how to inspire discussion as they read with their children. Please remember, however, that the discussion questions are only for the purpose of stimulating ideas, not to create a highly structured "oral exam" atmosphere while reading. The key is to keep the discussion dynamic and student-driven, using the sample questions when needed and adapting/rephrasing them as appropriate for the age and personality of the child. In the course of a vibrant discussion, you and your child will, no doubt, come up with questions and topics that were not mentioned in this book. Here are some suggestions for raising interesting and thought-provoking questions:

- Take turns reading the translations, going in a circle. This keeps the child's attention, because children eagerly await their turn. If your child cannot read, you should read and pause frequently to paraphrase the story at the child's level. Ask your child to tell the story in his or her own words.
- Whenever possible, ask "why" and "how" questions rather than "what" (factual) questions, thus encouraging your child to think and reason.
- Don't be afraid to ask open-ended questions that do not have a clear-cut answer. These questions often lead to beneficial discussions.
- Analogies are good opportunities to connect the *Śrīmad-Bhāgavatam* to your child's experience and imagination. The *Śrīmad-Bhāgavatam* is full of vivid analogies and metaphors, so utilize these for your discussions.
- Frequently encourage your child to make comments and raise questions. When your child raises a question for which you don't know the answer, don't be afraid to say so. Discuss his or her question thoroughly, read through purports to find guidance, and you will see many fresh realizations arise.
- Try to relate the story to daily life: "Why did Parīkṣit Mahārāja not retaliate against the boy's curse?" "What can we learn from Parīkṣit Mahārāja's behavior?" However, don't put your child on the spot by pointing fingers: "How should you have behaved with your friend Johnny the other day?" Such finger-pointing destroys the discussion and intimidates the child.
- Draw connections with other stories from the scriptures that your child may already know: "The boy Śṛṅgi showed anger in an inappropriate way, but when is it okay to show anger? Can you give an example?"
- Some sections will be more interesting to a child than others. If a particular section doesn't raise discussion, don't worry – just keep taking turns reading until you come to a translation that raises a question or comment.

- Have a "realizations session" at the end of a chapter, where your child can tell you what they learned from the chapter, and you can tell your child what you learned. Or bring the family together and ask your child to give a short class on the chapter.
- Even if you have not read *Śrīmad-Bhāgavatam* before, that is okay. As a parent (or teacher), you have more life experience and you know your child, which will allow you to lead a discussion and engage your child.
- When you read with an older child (the specific age will vary based on the maturity of the child), take the stance of a fellow reader and learner. This will help your child open up and feel comfortable. Of course, as the teacher, you will still need to correct a mistaken line of reasoning or raise points that are important, but try to do it as a partner rather than as a master.
- Consider these readings/discussions as your time with *Śrīmad-Bhāgavatam*. Stay focused and become absorbed in *Śrīmad-Bhāgavatam*. Just because your study partner is a 7-year old child does not mean that you will gain any less from studying *Śrīmad-Bhāgavatam*.

(B) *Written and Oral Exercises*
Once you have read a chapter of the *Bhāgavatam* translations together, you can use a variety of exercises provided in the book to teach language skills – including writing, comprehension, vocabulary and grammar – which will help in understanding the chapter.

This book provides comprehension questions, key themes, character descriptions, word searches, language puzzles, and many other activities. There is also a section in each chapter dedicated to arts, crafts, and songs. The goal is to provide parents with a practical way to make *Śrīmad-Bhāgavatam* a central part of their children's education. Regardless of whether parents are homeschooling or sending their children to school, we hope they will find renewed confidence in studying this great literature.

Here are the different kinds of departments and activities you will find:

- Story Summary
- Key Messages and Character Descriptions
- Discussion Questions and Higher-Thinking Questions
- Language and Vocabulary Activities
- Puzzles, Games and Quizzes
- Analogy Activities
- Arts, Crafts, Drama and other Hands-On Activities
- Songs
- Answers (includes answers to questions and quizzes and solutions to the puzzles)

The instructions for each activity are addressed directly to the child, but we assume that parents will still need to explain and supervise the activities, especially if the child is younger.

LEARNING OUTCOMES
The book's main objective is to provide children from the ages of 6–12 with spiritual knowledge from the *Śrīmad-Bhāgavatam* and

the opportunity for personal realization.

The primary process for doing this is by reading chapter translations with the children, discussing the stories and philosophical content of the chapter, and providing the children with the opportunity to make their own inquiries and share their personal experiences.

In addition, the activities in this book develop the key themes and philosophical points presented in each chapter, by accommodating a range of different learning styles, in a range of learning modes (visual, auditory and kinesthetic).

The activities also meet the following cognitive and language objectives:

- Thinking skills (based on Bloom's *Taxonomy of Educational Objectives*):
- Acquiring knowledge
- Developing comprehension skills
- Applying knowledge
- Using knowledge to be creative
- Analyzing information
- Self-evaluating

Language objectives:

- Written language (includes reading and writing)
- Visual language (includes communicating through the visual arts, such as drama and static imagery)
- Oral language (includes communication through speaking)

This book works to supplement any existing curriculum that parents or teachers may use to teach language skills. This is not a course designed to teach reading and writing in itself, but it can work together with a formal curriculum to further develop language skills, while providing children with a resource for studying *Śrīmad-Bhāgavatam*.

Śrīmad-Bhāgavatam lies at the heart of Śrī Caitanya Mahāprabhu's philosophy and movement. I pray that this book will help children and their parents develop a lifelong love for this great literature, following in the footsteps of Śrīla Prabhupāda and our previous *ācāryas*. *Śrīmad-Bhāgavatam* is very profound, and this book only skims the surface. I humbly request the readers to forgive any faults and shortcomings herein.

Aruddhā Devi Dasi
Nityānanda Trayodaśī, January 29, 2018
New Biharvan, Boise, Idaho
USA

1

The First Step In God Realization

Story Summary

Śukadeva Gosvāmī had come to meet King Parīkṣit, who was about to meet his death within seven days. The King approached Śukadeva Gosvāmī respectfully, and asked him a very important question: "What is the best thing in life that each person should do, and especially what is the best thing a dying person should do?"

Śukadeva Gosvāmī congratulated King Parīkṣit on asking such a perfect question.

"This is a very good question King Parīkṣit," began Śukadeva. "In fact, all kinds of people who hear the answer to your wonderful question will greatly benefit. All transcendental people think so. Shall I tell you why this is such a good question, my dear King?"

The King nodded, waiting patiently for the great Śukadeva to explain.

Śukadeva Gosvāmī hung his head low and shaking it, replied, "Not many people ask this question. They are too materialistic and waste their lives talking about useless subject matters. They are just busy with nonsense! They waste their nights sleeping or enjoying their senses, and waste their day striving to earn more and more money and simply maintaining their families – all the while forgetting to ask important questions like the one you have just asked. They don't care about these questions because they are too attached to everything material. Such materialistic people are attached to their bodies and their families, and although they see others dying around them, they foolishly think that they will live forever. Therefore, they don't try to find out what the goal of life is, or what a dying person should do. This is why I think your question is very good. Now let me tell you, my dear King, the best thing in life that each person should do, and the best thing a dying person should do."

King Parīkṣit leaned forward in great anticipation. The answer to this question was going to benefit not only him, but the whole world, including you and me.

"The best thing one can do in life," started Śukadeva, "is to hear about Kṛṣṇa, talk about Kṛṣṇa and remember Kṛṣṇa. This is the only way to free a person from miseries. Whatever spiritual process one decides to follow, the highest goal is to remember Kṛṣṇa at the time of one's death. Though there are different spiritual processes that free us from this world, pure devotees relish talking about Kṛṣṇa."

Śukadeva Gosvāmī continued: "Before this gloomy Age of Kali began, I studied the *Śrimad-Bhāgavatam* from my father Vyāsadeva. Though my father trained me well in spiritual perfection, I still liked to hear these stories about Kṛṣṇa because these stories aren't material; they are spiritual. This same *Śrimad-Bhāgavatam* I will recite to you because you are the most sincere devotee of Kṛṣṇa. Anyone who pays attention and respectfully hears *Śrimad-Bhāgavatam* will achieve strong faith in Lord Kṛṣṇa."

He reminded the King that the best thing any person can do in life is to always talk about Kṛṣṇa and chant His holy names as heard from authorities. Constant chanting of the holy names of the Lord will help not only materialistic people, but even those who do not have any material desires, as well as the spiritual personalities who are satisfied with themselves. All these different types of people will greatly benefit from chanting Kṛṣṇa's holy names and talking about Him.

"If someone has a long life but doesn't hear, chant, or remember Kṛṣṇa, then it is wasted. It is better to have just one moment of Kṛṣṇa consciousness than a long life with no Kṛṣṇa consciousness." Śukadeva Gosvāmī asked: "Do you remember the story of King Khaṭvāṅga?"

"Oh yes," beamed King Parīkṣit. "The demigods awarded King Khaṭvāṅga a boon. He asked how long he had to live, and they told him he only had a moment left! Hearing

this, he immediately stopped all his material activities and took shelter of Lord Kṛṣṇa."

"Yes!" replied Śukadeva Gosvāmī. He continued: "You only have seven days left to live, so during this time you must perform the rituals to prepare for your next life."

King Parīkṣit gravely took a deep breath and waited for Śukadeva Gosvāmī to guide him.

"Firstly, one must not be afraid of dying," he instructed. "A dying person must leave their home immediately and control their senses. They should go to a holy place and bathe before sitting alone in a clean area and meditating on the sacred three syllables: A-U-M. They must also control their breathing through *prāṇāyāma*. This is the mystic yoga process. As the mind becomes spiritualized, it can be pulled away from the senses and one can then begin to meditate on the limbs of Viṣṇu without forgetting Him as a person. In this way, the mind stops thinking about anything else but Lord Viṣṇu and it becomes best friends with the Lord.

He continued: "This mystic process is a lot of hard work, though, King Parīkṣit. Especially for someone who has a materialistic mind, this process does not really work well. Instead, one can also just engage one's mind in serving Kṛṣṇa and easily become fixed in Kṛṣṇa consciousness.

"You see, my dear King, material nature really agitates the mind because it makes the mind dirty, but if the mind thinks about Lord Kṛṣṇa, He makes the mind feel happier because He cleans all the dirt that material nature created. By remembering Kṛṣṇa and developing the habit of seeing Him everywhere, one can soon attain devotional service under His shelter."

King Parīkṣit asked further, "How do I think of Lord Kṛṣṇa so that all dirty things in my mind can be cleaned away?"

"Well," Śukadeva answered, "You can sit properly, breathe properly through *prāṇāyāma* yoga, and in a service mood, meditate on Lord Kṛṣṇa's universal form from His feet upwards. You see, my dear King, this material world is the personal body of Lord Kṛṣṇa, capturing all past, present and future. There is nothing higher than this in the material world. One must therefore concentrate one's mind on Him otherwise there is a danger of being misled and becoming degraded."

Key Messages

In this section we have summarized the Key Messages in this chapter. Use this list as a quick reference guide to the verses listed. Have you looked them all up in your *Śrīmad-Bhāgavatam?* Using your own words, you can memorize these Key Messages and the verses supporting them so you will always know where to find what you are looking for in *Śrīmad-Bhāgavatam*. You can go through this list and discuss each topic further. Can you think of examples in your personal life that relate to these Key Messages?

Theme	References	Key Messages
Gṛhastha vs. *gṛhamedhī*	2.1.2–4	Being a *gṛhastha* means to make spiritual advancement as a Kṛṣṇa conscious family. The *gṛhamedhīs* are very selfish and don't care about making spiritual advancement.
Three steps to freedom from miseries	2.1.5	The first step is to hear about the Lord. When one has carefully heard about Him, one will be able to glorify His name and activities. Then it will be possible to remember Him constantly.
Perfection of life – remember the Lord	2.1.6	Remembrance of the Lord is the goal and the perfection of life. It can be achieved following any of the three recommended paths.
How to receive spiritual knowledge	2.1.10	Understanding the *Bhāgavatam* depends on the mercy of the spiritual master, not on one's personal ability. If we have the right attitude, it will attract his mercy.
Whatever your desires, chant for ultimate success	2.1.11	If you are free from all material desires, have many desires, or are self-satisfied because you have transcendental knowledge, for ultimate success you should chant the holy name.
Use time wisely – human form of life	2.1.12–14	There is no value in having a long life if we don't use it to inquire about the Lord and take His shelter. Better to live for one moment in full Kṛṣṇa consciousness than a lifetime without Kṛṣṇa consciousness.
Preparing to leave this world	2.1.15–18 2.1.21	Understanding that we can't take anything with us when we leave this world, we must prepare to be detached and focus only on the Lord.
Seeing the Lord everywhere	2.1.23–38	The Lord can be perceived all around us in this material world by His universal form. Everything in creation can be used to remind us of the Lord.

Character Descriptions

Have you heard of any of these characters before? What do you know about them? Share what you know with a partner, then read the descriptions below.

Śukadeva Gosvāmī

- He was the son of the great sage *Vyāsadeva.*
- He spoke the *Śrīmad-Bhāgavatam* to *Mahārāja Parīkṣit.*
- His position in the spiritual world is as the parrot of *Śrīmatī Rādhārāṇī.*
- He was a lifelong *Brahmacārī.*
- He stayed in the womb of his mother for 12 years because he did no want to be influenced by *māyā.*
- He was only 16 years old when he recited the *Bhāgavatam.*

Mahārāja Parīkṣit

The famous king had been cursed to die in seven days. Mahārāja Parīkṣit decided to head to the River Ganges to meet the great saint Śukadeva Gosvāmī who could tell him all about Lord Kṛṣṇa's glories in the *Śrīmad-Bhāgavatam.*

- Son of Abhimanyu and Uttarā.
- Grandson of Arjuna and Subhadrā (Kṛṣṇa's sister).
- He was saved by Kṛṣṇa while in the womb of his mother.
- His name means "examiner" because he is always examining everyone to find the person that he first saw in the womb.
- He was crowned King after Mahārāja Yudhiṣṭhira.
- His son is Mahārāja Janamejaya.
- He attained salvation simply by hearing.

Understanding the Story

Now it's time for you to check how well you understood the story by answering these multiple-choice questions. (Answers at the end of the chapter.)

1. What question did King Parīkṣit ask Śukadeva Gosvāmī when they first met?
   a) How long do I have left to live?
   b) What is the best thing in life that each person should do?
   c) What is the best thing a dying person should do?
2. Why did Śukadeva Gosvāmī think Parīkṣit Mahārāja asked a very good question?
   a) Most people don't ask these questions as they are too attached to their lives, bodies, and families.
   b) Because he knew the answer.
   c) Although seeing others dying around them, people still foolishly think they will live forever and don't usually ask questions like this.
3. What is the highest goal of life?
   a) To remember our family as we leave our body.
   b) To remember our homes as we leave our body.
   c) To remember Kṛṣṇa as we leave our body.
4. There are different ways to remember Kṛṣṇa as we leave our body, but which type of people actually like to talk about Kṛṣṇa?
   a) Impersonalists
   b) Devotees
   c) *Jñānīs*
5. Who did Śukadeva Gosvāmī study the *Śrīmad-Bhāgavatam* from?
   a) His father Vyāsadeva
   b) King Parīkṣit
   c) Sūta Gosvāmī
6. Why did Śukadeva Gosvāmī decide to recite the *Śrīmad-Bhāgavatam* to King Parīkṣit?
   a) Because he wanted to tell somebody.
   b) Because King Parīkṣit was the most sincere devotee of Kṛṣṇa.
   c) Because King Parīkṣit was the most fallen.
7. If we pay attention and respectfully hear the *Śrīmad-Bhāgavatam*, what will happen to our faith?

   a) It will dwindle and break.
   b) It will become so strong that nothing can break it.
   c) It will turn into doubt.

8. According to Śukadeva Gosvāmī, what is better?
   a) A long life with no Kṛṣṇa consciousness.
   b) A moment with full Kṛṣṇa consciousness.
9. Which personality did Śukadeva Gosvāmī use to illustrate this? Can you remember what he did?
   a) King Parīkṣit
   b) King Yudhiṣṭhira
   c) King Khaṭvāṅga
10. How long did King Parīkṣit have left to live?
   a) Seven days
   b) A moment
   c) One day

Higher-Thinking Questions

Now it's time to deepen your understanding of Chapter 1 by delving into Śrīla Prabhupāda's purports for this chapter and reflecting upon the following questions.

1. What question did Mahārāja Parīkṣit ask Śukadeva Gosvāmī? Why was it glorified as the "best question"?
2. How might a Kṛṣṇa conscious person spend his day compared to a materialistic person?
3. How did Śukadeva Gosvāmī respond to the question "What should a dying person do"?
4. Can *Śrīmad-Bhāgavatam* be recited to anyone? What do you think should be the qualities of a person who would hear the *Śrīmad-Bhāgavatam* recited?
5. Who can benefit from chanting the holy names of the Lord? Can anyone, including a materialistic person, benefit? Can you think of any examples to support your answer?
6. "If someone has a long life but doesn't hear, chant, or remember Kṛṣṇa, then it is wasted." Do you agree? What reasons do you have for your answer?
7. Why do you think King Khaṭvāṅga accepted the invitation from the demigods to fight the demons in the higher planets?

8. What did King Khaṭvāṅga do when he came to know the news of his death? What do you think you would do if you came to know about your own death?
9. Do you think the mystic process given by Śukadeva Gosvāmī is easy to follow in the modern world? Give reasons to support your answers.
10. What was the alternative to the mystic process, as given by Śukadeva Gosvāmī? Can you think of five ways you might develop this type of consciousness?
11. How did Śukadeva Gosvāmī answer the question "How do I think of Lord Kṛṣṇa so all dirty things in my mind can be cleansed away?"
12. "Material nature really agitates the mind". Have you ever experienced this? When did you realize it? How did you overcome it? What care did you take not to repeat it again?
13. What is *prāṇāyāma*? Have you ever practiced it? How does it feel? What are its benefits?

ACTIVITIES

In this section you will find many exciting things to do! They will get you thinking, moving, drawing, acting, and most importantly, having loads of fun!

Action Activities . . . to get you moving!

UNIVERSAL FORM POINTING GAME

Description: Split up into two teams. Team 1 sends one member to the front. He or she takes a card and points to a part of their body, while the rest of the team members guess what that part is represented by in the universal form. They can give the choice of a, b, c, or d. If the team members can't guess correctly, Team 2 can have a go. (See **Resource 1**.)

Analogy Activities . . . to bring out the scholar in you!

"As long as one is engaged in hearing such transcendental activities of Kṛṣṇa, he remains aloof from the conditional life of material existence. The topics of Lord Kṛṣṇa are so auspicious that they purify the speaker, the hearer and the inquirer. They are compared to the Ganges waters, which flow from the toe of Lord Kṛṣṇa. Wherever the Ganges waters go, they purify the land and the person who bathes in them. Similarly, *kṛṣṇa-kathā*, or the topics of Kṛṣṇa are so pure that wherever they are spoken, the place, the hearer, the inquirer, the speaker, and all concerned become purified."

FACT FINDING MISSION

1. In which country can we find the River Ganges? You can check a map or an atlas.
2. Where does the River Ganges begin?

3. How long is the River Ganges?
4. Which cities does the River Ganges flow through?

Discussion Points:

- Why is the River Ganges considered sacred and special?
- What should one do when one is at the River Ganges?
- In what way is the River Ganges like the topics of Lord Kṛṣṇa?
- Does bathing in the Ganges purify one's heart? Does discussing the topics of Lord Kṛṣṇa purify one's heart?
- Why do you think the topics of Kṛṣṇa cleanse our hearts?

THE OCEAN OF MATERIAL EXISTENCE

"The great ocean of material nature is tossing with the waves of time, and the so-called living conditions are something like foaming bubbles, which appear before us as bodily self, wife, children, society, countrymen, etc."

– Śrīmad-Bhāgavatam 2.1.4 purport.

Description: Make a painting using water colors or another medium of your choice to illustrate the above analogy! Complete the following table to understand the analogy better.

What are each of the following compared to in the analogy?

Material nature	
Time	
Foaming bubbles	

In your own words, explain what you understand from the analogy.

Critical Thinking Activities
. . . to bring out the spiritual investigator in you!

UNIVERSAL RESEARCH

Description: Look at Chapter 11 of the *Bhagavad-gītā* to research the universal form. (Answers are on **Resource 2**.)

TEN OFFENSES ACTION PLAN

Description: List the ten offenses to the holy name. (HINT: Consult the purport to verse 11 in this chapter.) Do you think there are things that you currently do which offend the holy name? What can you do to correct such behaviors? Devise a plan of action and find a buddy who will also take up the same challenge. Help each other to check that you are keeping yourselves free from offenses. After a week, think about the following:

- Which offenses were the hardest to avoid?
- What helped the most in order to avoid committing the offenses?
- If someone commits an offense in front of you, what should you do? Go through each of the offenses and think about how you could react to:
  - Help the person committing the offense.
  - Not entangle yourself in the offense.
  - Avoid committing that offense in the future.

Introspective Activities
. . . to bring out the reflective devotee in you!

PERCEIVE THE LORD AROUND US

Description: Write a diary entry addressed to the Deities in your home or the temple, telling them how you were reminded of the Lord throughout the day through His universal form.

HEAR TODAY AND TOMORROW

Description: Think of all the things that devotees like to listen to. Why do they take pleasure in hearing these things, and what are the respective results? Think about the things that materialistic people like to listen to. Why do they like hearing these things, and what are the respective results? Create a mind-map to illustrate your thoughts.

CUTTING OFF MATERIAL ATTACHMENTS

Description: Draw a stick-man in the middle of the page. Around him, write down things that he may be attached to that could occupy his mind at the time of death. Then, one-by-one, cut away those things that he can't take with him.

TARGET FOR THE WEEK – HEAR, CHANT, AND GLORIFY

Description: Find a buddy with whom you can discuss how you have heard about, glorified, and remembered the Lord. Think of different ways that you can apply this. Be creative! Complete a spider diagram to help you brainstorm all sorts of ways to hear about, glorify, and remember the Lord and then put it into practice. Share your progress with your buddy.

DESIRES OF THREE KINDS

Description: Create a character profile of each of the types of people that could fit into these categories:

- Free from material desires
- All material desires
- Self-satisfied

Writing Activities . . . to bring out the writer in you

BREAKING NEWS!

Description: Write a news report on King Khaṭvāṅga. Remember to include the following:

- A good headline.
- A suitable picture with a caption.
- An interview "at the scene."
- The correct column layout of a newspaper article.

JUST A MOMENT

Description: Imagine that you are King Khaṭvāṅga, and write a narrative on how you feel when you are told that you only have a moment left to live.

SPELLING ERRORS

There is a spelling mistake in each sentence below. Write the correct spelling of each word in the space provided.

1. In fact, any type of person in this world who hears the answer to your wunderful question will really benefit. ____________________
2. They are too materiallistic and they waste their lives talking about useless subject matters. ____________________
3. King Parīkṣit leened forward in great anticipation. ____________________
4. This same *Śrīmad-Bhāgavatam* I will resite to you. ____________________
5. It is better to have just one moment of Kṛṣṇa conscoiussness, than a long life with no Kṛṣṇa conscoiussness. ____________________
6. King Parīkṣit graively took a deep breath. ____________________
7. They must also control there breathing through *prāṇāyāma.* ____________________

8. You see my dear King, material nature really aggitatees the mind because it makes the mind dirty. ____________________

9. By remembering Kṛṣṇa and developing the habit of ceeing Him everywhere, one can soon attain devotional service under His shelter. ____________________

10. One must therefore consentraet his mind on Him otherwise there is a danger of being misled. ____________________

GET THE WORDS RIGHT

Look at the following passages selected from the Story Summary. Some words in the sentences are scrambled. Try to unscramble the words.

1. Śukadeva Gosvāmī hnug ________his head low and shaking it replied, "Not many people ask this question.

2. They are too mlaetriasitic_________________and they waste their lives talking about useless subject matters. They are just busy with eennsson__________________!

3. At night, they waste their lives glspenei_________________or enjoying their senses, and during the day they waste their lives earning more and more yomen__________________ and simply maintaining their families – all the while forgetting to ask important questions like the one you have just asked.

4. They don't care about these questions because they're too detcatah________________to their lives. Such materialistic people are attached to their bodies and their families, and although they see others gindy ________________around them, they foolishly think that they will live forever. Therefore, they don't try to find out what the goal of life is or what a dying person should do.

5. Now let me tell you, my dear King, the best thing in life that each psoren ______________ should do, and the best thing a dying person should do."

SEQUENCING

Given below are the events that happened in the story of King Khaṭvāṅga. They are all mixed up. Read and refer to *Śrīmad-Bhāgavatam* 2.1.13 purport, and try to arrange them in the correct order.

1. Demigods, fully satisfied, gave him benedictions.
2. Instead of material enjoyment, he inquired about the duration of his life.
3. He came down to earth and took shelter of the Supreme Personality of Godhead.
4. Mahārāja Khaṭvāṅga was a saintly king.
5. The King left the heavenly kingdom, which is full of material enjoyment.
6. Demigods informed Mahārāja Khaṭvāṅga that his life would last only a moment longer.
7. Mahārāja Khaṭvāṅga was invited by the demigods to fight the demons.
8. He fought the battles to the full satisfaction of the demigods.
9. Even an attempt for a moment by the saintly king was successful because he was always alert to his prime duty.
10. This shows us how much he was preparing himself for his next life.
11. He was successful in his attempt and achieved liberation.

GṚHASTHA OR GṚHAMEDHĪ?

Description: According to the purport to Verse 2 of this chapter, there are two different ways to define householders - gṛhastha and gṛhamedhī. Gṛhasthas are those who understand that the purpose of family life is to engage everything and everyone in the family in the service of Kṛṣṇa and live transcendentally. Gṛhamedhīs are householders who are too engrossed in materialistic activities. They spend all their time and energy in the pursuit of sense gratification and have no time or interest in spiritual life.

Consider each activity in the following list and label it as gṛhastha or gṛhamedhī in the space provided.

____________ Lives only for the benefit of his family.
____________ Offers food to the Lord and eats only prasādam.
____________ Is not interested in finding the solution to the miseries of life such as birth, death, old age, and disease.
____________ Does not raise Kṛṣṇa Conscious children.
____________ Holds a job to support his family and compete with his neighbors.

____________ Controls the tongue, the belly and genitals through regulation.
____________ Acquires material things only to use them for the service of the Lord.
____________ Performs ārati and serves the Deities in the home.
____________ Eats tasty foods to satisfy the tongue and does not offer food to Kṛṣṇa.
____________ Seeks the shelter of the Supreme Person.
____________ Takes pleasure in inquiring and talking about material subjects that are unrelated to Kṛṣṇa or His devotees.
____________ Has children with the objective of raising them to be devotees of Kṛṣṇa.
____________ Acquires material things for own sense enjoyment.
____________ Inquires and hears about Lord Kṛṣṇa's pastimes.
____________ Busy with sense gratification without following Vedic rules and regulation.
____________ Seeks fame and prestige.

WHAT WORDS FIT THE CLUES?

Read the sentence clues in the table and identify the correct corresponding word or phrase from the box to make both sentences true.

Śrīla Vyāsadeva
Material nature
The mystic yoga process
Materialistic people
Hear about Kṛṣṇa, talk about Kṛṣṇa, and remember Kṛṣṇa

Clues	Answer (from the box above)
Was Śukadeva's father. An incarnation of the Lord	
Waste their time sleeping and enjoying their senses. Do not care about questions related to self-realization, thinking they will live forever.	
The best thing a dying person can do. The best thing a living person should do.	
Involves sitting alone in a clean area and meditating on AUM. Involves leaving the home, controlling the senses and breathing through prāṇāyāma.	
Really agitates the mind. Creates dirt (contamination) in the mind.	

PUNCTUATION PRACTICE

Description: The following passage is from the Story Summary, but someone forgot to punctuate it! Edit it, using punctuation marks: periods, commas, apostrophes, and quotation marks. Add capital letters. Check your answer against the edited version in the answer section.

this is a very good question king parīkṣit began śukadeva in fact all kinds of people who hear the answer to your wonderful question will greatly benefit all transcendental people think so shall i tell you why this is such a good question my dear king
the king nodded waiting patiently for the great śukadeva to explain
śukadeva Gosvāmī hung his head low and shaking it replied not many people ask this question they are too materialistic and waste their lives talking about useless subject matters they are just busy with nonsense they waste their nights sleeping or enjoying their senses and waste their day striving to earn more and more money and simply maintaining their families all the while forgetting to ask important questions like the one you have just asked they don't care about these questions because they are too attached to everything material such materialistic people are attached to their bodies and their families and although they see others dying around them they foolishly think that they will live forever therefore they don't try to find out what the goal of life is or what a dying person should do this is why i think your question is very good now let me tell you my dear king the best thing in life that each person should do and the best thing a dying person should do

KEYWORDS

- Explain the meanings of the following keywords from the summary.
- Use each word in a sentence (either in oral or written form).
- Find at least one synonym and one antonym.
- Identify the word's part of speech (noun, verb, adjective, pronoun, or adverb).

Key Word *(part of speech)*	**Definition**	**Synonym & Antonym**
agitate (________________)		**Syn.** **Ant.**
degraded (________________)		**Syn.** **Ant.**

materialistic (________________)		**Syn.** **Ant.**
benefit (verb) (________________)		**Syn.** **Ant.**
forever (________________)		**Syn.** **Ant.**
especially (________________)		**Syn.** **Ant.**

WHAT DO YOU THINK?

Tick the statements that you think are correct.

1. Mahārāja Parīkṣit asked Sūta Gosvāmī a very important question.
2. The best thing for a dying person to do is to seek shelter of his family and seek their protection.
3. Chanting the holy names of the Lord will help not only materialistic people, but also those who do not have material desires.
4. So many people ask the same question Mahārāja Parīkṣit asked.
5. The best thing any person can do in their life is to hear about, talk about and remember Kṛṣṇa.
6. After hearing that he had only one moment left to live, King Khaṭvāṅga immediately took shelter of Lord Kṛṣṇa.
7. Before Kali Yuga, Śukadeva Gosvāmī studied the Śrīmad-Bhāgavatam from his father, Lord Brahmā.

DEVOTIONAL BUCKET LIST

Description: A "bucket list" is a list of things a person wants to do before they die. Most people's bucket list includes items such as going for their dream vacation, sky diving or other adventure sports, meeting celebrities, etc. In contrast, when Mahārāja Parīkṣit was told he had only seven days to live, the only thing on his bucket list was to inquire from the great sages about the meaning and purpose of life.

We want to be as focused as Mahārāja Parīkṣit but for some of us, it takes time to reach that stage of bhakti. Therefore, we first learn to dovetail all our desires with the pleasure of the Lord. In this activity, we will practice aligning our greatest material desires with the transcendental service and remembrance of Lord Krsna.

1. Think of 4-6 items for your bucket list and add them in the left column of the table below - for example, attending a music concert, writing a book, learning to play a musical instrument, going on vacation to some faraway place, etc. To the right of each item, describe how you can dovetail these activities and make them Kṛṣṇa conscious. For example, if you are going on a tour of Europe, perhaps you can visit one or more temples and take darshan of the Deities, or join local devotees for public hari-nāma! The table has a few examples to help get you started.
2. Now choose one of the items on your bucket list and write a short reflective story about it to an audience of your choice, using the questions below as a guide. If you have already done this activity, some of the questions will be easier to answer. If you have not yet accomplished that goal, then envision how it would feel to have completed the activity and then write the story!
    - Who were you with?
    - What did you do?
    - How did you connect your activity to Kṛṣṇa?
    - How did this benefit your spiritual life?
    - What lessons did you derive from doing this?
    - Would you do it again?

Give an oral presentation to your friends and family.

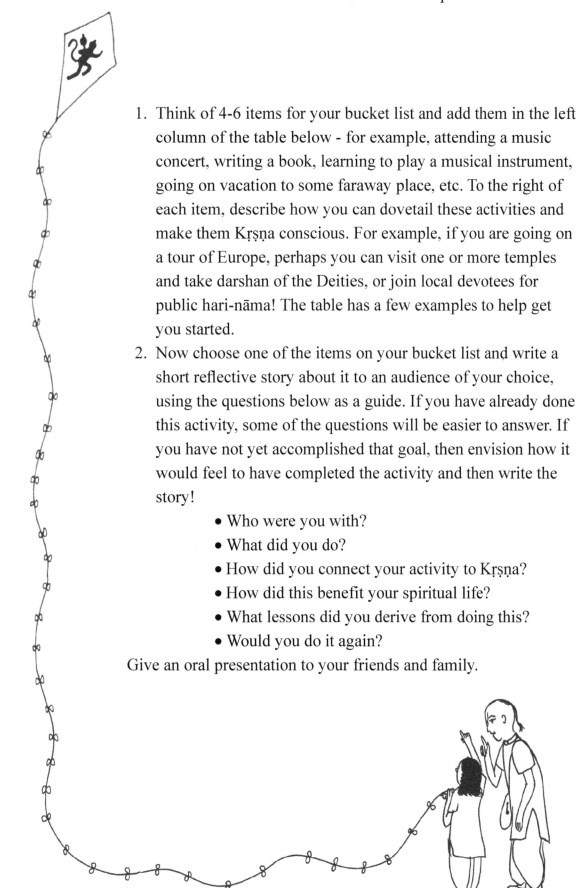

Bucket List Item	How to make the activity Kṛṣṇa conscious?
Example: Learn How to Dance	Find some devotees who are interested in also learning how to dance. Dance to nice devotional music.
Example: Learn How to Fly a Kite	Try to find a devotee who can teach you how to fly a kite. Paste a picture of Kṛṣṇa, or Hanumān, on the kite!

A LETTER TO THE SPIRITUAL MASTER

Description: By narrating how Mahārāja Khaṭvāṅga took complete shelter of the Lord when he had just one moment left to live, Śukadeva Gosvāmī encouraged Mahārāja Parīkṣit to do the same for the seven remaining days of his life.

Imagine you are Mahārāja Parīkṣit. Write a letter of gratitude to Śukadeva Gosvāmī, thanking him for the encouragement. Remember to include the following details:

- How you are grateful to have met a bonafide spiritual master at such a crucial time.
- How the words of encouragement you received have helped you.
- How Mahārāja Khaṭvāṅga's example has inspired you.
- How you plan to follow in his footsteps.

Resource 1: UNIVERSAL FORM POINTING GAME

Point to your: **Nails**

Read out the question:
"Is it:
a) Birds
b) Rivers
c) Yama, the God of death
d) Horse, mule, camel, elephant?"

Answer:
d) Horse, mule, camel, elephant

Point to your: **Hairs on your head**

Read out the question:
"Is it:
a) Clouds which carry water
b) Rivers
c) Trees
d) Religion?"

Answer:
a) Clouds which carry water

Point to your: **Chin**

Read out the question:
"Is it:
a) Hankering
b) Rudradeva
c) Direction of water
d) Satyaloka?"

Answer:
a) Hankering

Point to your: **Nostrils**

Read out the question:
"Is it:
a) Aśvinī-Kumāras
b) Vedic hymns
c) Religion
d) Ocean?"

Answer:
a) Aśvinī-Kumāras

Resource 1: UNIVERSAL FORM POINTING GAME (*continued*)

Point to your: **Ears**

Read out the question:
"Is it:
a) Modesty
b) Material fragrance
c) Ten directions
d) Moon?"

Answer:
c) Ten directions

Point to your: **Jaws of teeth**

Read out the question:
"Is it:
a) Air
b) Rudradeva
c) Yama, the God of death
d) *Brāhmaṇas*?"

Answer:
c) Yama, the God of death

Point to your: **Movements**

Read out the question:
"Is it:
a) Day and night
b) Blazing fire
c) Outer space
d) Passing of the ages?"

Answer:
d) Passing of the ages

Point to your: **Hairs on your body**

Read out the question:
"Is it:
a) Trees
b) Rivers
c) Modesty
d) Birds?"

Answer:
a) Trees

Point to your: **Sense of smell**

Read out the question:
"Is it:
a) Day and night
b) Blazing fire
c) Outer space
d) Passing of the ages?"

Answer:
d) Passing of the ages

Point to your: **Tongue**

Read out the question:
"Is it:
a) Birds
b) Juice or essence of everything
c) Vedic hymns
d) Day and night?"

Answer:
b) Juice or essence of everything

Resource 1: UNIVERSAL FORM POINTING GAME (*continued*)

Point to your: **Belt zone**

Read out the question:
"Is it:
a) Horse, mule, camel, elephant
b) Humanity
c) Wild animals and all quadrupeds
d) Rivers?"

Answer:
c) Wild animals and all quadrupeds

Point to your: **Navel depression**

Read out the question:
"Is it:
a) Outer space
b) Rivers
c) Religion
d) Moon?"

Answer:
a) Outer space

Point to your: **Breath**

Read out the question:
"Is it:
a) Vedic hymns
b) Rivers
c) Air
d) Moon?"

Answer:
c) Air

Point to your: **Back**

Read out the question:
"Is it:
a) Śūdras
b) Satyaloka
c) Yama, the God of death
d) Irreligion?"

Answer:
d) Irreligion

Point to your: **Smile**

Read out the question:
"Is it:
a) Clouds which carry water
b) Illusory material energy
c) Art of affection
d) Hankering?"

Answer:
b) Illusory material energy

Point to your: **Eyelids**

Read out the question:
"Is it:
a) Day and night
b) Rivers
c) Ocean
d) Manu?"

Answer:
a) Day and night

Resource 2: DESCRIPTION OF THE UNIVERSAL FORM

BG 11.10–11
- Unlimited mouths
- Unlimited eyes
- Unlimited wonderful visions
- Decorated with celestial ornaments
- Many divine upraised weapons
- Celestial garlands
- Celestial garments
- Divine scents
- Wondrous
- Brilliant
- Unlimited
- All-expanding

BG 11.12
- Effulgence similar to hundreds of thousands of Suns

BG 11.13
- Unlimited expansions of the universe
- Thousands of planets made of earth, gold, jewels

BG 11.15
- All demigods
- Various living entities
- Brahmā sitting on the lotus
- Lord Śiva and all sages
- Divine serpents

BG 11.16
- Unlimited arms
- Unlimited bellies
- Unlimited mouths
- Unlimited eyes
- No end, middle, or beginning

Resource 2: DESCRIPTION OF THE UNIVERSAL FORM (*continued*)

BG 11.17

- Glaring effulgence in all directions
- Effulgence like blazing fire
- Effulgence like the immeasurable radiance of the sun
- Glowing form everywhere
- Adorned with crowns, clubs, and discs

BG 11.19

- Without origin, middle, or end
- Unlimited glory
- Numberless arms
- Sun and moon are eyes
- Blazing fire coming from mouth
- Burning the entire universe with radiance

BG 11.20

- One, but spread throughout the sky, planets, and all space between
- Wondrous and terrible form

ANSWERS

Understanding the Story (pages 7-8)

1) b, c, 2) a, c, 3) c, 4) b, 5) a, 6) b, 7) b, 8)b, 9) c, 10) a

The ocean of material existence (page 11)

Material nature : ocean

Time : waves

Foaming bubbles : living conditions

From the analogy, we understand the nature of material existence. It is built on an illusory platform like the waves and it is temporary like the bubbles. We should not get too carried away by it because just like bubbles are formed and soon dissipate, all material existence is bound to come to an end.

Spelling Errors (pages 14–15)

1. wonderful
2. materialistic
3. leaned
4. recite
5. consciousness
6. gravely
7. their
8. agitates
9. seeing
10. concentrate

Get the Words Right (page 15)

1. hung
2. materialistic, nonsense
3. sleeping, money
4. attached, dying
5. person

Sequencing (pages 15-16)

1. Mahārāja Khaṭvāṅga was a saintly king.
2. Mahārāja Khaṭvāṅga was invited by the demigods to fight the demons
3. He fought the battles to the full satisfaction of the demigods.
4. Demigods fully satisfied gave him benedictions.
5. Instead of material enjoyment, he inquired about the duration of his life.
6. Demigods informed Mahārāja Khaṭvāṅga that his life would last only a moment longer.
7. The King left the heavenly kingdom which is full of material enjoyment.
8. He came down to earth and took shelter of Supreme Personality of Godhead.

9. He was successful in his attempt and achieved liberation.
10. Even an attempt for a moment by the saintly king was successful because he was always alert to his prime duty.
11. This shows us how much he was preparing himself for his next life.

Gṛhastha or Gṛhamedhī? (pages 16-17)

Gṛhamedhī — Lives only for the benefit of his family.
Gṛhastha — Offers food to the Lord and eats only prasādam.
Gṛhamedhī — Is not interested in finding the solution to the miseries of life such as birth, death, old age, and disease.
Gṛhamedhī — Does not raise Kṛṣṇa Conscious children.
Gṛhamedhī — Holds a job to support his family and compete with his neighbors.
Gṛhastha — Controls the tongue, the belly and genitals through regulation.
Gṛhastha — Acquires material things only to use them for the service of the Lord.
Gṛhastha — Performs ārati and serves the Deities in the home.
Gṛhamedhī — Eats tasty foods to satisfy the tongue and does not offer food to Kṛṣṇa.
Gṛhastha — Seeks the shelter of the Supreme Person.
Gṛhamedhī — Takes pleasure in inquiring and talking about material subjects that are unrelated to Kṛṣṇa or His devotees.
Gṛhastha — Has children with the objective of raising them to be devotees of Kṛṣṇa.
Gṛhamedhī — Acquires material things for own sense enjoyment.
Gṛhastha — Inquires and hears about Lord Kṛṣṇa's pastimes.
Gṛhamedhī — Busy with sense gratification without following Vedic rules and regulation.
Gṛhamedhī — Seeks fame and prestige.

What Words Fit The Clues? (pages 18)

Śrīla Vyāsadeva
Materialistic people
Hear about Kṛṣṇa, talk about Kṛṣṇa, and remember Kṛṣṇa
The mystic yoga process
Material nature

Punctuation Practice (page 19)

"This is a very good question King Parīkṣit," began Śukadeva. "In fact, all kinds of people who hear the answer to your wonderful question will greatly benefit. All transcendental people think so. Shall I tell you why this is such a good question, my dear King?"

The King nodded, waiting patiently for the great Śukadeva to explain.

Śukadeva Gosvāmī hung his head low and shaking it, replied, "Not many people ask this question. They are too materialistic and waste their lives talking about useless subject matters. They are just busy with nonsense! They waste their nights sleeping or enjoying their senses, and waste their day striving to earn more and more money and simply maintaining their families — all the while forgetting to ask important questions like the one you have just asked. They don't care about these questions because they are too attached to everything material. Such materialistic people are attached to their bodies and their families, and although they see others dying around them, they foolishly think that they will live forever. Therefore, they don't try to find out what the goal of life is, or what a dying person should do. This is why I think your question is very good. Now let me tell you, my dear King, the best thing in life that each person should do, and the best thing a dying person should do."

Keywords (pages 19-20)

Key Word *(part of speech)*	**Definition**	**Synonym & Antonym**
agitate (verb)	a. stir or disturb something b. make someone troubled or nervous	**Syn.** Disturb, shake, trouble **Ant.** Soothe, tranquilize, comfort
degraded (adjective)	a. treated or regarded with contempt or disrespect. b. Broken down chemically.	**Syn.** Degenerated, cheapened **Ant.** Improved, pure, moral
materialistic (adjective)	a. excessively concerned with material possessions; money-oriented. b. Person who follows a doctrine that the only or the highest values in life lie in material well-being of an individual.	**Syn.** Greedy, consumerist **Ant.** Spiritual, thrifty
benefit (verb)	a. help or give advantage to someone or something.	**Syn.** Gain, profit, aid **Ant.** Hurt, injure, obstruct
forever (adverb)	a. for all future times b. for a very long time	**Syn.** Always, eternally **Ant.** Never, temporarily

especially (adverb)	a. used to single out one person or thing over all others. b. To a great extent; very much.	**Syn.** Exclusively, specifically **Ant.** broadly, ordinarily

What Do You Think? (page 20)

1. False
2. False
3. True
4. False
5. True
6. True
7. False

2

The Lord in the Heart

STORY SUMMARY

King Parīkṣit sat on the bank of the sacred River Ganges, listening very attentively to the wise words of Śukadeva Gosvāmī. The King, who would die in seven days, had just heard from his spiritual master that by meditating on Lord Kṛṣṇa's universal form, all impure things in the mind would be cleared away. But King Parīkṣit was confused. "How are they cleared away?" he wondered.

"Let me give you an example, my dear King," began the great sage. "When the material world was destroyed, it was Lord Brahmā's job to create it again. But the problem was that Lord Brahmā had completely forgotten how to do this! So he turned to Lord Kṛṣṇa and sat meditating on His universal form.

Lord Kṛṣṇa was indeed pleased with this. He cleared away the forgetfulness in Lord Brahmā's mind, and awarded him the ability to remember how to recreate the world."

It is amazing that forgetfulness of our eternal relationship with the Lord is cleared away just by meditating on Lord Kṛṣṇa's universal form. Even more amazing however, is that this is only the first step in understanding who Lord Kṛṣṇa really is. Śukadeva Gosvāmī prepared to explain to his disciple the next step in understanding Lord Kṛṣṇa – seeing the Lord in the heart.

"Did you know that some parts of the *Vedas* talk about all the pleasures you can get in the heavenly planets?" began Śukadeva. "Many people are attracted to this, so they really want to go there after they die. But don't let this fool you, my dear King. These are false pleasures because they are temporary. There is actually no eternal happiness there, so please don't desire to go to heaven when you die."

"Hmm," thought King Parīkṣit to himself, ". . . my spiritual master is hinting that I must meditate on Lord Kṛṣṇa's lotus feet instead."

Śukadeva Gosvāmī continued: "This is why people who know the truth should be satisfied with the bare necessities of life, and always remember that Lord Kṛṣṇa protects us and gives us what we need.

"Now you see my dear King, only people who are enlightened can serve the Lord in the heart. These people begin by meditating on Lord Kṛṣṇa's lotus feet and go upwards to His calves, then His thighs, then higher and higher until they reach the smiling face of the Lord. As they do this, their intelligence becomes more and more purified.

"But, if someone has too many material desires and just can't lovingly serve the Lord as a person, they must continue to do their duty in this material world and meditate on the Lord as His universal form until they are purified enough to see Him in the heart."

Śukadeva Gosvāmī had explained the best thing in life a materialistic person and an enlightened person should do. He now prepared to explain the best thing a dying person should do.

"A yogī does not need to worry about the right time to die. He should just sit down comfortably, breathe properly, control his senses, and then engage his spirit soul in serving the Lord in his heart. This is a very happy stage. It's called *labdhopaśānti*. At this stage, nothing in the material world can disturb him – not even the body dying! He does not get disturbed by anything because he is always serving Lord Kṛṣṇa's lotus feet in his heart and avoiding things that are not related to Kṛṣṇa.

"At the time of death, the yogī blocks the lowest hole in his body with his heel and then moves the life air up through his body until it leaves through a higher hole in the head. A yogī with no material desires goes straight back to Kṛṣṇa, but if a yogī still has some material desires, he goes to a higher material planet to fulfil his last remaining material desires.

"Such mystics travel over the Milky Way and stop at the planet of fire to clear

out the last of their material contaminations before arriving at Lord Brahmā's planet called Brahmaloka. They then travel to Lord Viṣṇu's planet at the pole star before going to Maharloka where they live for a very long time until the time of the final devastation of the universe. At this time, fire from Lord Ananta Śeṣa's mouth at the bottom of the universe burns up all the planets. When the yogī sees this, he travels on an airplane to Satyaloka to live there for a very long time.

"Satyaloka is a nice place. There no one feels unhappy, no one gets old and dies, or feels any pain. The purified devotees only feel sad for the suffering souls in lower planets who do not know about the power of serving Kṛṣṇa. Eventually, in Satyaloka, the devotees' bodies change from earthly to watery, fiery, glowing and airy, until they reach the ethereal stage. At this point, they can start moving further and further out of the material creation. They finally leave behind their false ego and become pure souls. Only pure souls that are this perfect can be with Kṛṣṇa in the spiritual world in a happy state. Once they get there, they will never return to the material world.

"You know Parīkṣit, this is all described in the Vedas," Śukadeva Gosvāmī continued. "Lord Kṛṣṇa had explained this to Lord Brahmā and then Lord Brahmā studied the *Vedas* three times. Do you know what he concluded?"

King Parīkṣit waited in anticipation for the answer.

"That loving Lord Kṛṣṇa is the highest goal!" answered Śukadeva enthusiastically. "This is why, my dear King, it is very important that every living being hears, glorifies and remembers Lord Kṛṣṇa always. Those who hear the messages of Lord Kṛṣṇa from His devotees will have their material desires cleared away completely, and they will go straight back to Lord Kṛṣṇa in the spiritual world."

The point made by Śukadeva Gosvāmī is a very important one. There is no need to try and meditate on the universal form, or even the Supersoul in the heart. These are very complicated processes. As long as we always hear, chant and remember Lord Kṛṣṇa, our material desires will be completely cleared away and we can go back to the spiritual world simply by this process.

Key Messages

- Look them up in your *Śrīmad-Bhāgavatam.*
- Put them in your own words to help you memorize them.
- Discuss each one further.
- Apply them in your life.

Theme	References	Key Messages
The bare necessities of life will come to you	2.2.3–5	Sometimes people work very hard for temporary things that will not ultimately benefit them. They should not waste their time in this way, but lead a simple life so that they have time to pursue spiritual goals.
The Lord in the heart	2.2.6 2.2.8–13	Kṛṣṇa resides in all of our hearts as the Supersoul. If we turn to Him, we can end all types of material suffering. Everything else in this world is temporary, even the body that we are in, but the soul and our dear Lord as the Supersoul are eternal.
Easy journey to other planets?	2.15–21 2.24–30	Previously, expert yoga practice involved control of the mind and senses and precise regulation of the life air to transfer oneself to the spiritual world. In this Age of Kali, a much easier, practical and effective process has been recommended. If we engage our mind and senses in the service of the Lord and chant His holy name, we can make a swift journey back to the Lord.
Don't get distracted	2.22	Even on the journey back home to Godhead, we may be led astray by lingering desires to enjoy. Therefore, we should engage ourselves fully in devotional service to mold our desires so that they don't cause a distraction, but actually help us to achieve the Lord.
Compassion	2.27	Devotees are naturally compassionate. They don't desire just their own salvation but want others to take to the process of devotional service so that they too get the utmost benefit.
Back to the basics	2.31 2.36–37	As long as we are in the material world, we are contaminated. To wash away this contamination, we need to hear about, glorify and remember the Lord. This simple process will cleanse our hearts and make us eligible to go back to the Lord.

Understanding the Story

Now it's time for you to check how well you understood the story by answering these multiple-choice questions. (Answers at the end of the chapter.)

1. Where did Mahārāja Parīkṣit sit to listen to Śukadeva Gosvāmī?
   a) On the bank of the sacred River Ganges.
   b) In his palace.
   c) On top of Mount Meru.
2. Who was the spiritual master of Mahārāja Parīkṣit?
   a) Sūta Gosvāmī
   b) Lord Brahmā
   c) Śukadeva Gosvāmī
3. How can impure things in one's heart be cleared away?
   a) By performing *aśvamedha yajña.*
   b) By meditating on Kṛṣṇa's universal form.
   c) By praying to demigods.
4. Who creates and recreates this material world?
   a) Lord Brahmā
   b) Lord Śiva
   c) Goddess Durgā
5. What is the warning against the *Vedas* that Śukadeva Gosvāmī is giving to Mahārāja Parīkṣit?
   a) Some parts of *Vedas* entice people to aim to go to the heavenly planets instead of the Vaikuṇṭha planets after they die.
   b) People lose interest in spiritual life after studying the *Vedas,* as they find them difficult to understand.
   c) Study of *Vedas* reduces our desire to eat and sleep.
6. How should the people who know the truth lead their life?
   a) Live opulently so people who do not know the truth can get attracted to the truth.
   b) They should live a simple life and remember that Kṛṣṇa will give them what they need.
   c) Live any way they like, as it does not affect their knowledge of the truth.
7. How should one take the *darśana* of the Supreme Lord?
   a) By meditating on the ground in front of the Deities.
   b) Only meditate on the feet of the Lord, as looking anywhere else is offensive.

c) Begin by meditating on the feet and go upwards until one reaches the smiling face of the Lord.

8. What type of souls can enter into the spiritual world to be with Kṛṣṇa?
   a) Pure souls whose only interest is to love Kṛṣṇa.
   b) Souls that like to enjoy on the earth planet and also like to visit Kṛṣṇa on His planet.
   c) Only souls within bodies of demigods can enter the spiritual world.
9. What was the conclusion of Lord Brahmā upon studying *Vedas*?
   a) That the goal of life is to work hard so you can look after your family.
   b) Loving Lord Kṛṣṇa is the highest goal of life.
   c) It is very difficult to become a devotee of the Lord.
10. What is the simple process by which we can go back to the spiritual world?
   a) Study the *Vedas* multiple times.
   b) Stand on one leg and control one's breathing for long periods of time.
   c) Completely clear away one's material desires by always hearing, chanting, and remembering Lord Kṛṣṇa.

Higher-Thinking Questions

Now it's time to deepen your understanding of Chapter 2 by delving into Śrīla Prabhupāda's purports for this chapter and reflecting upon the following questions.

1. In verse 6, Śrīla Prabhupāda talks about illusion. Explain with examples what you think illusion is.
2. In verse 8, many names of Kṛṣṇa are listed and the *śāstras* say that Lord Kṛṣṇa has hundreds and millions of names. Why does Lord Kṛṣṇa have so many names?
3. Verse 3 talks about the minimum necessities of life. As a young Vaiṣṇava, think about all the things you have – toys, books, clothes, games, etc. Which of those are necessities and why?
4. Can you describe the process of looking at the Deity form of the Lord? Where should we start? (2.2.13)
5. "Every living being is serving the dictates of desire, he is perpetually unhappy." Explain this verse 2.2.16, and give some examples of what you think it means.
6. Read the purport of the verse 2.2.5. Can you identify the qualities, duties, and responsibilities of a *sannyāsī*? Discuss how Śrīla Prabhupāda met the requirements of a *sannyāsī*.
7. How can we make the seed of *bhakti-yoga* sprout in our heart? How can we water the

creeper of *bhakti-yoga* to ensure it reaches Kṛṣṇa's lotus feet in Goloka Vṛndāvana? How can we ensure that our *bhakti-yoga* creeper is not cut down? (verse 2.2.30)

8. Look at verse 2.2.35. List our (a) five perceptive senses, (b) five senses of action, and (c) three subtle senses. Can you explain what they are? How can the knowledge of our senses help us determine that we are not this body?
9. Based on the description provided in verses 2.2.8–12, draw an image of the Personality of Godhead residing in your heart. How do you feel upon knowing that there is such a beautiful personality in your heart who watches everything that you do and knows all your thoughts?
10. The Personality of Godhead residing in our heart has 24 different forms. Can you name some of them? (Refer to verse 2.2.8)

ACTIVITIES

In this section you will find many exciting things to do! They will get you thinking, moving, drawing, acting, and most importantly, having loads of fun!

Critical Thinking Activities
. . . to bring out the spiritual investigator in you!

LIFESPAN ACTIVITY

Sometimes when you read about the duration of life on other planets being 15,480,000,000,000 years, it might seem like an exaggeration. Try to investigate the duration of life of different species using **Resource 1**. When you have done this, think about how you found it so difficult to believe

THE ORIGINAL VARṆĀŚRAMA

"It is said that one should become a brāhmaṇa before one can understand the Vedic statements, and this stricture is as important as the stricture that no one shall become a lawyer who has not qualified himself as a graduate."

– *Śrīmad-Bhāgavatam 2.2.27 purport.*

In today's India, the caste system by birthright is prevalent. Our scriptures are clear, however, that the idea of varṇa or caste simply by birthright is wrong and was never practiced in ancient India.

Imagine you are attending a conference where you have been asked to speak about the Indian caste system. Carefully research your points and come up with a talk that properly explains the Vedic concept of varṇa to the audience.

Make sure you research the following:

- What is the Vedic varṇāśrama system?
- What are the qualifications of different varṇas?
- Examples of people in Vedic culture who were born in one varṇa but later were considered to belong to some other varṇa.

- How the Vedic varṇāśrama system degraded into the modern caste system.
- Reasons and analogies why birthright cannot be considered the criteria for a person to belong to a particular caste.
- A strong conclusion.

Take the help of your mentor to understand this. You can give this talk to your Bhāgavatam group.

THE KEY TO HAPPINESS

We are surrounded by advertisements that entice us to buy luxurious items – cars, houses, clothes, jewelry, etc. A comfortable and luxurious life is considered to be the basis of our happiness and everyone in this material world is chasing after such happiness.
Verses 3 -5 of this chapter present a surprisingly contrarian point of view: "The civilization which aims at this utmost perfection never indulges in creating unwanted things, and such a perfect civilization prepares men *only to accept the bare necessities of life* or to follow the principle of the best use of a bad bargain." SB 2.2.3 purport.
Within your group, discuss the meaning of the above statement, and whether we can be happy if we don't own or enjoy a lot of luxurious things. Write down your points.
Finally create an advertisement that urges adoption of a simple life, pointing out its advantages over a life full of unnecessary luxuries. Make sure to bring out that a simple life can also be a lot of fun!.

Introspective Activities
. . . to bring out the reflective devotee in you!

DEITY DARSAN

Description: Next time you go to the temple, try to meditate upon the Lord as described in these verses – starting from His lotus feet. When you get home, see if you can remember what the Lord looked like. Fill in the sheet (**Resource 2**). You may add or change some of the headings according to your local Deities.

LABEL THE SUPERSOUL

Label the Supersoul in **Resource 3** using the description given in Chapter 2.

Action Activities . . . to get you moving!

CAMPING ESSENTIALS

Description: Go camping! Be sure to pack the things that are necessary. Read verses 2.2.3 – 2.2.5 for some ideas of what this means. Try to apply as many of the points from the verses as possible.

For example:

- Arms to sleep on.
- Palms of hands to eat from, and as utensils.
- Tree shade for covering.
- Visit a river to see what animals are maintained by it.
- Visit a cave or a mountain to see which animals are maintained by it.

While you are out there, try to keep a journal to document your experience and collect things from nature along your way, such as twigs, leaves etc. You can stick these into your book or place them in a box.

Artistic Activities
. . . to reveal your creativity!

MEDITATION FLOW CHART

Description: Can you make a flow chart to show the process of meditating upon the Lord's form? Be as creative as you like!

CREATE THE SUPERSOUL

Description: Draw and paint a picture of the Personality of Godhead in the heart and decorate it using the description provided in the chapter. Use different materials to make your picture even more attractive. You can embroider with beads or use yarn for the hair, etc. Or perhaps you can create a 3D model of the Supersoul using clay or any other appropriate material, and decorate it using the description provided.

SUPERSOUL T-SHIRT

Description: On a plain T-shirt, use fabric paint to create a picture of the Supersoul on the area of the heart.

Theatrical Activities
. . . to bring out the actor in you!

REACH YOUR GOAL

Description: Create a "football commentary" on how the soul is *going, going, gone* back to the spiritual world, and has reached the final "goal"! You can do this alone or with a group while acting it out, with a co-presenter giving you up-to-the-minute feedback! Remember use of expression and emphasis.

Writing Activities . . . to bring out the writer in you!

HARRY THE HOARDER

Description: Write your own short story about a character called Harry the Hoarder. What does his name mean? What might his life journey be like? Younger students may take ideas from the plots below to start them off. Older students should be encouraged to create an original story.

- He wins the lottery
- He ends up homeless
- He meets a devotee on book distribution

SPELLING PRACTICE

Description: A list of words from different verses has been given in **Resource 4**. These can be used for spellings, synonyms and antonyms. Parents can select them as they wish, depending on the capacity of their child.

WHAT GOES WHERE

Description: Fill in the blanks in the Story Summary, choosing words from below.

labdhopaśānti	die	Ananta Śeṣa's
higher material planet	Lord	senses
body	material	Brahmaloka
Milky Way	lowest	lotus feet
materialistic	Satyaloka	planets
pole	dying	higher

Śukadeva Gosvāmī had explained the best thing in life a________________ person and an enlightened person should do. He now prepared to explain the best thing a _________ person should do: "A yogī does not need to worry about the right time to _________. He should just sit down comfortably, breathe properly, control his __________, and then engage his spirit soul in serving the _________ in his heart. This is a very happy stage. It's called _______________. At this stage, nothing in the material world can disturb him – not even the ____________ dying! He doesn't get disturbed by anything because he is always serving Lord Kṛṣṇa's _______________ in the heart, and avoiding things that are not related to Kṛṣṇa. At the time of death, the yogī blocks the_________ hole in his body with his heel and then moves the life air up through his body until it leaves through a __________hole. A yogī with no ______________desires goes straight back to Kṛṣṇa, but if a yogī still has some material desires, he goes to a _________________ _________ to fulfil his last remaining material desires. Such mystics travel over the ________________and stop at the planet of fire to clear out the last of their material contaminations before arriving at Lord Brahmā's planet called __________________. They then travel to Lord Viṣṇu's planet at the _________star before going to Maharloka where they live for a very long time until the time of the final devastation of the universe.

At this time, fire from Lord __________________mouth at the bottom of the universe burns up all the _________, and when the yogī sees this, he travels on an airplane to __________________to live there for a very long time."

SPELLING ERRORS

There is a spelling mistake in each sentence below. Write the correct spelling of each word in the space provided.

1. King Parīkṣit sat on the bank of the sacred River Ganges, listening very atenttively to the wise words of Śukadeva Gosvāmī. ____________________
2. When the material world was destroyed, it was Lord Brahmā's job to rekriate the world again. ____________________
3. It is amasing that forgetfulness of our eternal relationship with the Lord is cleared away just by meditating on Lord Kṛṣṇa's universal form. ____________________
4. Śukadeva Gosvāmī prepared to explain to his dissiple the next step in understanding Lord Kṛṣṇa. ____________________
5. Many people are atrracted to this so they really want to go there after they die. ____________________
6. My spiritual mastar is hinting that I must stay focused on going to Lord Kṛṣṇa's lotus feet instead. ____________________
7. "This is why people who know the truth should be satisfied with the bear necessities of life, and always remember that Lord Kṛṣṇa protects us and gives us what we need. ____________________
8. Śukadeva Gosvāmī had just explained the best thing in life a matteriallistic person and an enlightened person should do. ____________________
9. At this stage, nothing in the material world can disturb him – not even the body dieng! ____________________
10. They only feel sad for the sufering souls in lower planets who don't know about the power of serving Kṛṣṇa. ____________________
11. Only pure souls that are this purfect can be with Kṛṣṇa in the spiritual world in a happy state. ____________________
12. "That loving Lord Kṛṣṇa is the highest goal!" answered Śukadeva enthuciastikally. ____________________

GET THE WORDS RIGHT

Description: Look at the following passages selected from the Story Summary. Some words in the sentences are scrambled. Try to unscramble the words.

King Parīkṣit sat on the bank of the sacred River Gengas______________, listening very attentively to the wise words of Śukadeva Gosvāmī. The King, who would die in seven days, had just heard from his spiritual master that by meditating on Lord Kṛṣṇa's uasrevinl______________form, all impure things in the heart would be cleared away. But King Praikīṣt ______________ was confused. "How are they crealed ______________ away?" he wondered.

"Let me give you an example my dear King," began the great sage. "When the mriaatel______________world was destroyed, it was Lord Brahmā's job to create it again. But the pbelorm______________was that Lord Brahmā had completely forgotten how to do this! So he turned to Lord Kṛṣṇa and sat meditating on His universal form. Lord Kṛṣṇa was indeed pleased with this, so He cleared away the forgetfulness in Lord Brahmā's mind, and aewardd______________him the ability to remember how to recreate the world."

It is amazing that forgetfulness of our eternal relationship with the Lord is cleared away just by meditating on Lord Kṣṛaṇ's______________universal form. Even more ainazmg ______________, however, is that this is only the first step in understanding who Lord Kṛṣṇa really is. Śukadeva Gosvāmī prepared to explain to his disiclpe______________the next step in understanding Lord Kṛṣṇa – seeing the Lord in the hraet______________.

KEYWORDS

- Explain the meanings of the following keywords from the summary.
- Use each word in a sentence (either in oral or written form).
- Find at least one synonym and one antonym.
- Identify the word's part of speech (noun, verb, adjective, pronoun, or adverb).

Key Word *(part of speech)*	**Definition**	**Synonym & Antonym**
attentively (________________)		**Syn.** **Ant.**

impure (________________)		**Syn.** **Ant.**
temporary (________________)		**Syn.** **Ant.**
hint (________________)		**Syn.** **Ant.**
further (________________)		**Syn.** **Ant.**
process (________________)		**Syn.** **Ant.**

THE WAY TO GOLOKA VṚNDĀVANA

As described in this chapter, a pure yogī will go straight to the Lord at the time of death, but a yogī with residual material desires will first go to the higher planetary system to enjoy before he reaches the ultimate destination, Goloka Vṛndāvana.

In this activity, you are going to describe the yogī's journey back to Godhead. Different steps in the yogī's progress towards the spiritual world are listed below but they are not in the correct sequence. Organize the yogī's steps in the correct sequence, starting with the first step and traveling all the way up to Goloka Vṛndāvana.

If you would like to draw the yogī's journey using your imagination, create a poster with the first step at the bottom, and successive steps leading to the top. Describe and draw different planets all the way to Goloka Vṛndāvana illustrated at the top of your poster!

[Older children] After completing the above, write a short story about a yogī who makes his way to Kṛṣṇa. Create your own yogī character and try to be as descriptive as possible. What is his name? Where is he from? What sorts of desires does he still have? How does he finally become Kṛṣṇa conscious in the end? Narrate this story to your family and friends.

Stops at the planet of fire to get purified
Goes to Satyaloka
Leaves his body
Leaves behind the false ego

Ananta Śeṣa's fire burns all the planets, including Maharloka
Goes to Maharloka and lives for a long time
Reaches the ethereal state
Reaches Goloka Vṛndāvana
Body goes through many elemental changes
Reaches the pole star to relate with Lord Hari

MISSING WORDS ACTIVITY SHEET

Directions: After reading the story summary, choose the correct word from the box below to complete the sentences.

feet	happy	meditating	universal form	spiritual world	
higher	Supersoul	labdhopaśānti	dying	calves	
thighs	face	Vedas	lower	heavenly	forgetfulness
eternal	cleared	hear, chant and remember			

- At the time of death, the yogī blocks the ____________ hole in his body with his heel and then moves the life air up through his body until it leaves through a ___________ hole in the head.
- It is amazing that ___________________ of our ____________ relationship with the Lord is _____________ away just by meditating on Lord Kṛṣṇa's universal form.
- As long as we always ___________________________ Lord Kṛṣṇa, our material desires will be completely cleared away and we can go back to the ____________________ simply by this process.
- These people begin by ____________________ on Lord Kṛṣṇa's lotus ________ and go upwards to His __________, then His _________, then higher and higher until they reach the smiling _________ of the Lord.
- Did you know that some parts of the ___________ talk about all the pleasures you can get in the ________________ planets?" began Śukadeva.
- There is no need to try and meditate on the_________________, or even the _________________ in the heart.
- This is a very _________ stage. It's called ____________________. At this stage, nothing in the material world can disturb him—not even the body ____________!

FIRST LETTER QUESTION GAME

Description: In this game, the letter in the question on the left is the first letter of the answer. Ask your partner the questions in the left column. At first, you may need to rephrase the questions so your partner understands the game – e.g., "What word starting with the letter "N" is the name of the person who said Kṛṣṇa would soon be returning to the spiritual world?"

Question	Answer
What Y is the name of a person who undergoes austerity and a process of self realization?	
What B is the name of Lord Brahmā's residence?	
What S is the name of a pure land above Maharloka where souls live for a very long time?	
What souls P are perfect and can be with Kṛṣṇa in a happy state?	
What L is the highest goal one can achieve?	
What M will be cleared away as we hear, chant and remember Kṛṣṇa?	
What H pleasures are temporary and false, according to the chapter summary?	
What U does Lord Brahmā forget how to create after each devastation?	

WRITING A LETTER ABOUT KṚṢṆA!

Write a letter to a non-devotee person. In the letter, describe how hearing, chanting and remembering Kṛṣṇa will benefit us in ways we can only imagine. Tell him/her about Kṛṣṇa – What does He look like? What are His qualities? Who are some of His famous devotees? How many names does He have and what are they? What steps can one take to learn about and remember Kṛṣṇa?

Your purpose is to glorify Kṛṣṇa so that your own attraction to Him increases and the reader also becomes attracted to Him. Draw an attractive picture to go along with your letter.

Make this a preaching effort! Seek help from an adult to visit a nursing home or other appropriate venue. Chant the mahā-mantra, distribute prasādam, distribute books, and talk to anyone who is interested in hearing about Lord Kṛṣṇa.

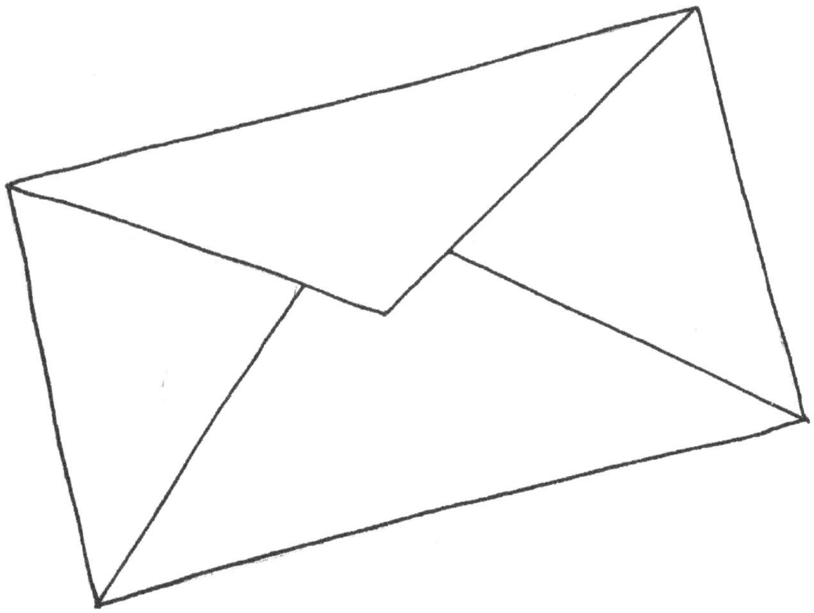

PLAIN LIVING AND HIGH THINKING

In the purport to Verse 37 of this chapter, Śrīla Prabhupāda says: "Life is never made comfortable by artificial needs, but by plain living and high thinking." A few scenarios are described in the table below. Some of them might easily qualify as 'plain living and high thinking' category, others would obviously not. There may be some scenarios that are not so clear! For such ambiguous scenarios, describe under what circumstances could they be considered as 'plain living and high thinking'.

Answers are not provided for this activity. As you fill out the table below, keep the following in mind:

- Simply renouncing material possessions has no value, unless it is accompanied with progressive attachment to Kṛṣṇa and engagement in His loving devotional service.
- Following the four regulative principles is important for Kṛṣṇa's devotees. If you do not know these principles, ask a devotee and find out!
- Even material opulence can be utilized in Kṛṣṇa's service.
- One should understand what is essential to lead a comfortable life and what can be considered excessive and therefore having the potential to negatively affect our devotional life.

Essay writing: Write an essay about what it means to be satisfied with the bare necessities of life. You may find it helpful to study the purports to Verses 2, 3, 4, and 37. Your essay should include the following:

- What is the purpose of human life?
- What are considered the bare necessities of human life?
- What must a family do to overcome material desires and live transcendentally?
- What's wrong with fulfilling our material desires?

Resource 1

LIVING THING	LIFE SPAN
Human	
Rabbit	
Giant tortoise	
Bee	
Ant	
Crocodile	
Mayfly	
Dragonfly	
English oak tree	

- Which has the longest lifespan?
- Convert the lifespan into the same units – for example, minutes or hours or days, and then compare them.
- If you were the species with the shortest lifespan and you were told the lifespan of the species with the longest, would you believe it?
- Śrīla Prabhupāda uses a very famous example of the frog in a well.
- Research how this example of the frog in a well relates to this topic.

Resource 2: DEITY DARŚANA

What You Observed	Sun	Mon	Tue	Wed	Thu	Fri	Sat
How were the Lord's lotus feet decorated?							
What colors were the Deities wearing?							
What were the Deities holding? (Flowers, cāmara, garland, etc.)							
What type was Kṛṣṇa's flute? (Gold, silver or wooden.)							
Did the Deities have any *gopī* dots on their faces?							
What were the Deities wearing on Their heads? (Crowns, turbans, top knots, etc.)							
What did the background look like?							
Was there anything else extra-special that you liked about the way they were dressed?							

Resource 3

Resource 4: SPELLING PRACTICE

VERSE 3
Scarcity
Budge
Stark

VERSE 4
Ample
Paraphernalia
Nullify
Phenomenon
Phantasmagoria
Yore
Amenities
Groves
Detrimental
Renunciation
Abnegation

VERSE 5
Parasite
Sycophant
Mendicants
Magnanimous
Aural
Assimilation

VERSE 6
Omnipotency
Overwhelmed
Pervading
Extricate
Anomaly
Illusion
Mirage

VERSE 10
Whorls
Mystic
Engraved
Torso
Variegatedness

VERSE 11
Wreath

VERSE 12
Magnaminous
Benedictions
Authentic
Entanglements
Altruistic
Philanthropic
Deliberation
Cessation
Assimilating

VERSE 13
Void
Gigantic
Transcendental
Manifested
Detachment
Impersonalists
Voidists

VERSE 14
Unfettered

VERSE 15
Empirical
Speculation

VERSE 16
Eternity
Unalloyed
Perpetually
Hankering

VERSE 17
Conspicuous
Satanic
Entourage

VERSE 22
Whimsically
Expedient
Ambitious

VERSE 23
Endeavor
Futile

VERSE 26
Flaws
Authentic

VERSE 27
Bereavement
Anxieties
Compassion
Unsurpassable
Miseries
Temperament
Authorized
Authentic
Literature
Stricture
Impediment
Paraphernalia
Myth

ANSWERS

Understanding the Story (pages 38–39)

1) a, 2) c, 3) b, 4) a, 5) a, 6) b, 7) c, 8) a, 9) b, 10) c

What Goes Where (pages 45-46)

Śukadeva Gosvāmī had explained the best thing in life a materialistic person and an enlightened person should do. He now prepared to explain the best thing a dying person should do.

"A yogī does not need to worry about the right time to die. He should just sit down comfortably, breathe properly, control his senses, and then engage his spirit soul in serving the Lord in his heart. This is a very happy stage. It's called ***labdhopaśānti***. At this stage, nothing in the material world can disturb him – not even the body dying! He doesn't get disturbed by anything because he is always serving Lord Kṛṣṇa's lotus feet in the heart and avoiding things that are not related to Kṛṣṇa. At the time of death, the yogī blocks the lowest hole in his body with his heel and then moves the life air up through his body until it leaves through a higher hole. A yogī with no material desires goes straight back to Kṛṣṇa, but if a yogī still has some material desires, he goes to a higher material planet to fulfil his last remaining material desires. They travel over the Milky Way and stop at the planet of fire to clear out the last of their material contaminations before arriving at Lord Brahmā's planet called Brahmaloka. They then travel to Lord Viṣṇu's planet at the pole star before going to Maharloka where they live for a very long time until the final devastation of the universe. At this time, fire from Lord Ananta Śeṣa's mouth at the bottom of the universe burns up all the planets, and when the yogī sees this, he travels on an airplane to Satyaloka to live there for a very long time."

Spelling Errors (page 46)

1. attentively
2. recreate
3. amazing
4. disciple
5. attracted
6. master
7. bare
8. materialistic
9. dying
10. suffering
11. perfect
12. enthusiastically

Get the Words Right (page 47)

1. Ganges
2. universal
3. Parīkṣit
4. cleared
5. material
6. problem
7. awarded
8. Kṛṣṇa's
9. amazing
10. disciple
11. heart

Keywords (pages 47-48)

Key Word *(part of speech)*	**Definition**	**Synonym & Antonym**
attentively (adverb)	a. while paying close attention b. very politely attending to the comfort or wishes of others	**Syn.** observantly, vigilantly **Ant.** carelessly, inattentively
impure (adjective)	a. mixed with foreign matter; adulterated b. ritually unclean	**Syn.** Alloyed, contaminated **Ant.** Unalloyed, fine, pure
temporary (adjective)	a. lasting for only a limited period of time b. not permanent	**Syn.** Brief, momentary, transitory **Ant.** Enduring, lasting, permanent
hint (noun)	a. a slight or indirect indication or suggestion b. a small piece of practical information or advice	**Syn.** indication, clue, inkling **Ant.** information, solution, answer
further (adverb, adjective, or noun)	a. (adv.) to a greater degree or extent b. (adj.) used to emphasize the difference between a suggested fact and the truth	**Syn.** farther, more unlike, additionally **Ant.** Fewer, less, alike
process (verb or noun)	a. (noun) a series of actions or steps taken in order to achieve a particular end b. (noun) a natural series of changes	**Syn.** practice, development, procedure. **Ant.** cessation, inaction, a decline

The Way to Goloka Vṛndāvana (pages 48-49)

Leaves his body

Stops at the planet of fire to get purified

Reaches the pole star to relate with Lord Hari

Goes to Maharloka and lives for a long time
Ananta Śeṣa's fire burns all the planets, including Maharloka
Goes to Satyaloka
Body goes through many elemental changes
Reaches the ethereal state
Leaves behind the false ego
Reaches Goloka Vṛndāvana

Missing Words Activity Sheet (page 50)

- At the time of death, the yogī blocks the lower hole in his body with his heel and then moves the life air up through his body until it leaves through a higher hole in the head.
- It is amazing that forgetfulness of our eternal relationship with the Lord is cleared away just by meditating on Lord Kṛṣṇa's universal form.
- As long as we always hear, chant, and remember Lord Kṛṣṇa, our material desires will be completely cleared away and we can go back to the spiritual world simply by this process.
- These people begin by meditating on Lord Kṛṣṇa's lotus feet and go upwards to His calves, then His thighs, then higher and higher until they reach the smiling face of the Lord.
- Did you know that some parts of the Vedas talk about all the pleasures you can get in the heavenly planets?" began Śukadeva.
- There is no need to try and meditate on the_universal form, or even the Supersoul in the heart.
- This is a very happy stage. It's called labdhopaśānti . At this stage, nothing in the material world can disturb him—not even the body dying!

First Letter Question Game (page 51)

Yogī
Brahmaloka
Satyaloka
Pure souls
Loving Kṛṣṇa
Material desires
Heavenly
Universe

3

Pure Devotional Service–The Change In Heart

Story Summary

The sages sitting in Naimiṣāraṇya were in awe upon hearing the great sage Sūta retell the transcendental conversation between Parīkṣit Mahārāja and Śukadeva Gosvāmī. Sūta described how the sages gathered on the banks of the River Ganges were eagerly listening to the wise answers of the great sage Śukadeva to King Parīkṣit.

"So there you have it." concluded Śukadeva Gosvāmī, "You asked what a dying person should do and I have answered you.

"You see, it depends on what people desire," he said. "If people desire something material, they generally worship the demgod in charge. For example, someone who wants to be powerful will worship the powerful demigod of fire, or if they want a strong body, they worship the very strong earth. If they want to be beautiful, they worship the beautiful Gandharvas, or if they want a lot of money, they worship the very wealthy Varuṇa. But, if they prefer to be spiritually happy and don't desire anything material, they worship the Supreme Personality of Godhead, Lord Kṛṣṇa.

"The person who is more intelligent worships Lord Kṛṣṇa directly – whether he has no material desires, is full of material desires, or just wants to be liberated and suffer no more. He worships Lord Kṛṣṇa because he is intelligent enough to know that everything comes from Him anyway."

Śukadeva Gosvāmī continued: "But my dear King Parīkṣit, the highest benediction — much more than all these material desires—is to always serve Lord Kṛṣṇa selflessly, with love. This means that the only reason you serve Lord Kṛṣṇa is because you love Him, and because you love Him so much, you want to serve Him all day and all night. This is a benediction which can only come by associating with Lord Kṛṣṇa's pure devotees, and no other way."

Śukadeva Gosvāmī advised that if one hears about Lord Kṛṣṇa from His pure devotees, one receives transcendental knowledge which has the power to cut away all desires and attachments of this material world and make the soul completely satisfied. "All the great souls approve of this, so who wouldn't be attracted to such a generous offer to hear about Lord Kṛṣṇa?" he said.

King Parīkṣit, the grandson of the Pāṇḍavas, had been a pure devotee since his childhood. Even while playing with his dolls, he would worship Lord Kṛṣṇa, imitating the way his family would worship their family Deity. Śukadeva Gosvāmī, the son of Vyāsadeva, was also a pure devotee. When devotees come together, they share their love for Kṛṣṇa by speaking about Him.

As the sun rises, a new day begins, and as

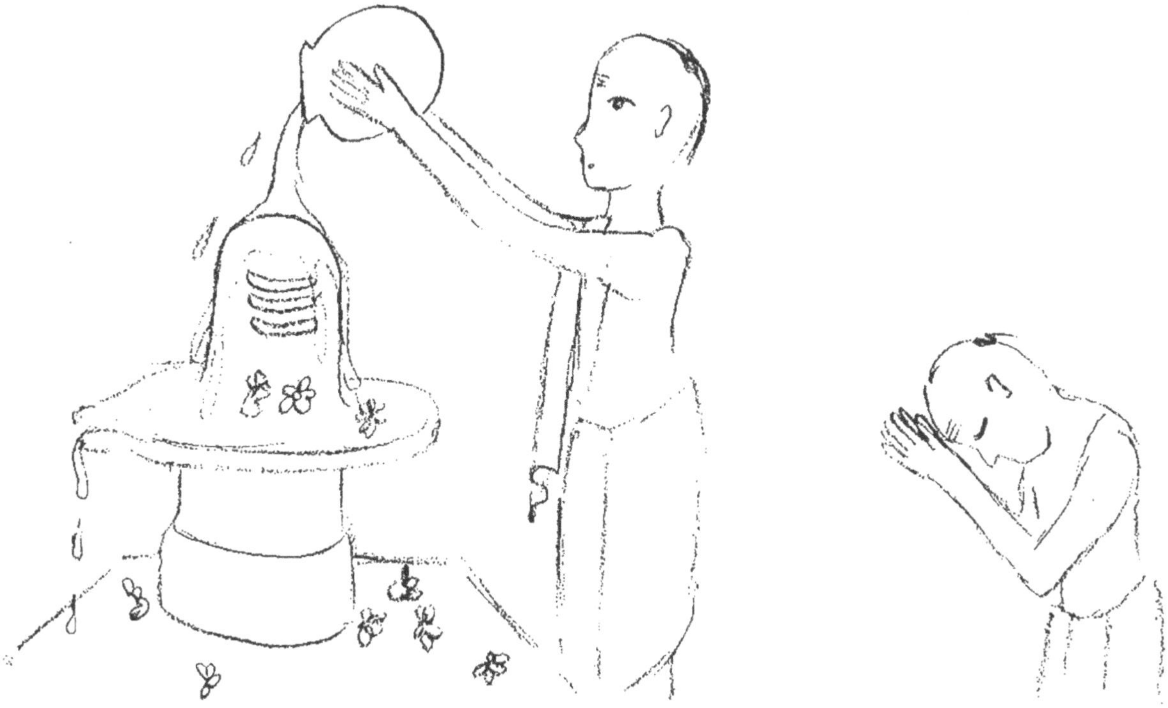

it sets, that day is lost. Life for all is shortened by one day, except for those who spend their time discussing and hearing topics of Lord Kṛṣṇa.

"Only men who are like dogs, hogs, camels, and asses praise those who never hear about Kṛṣṇa and His pastimes," said Śukadeva Gosvāmī. "For one who hasn't heard about Kṛṣṇa, his earholes are described as being like the holes where snakes live, and if he hasn't chanted 'Kṛṣṇa,' then his tongue is just like that of a frog.

"A head that is bedecked with a beautiful silk turban is simply a heavy burden if it's not used to bow down at Kṛṣṇa's lotus feet. Hands that are decorated with beautiful bangles are considered dead if not used for Kṛṣṇa, and eyes that don't look at Kṛṣṇa are just like the eyes on the plumes of a peacock.

"If the legs aren't used to travel to holy places, then they are as good as tree trunks, and if the head hasn't been touched by the dust of the lotus feet of a pure devotee or if the nose has not been used to smell *tulasī*, then the body is as good as dead. That heart is certainly steel-framed if in spite of one chanting the holy names with attention, it still doesn't melt!"

Key Messages

- Look them up in your *Śrīmad-Bhāgavatam.*
- Put them in your own words to help you memorize them.
- Discuss each one further.
- Apply them in your life.

Theme	References	Key Messages
The fire of material desire	2.3.2–10	People have so many desires that drive them. Ultimately, any desire apart from that of achieving the Lord will further entangle them within this material world.
Kṛṣṇa fulfills all desires	2.3.10	Kṛṣṇa is the intimate well-wisher of all. He is so kind that whatever people desire or don't desire, He is the refuge for all.
Pure devotees hold the keys	2.3–11	Only by the association and direction of pure devotees of the Lord can one achieve pure devotion, which is the highest perfection of human life.
Utilize time by discussing topics about Kṛṣṇa with devotees	2.3.14 2.3.16–17 2.3.20	Discussion about Lord Kṛṣṇa in the company of devotees is very powerful and potent. By utilizing our time in this way, we can quickly achieve devotional service to the Lord.
Use what we have for the Lord	2.3.17–24	Our bodies are gifts from the Lord to be used only in His service and not to fulfil our own selfish needs. If we fail to use what we have for the service of the Lord, it becomes useless.

Understanding the Story

Now it's time for you to check how well you understood the story by answering these multiple-choice questions. (Answers at the end of the chapter.)

1. The sages were gathered on the banks of the
   a) River Yamuna.
   b) River Sarasvatī.
   c) River Gaṅgā.
2. They were listening to the answers given by
   a) Vyāsadeva.
   b) Sūta Gosvāmī.
   c) Śukadeva Gosvāmī.
3. If people desire material things, they worship
   a) Lord Viṣṇu.
   b) demigods.
   c) Lord Kṛṣṇa.
4. If they want to be rich, they worship
   a) Varuṇa.
   b) Indra.
   c) Yama.
5. If they want to be spiritually happy, they worship
   a) Lord Viṣṇu.
   b) Lord Kṛṣṇa.
   c) demigods.
6. Who is intelligent?
   a) One who worships Kṛṣṇa for material or spiritual desires.
   b) One who worships demigods for their material benefits.
   c) One who worships demigods for liberation.
7. What is the highest benediction?
   a) To always selflessly serve Lord Kṛṣṇa.
   b) To serve Kṛṣṇa so that our desires are fulfilled.
   c) To serve demigods for fulfilling of our desires.
8. How does one get this highest benediction?
   a) By performing severe austerities.

   b) By praying to Kṛṣṇa.
   c) By associating with Lord Kṛṣṇa's pure devotees.

9. Parīkṣit Mahārāja and Śukadeva Gosvāmī are pure devotees of the Lord.
   a) False
   b) True
   c) Not sure
10. The earholes of people who don't hear about Kṛṣṇa are the same as
    a) holes where snakes dwell.
    b) frog holes.
    c) holes in animals.
11. For one who doesn't chant or sing about Lord Kṛṣṇa, his tongue is like a
    a) snake's tongue.
    b) frog's tongue.
    c) tongue of animals.
12. If the legs are not used to travel to holy places, then they are like
    a) tree trunks.
    b) tree branches.
    c) tree stems.
13. If one chants the holy names with attention and still his heart doesn't melt, then it is
    a) iron-framed.
    b) stone.
    c) steel-framed.

Higher-Thinking Questions

Now it's time to deepen your understanding of Chapter 3 by delving into Śrīla Prabhupāda's purports for this chapter and reflecting upon the following questions.

1. Śukadeva Gosvāmī explains how an intelligent person worships Kṛṣṇa for all his desires because Kṛṣṇa is the root of everything. Can you think of an example in the *Śrīmad-Bhāgavatam* where a devotee approached Kṛṣṇa for the fulfillment of his material desires, but later was ashamed?

2. How can we be engaged in Kṛṣṇa's service twenty-four hours a day? Discuss with the help of *Bhagavad-gītā* 10.9. What steps can you take to increase your remembrance and service of Kṛṣṇa during the day?
3. Why is the tongue that doesn't glorify Kṛṣṇa compared to the tongue of a toad? Refer to the purport of *The Nectar of Instruction*, Text 1, for Śrīla Prabhupāda's explanation.
4. Read verse 2.3.19 and write an essay on what kinds of people are referred to as dogs, hogs, camels, and asses.
5. Make a list of the qualities of a pure devotee using the purport of verse 2.3.13. Select some of these qualities and discuss how you can serve the Lord using these qualities.
6. What kind of benefits can demigods provide? Why do *śāstras* instruct us not to worship the demigods? How can a demigod-worshiper attain love of Kṛṣṇa? Refer to verses 2.3.2–11.
7. What is the purpose of life? How can one get love of Kṛṣṇa?
8. Discuss what the word "benediction" means. What is the greatest benediction for a devotee?

ACTIVITIES

In this section you will find many exciting things to do! They will get you thinking, moving, drawing, acting, and most importantly, having loads of fun!

Critical Thinking Activities

... to bring out the spiritual investigator in you!

ANNOUNCEMENT

Description: Find a fun way to help the people of the world learn about Kṛṣṇa! We can be as creative and dynamic as we want to tell the people of the world about the Lord!

You will need: Computer / Internet (Alternatively, pen and paper is just fine too!)

Create an advertisement for an event called "Back to Godhead" – anyone who attends this event will meet Kṛṣṇa! Think about what YOU would title the event. Is Back to Godhead appropriate? Can you think of an alternative title? Consider what advertising points you would put on the poster. What can you share that would inspire people to want to learn more about this wonderful personality called Kṛṣṇa? Would it be the *prasādam*? The *śāstric* evidence? For older children who are already familiar with social networking sites, the advertisement can be created in the form of a Facebook event, or an online e-newsletter.

Artistic Activities
... to reveal your creativity!

TELL THE PEOPLE OF THE WORLD ABOUT KṚṢṆA

Description: Make a megaphone to share the glories of Kṛṣṇa.
You will need: Thick craft paper, glue, tape, sequins, felt-tip pens, crayons, glitter, stickers.

Instructions:

1. Cut out a circle from the thick craft paper.
2. Make a small hole in the center of the circle.
3. Decorate the circle – you can draw or write anything you like! Maybe karatālas, a *mṛdanga*, musical notes, or even a verse from the scriptures.
4. Roll the circle into a cone shape and secure with glue or tape, making sure your decoration is on the outer side of the cone.
5. Now, you can go and tell the world about Kṛṣṇa with your megaphone!
   Prompt Question (for older children): Now that you have your megaphone, think about what your message is.

Introspective Activities
... to bring out the reflective devotee in you!

KEY INSTRUCTIONS TALLY CHART

Description: Try to keep track of how well you are following the instructions from Chapter 3. Use the tally chart (**Resource 1**) to document your progress.

Writing Activities . . . to bring out the writer in you!

GET THE WORDS RIGHT

Description: Look at the following passages selected from the Story Summary. Some words in the sentences are scrambled. Try to unscramble the words.

As the sun rises, a new day bniges ___________, and as it sets, that day is lost. Life for all is shortened by one day, epcxet ___________ for those who spend their time discussing and hearing topics of Lord Kṛṣṇa.

"Only men who are like dogs, hogs, camels, and sessas __________ praise those who never hear about Kṛṣṇa and His pastimes," said Śukadeva Gosvāmī.

"For one who hasn't hared ___________ about Kṛṣṇa, his earholes are described as being like the holes where snakes live, and if he hasn't chanted the names of Kṛṣṇa, then his egtnou __________ is just like that of a frog.

"A head that is beedkedc ________________ with a beautiful silk ubntra _________ is simply a heavy burden if it's not used to bow down at Kṛṣṇa's lotus feet. Hands that are decorated with btifueaul ________________ bangles are considered daed _______ if not used for Kṛṣṇa, and eyes that don't look at Kṛṣṇa are just like the eyes on the pmules ___________ of a peacock.

"If the legs aren't used to travel to holy places, then they are as good as tree rktuns ___________, and if the head hasn't been touched by the dust of the lotus feet of a pure etovede _______________ or if the nose has not been used to smell *tulasī*, then the body is as good as dead. That heart is certainly steel-framed if, in spite of one chanting the holy names with oteanittn ________________, it still doesn't melt!"

SEQUENCING

Given below are a few of the events that have happened in Chapter 3, Pure Devotional Service – The Lord in the Heart. They are all mixed up. Arrange them in the correct order, using the summary of the chapter.

1. If people desire something material, they generally worship the demigod in charge.
2. That heart is certainly steel-framed if, in spite of one chanting the holy names with attention, it still doesn't melt!
3. The highest benediction – much more than all these material desires – is to always serve Lord Kṛṣṇa selflessly with love.

4. Sūta described how the sages gathered on the banks of the River Ganges were eagerly listening to the wise answers of the great sage Śukadeva to King Parīkṣit.
5. But if they prefer to be spiritually happy, and don't desire anything material, they worship the Supreme Personality of Godhead, Lord Kṛṣṇa.
6. This means that the only reason you serve Lord Kṛṣṇa is because you love Him – and because you love Him so much, you want to serve Him all day and all night.
7. Life for all is shortened by one day, except for those who spend their time discussing and hearing topics of Lord Kṛṣṇa.
8. If they want a strong body, they worship the very strong earth.
9. If he hasn't chanted the names of Kṛṣṇa, then his tongue is just like that of a frog.
10. If they want a lot of money, they worship the very wealthy Varuṇa.
11. Eyes that don't look at Kṛṣṇa are just like the eyes on the plumes of a peacock.
12. If one hears about Lord Kṛṣṇa from His pure devotees, they receive transcendental knowledge, which has the power to cut away all material desires and attachments of this material world, and make the soul completely satisfied.
13. The person who is more intelligent worships Lord Kṛṣṇa directly – whether he has no material desires, or is full of material desires.
14. For one who hasn't heard about Kṛṣṇa, his earholes are described as being like the holes where snakes live.

YOUNGER KIDS' WORD SEARCH

S	A	N	F	A	U	A	L	E
A	N	K	I	N	D	G	R	A
N	F	I	X	E	A	R	C	V
E	S	A	E	Q	U	A	L	E
M	I	L	D	A	L	V	E	X
S	M	L	I	E	C	E	A	P
U	P	O	E	T	I	C	N	E
A	L	S	I	L	E	N	T	R
M	E	E	K	D	G	S	I	T

KIND	
MEEK	
SILENT	
FIXED	
POETIC	
CLEAN	

EQUAL	
MILD	
GRAVE	
EXPERT	
SIMPLE	

OLDER KIDS' WORD SEARCH

P	E	C	O	M	P	A	S	S	I	O	N	A	T	E
E	Q	S	H	I	V	A	T	T	A	C	A	P	F	L
A	S	U	T	A	A	T	H	A	L	D	T	Q	A	U
C	O	K	L	R	R	E	S	P	E	C	T	F	U	L
E	D	A	M	U	U	P	A	E	S	U	A	R	L	M
F	F	R	I	E	N	D	L	Y	Y	A	C	M	T	U
U	E	N	V	S	A	U	N	A	K	A	H	A	L	J
L	S	I	A	N	A	N	R	I	T	T	E	H	E	B
V	P	A	H	A	U	S	U	G	A	E	D	Y	S	I
A	E	D	E	G	A	N	D	H	A	R	V	A	S	K
B	E	N	E	V	O	L	E	N	T	N	I	S	U	N
R	T	C	H	A	R	I	T	A	B	L	E	T	R	I

SUTA	
PEACEFUL	
RESPECTFUL	
GANDHARVA	
SAUNAKA	
FAULTLESS	
CHARITABLE	

ATTACHED	
SHIVA	
SUKA	
BENEVOLENT	
FRIENDLY	
COMPASSIONATE	

CROSSWORD

ACROSS

1) Legs are like this if they aren't used to travel to the holy places.
2) Though our hands are decorated with these, we are as good as dead if we don't engage in the service of the Lord.
4) As it rises, a new day begins, and as it sets, that day is lost.
6) We may be croaking like this animal if we don't glorify the Lord.
7) If we don't listen to the pastimes of the Lord, our ears become like this reptile's hole.
8) A man who does not glorify the Lord is compared to the animal with a hump or two.

DOWN

1) A head wearing one of these will be a burden if it doesn't bow before the Lord.
3) We may as well be dead if we don't receive this from the feet of the devotees.
5) Our eyes could look as beautiful as this bird's feathers, but useless if we don't see the Lord's form.
7) The heart feels like it is encased in this metal if we don't feel ecstasy when chanting Kṛṣṇa's names.
9) A man who does not glorify the Lord is compared to this donkey-like animal.

Theatrical Activities

. . . to bring out the actor in you!

BHĀGAVATAM CHARADES

Description: Cut out the cards from the sheet (**Resource 2**). One at a time, pick a card and act out or draw the instructions described on the card. The rest of the group has to guess what is being described/drawn and what the spiritual message is.

THE GOD STORE

Description: Imagine that you work at the "God Store." You are showing some new people around who have no prior knowledge about worshiping gods. Describe to them briefly each of the gods according to the person's needs and desires. Who would you recommend overall, and why?

SING-ALONG

Description: Five little nosey frogs! Sing this fun song to the melody of "Five little speckled frogs."

Five little nosey frogs
Croaked too much on their log
Speaking a little *prajalpa* uh-oh
Along came a hungry snake
Then it became too late
Now there are four green curious frogs glug-glug

Four little nosey frogs . . .

Three little nosey frogs . . .

Two little nosey frogs . . .

One little Vaiṣṇava frog
Sang sweet songs for the Lord
While eating a *maṅgala-āratī* sweet yum-yum
He shared glories of the Lord
And he was never bored
Now he is a blissed out little frog glug-glug

WHAT DO YOU THINK?

Tick the statements that you think are correct.

1. Sūta Gosvāmī described how the sages gathered on the banks of the River Yamunā were eagerly listening to the wise answers of the great sage Śukadeva to King Parīkṣit.
2. The most intelligent person worships Lord Kṛṣṇa directly.
3. The highest benediction is to always serve Lord Kṛṣṇa selflessly, with all material desires.
4. Śukadeva Gosvāmī said if one hears about the demigods from their pure devotees, he can receive transcendental knowledge.
5. As the sun rises and sets, life is shortened by one day, except for those who spend their time discussing and hearing the topics of Lord Kṛṣṇa.
6. Only men who are like chickens, flies, geese and chimpanzees praise those who never hear about Kṛṣṇa and His pastimes.

PART-OF-SPEECH DETECTIVE

In this activity you will be identifying the different parts of speech (noun, verb, adjective, adverb, pronoun) in the given sentences.
First, let us define each part of speech so you know exactly what to look for.

Part of speech	Definition	Example
Noun	Person, place, or thing	The brown **cat** quickly jumped into his arms.
Pronoun	Someone or something, which can exist outside of the subject matter of a sentence.	The brown cat quickly jumped into **his** arms.
Verb	An action, state, or occurrence.	The brown cat quickly **jumped** into his arms.
Adjective	A word or phrase describing a noun.	The **brown** cat quickly jumped into his arms.
Adverb	A word or phrase describing or quantifying an adjective or verb.	The brown cat **quickly** jumped into his arms.

Now that you know how to identify each part of speech, practice by underlining the appropriate one in the sentences below!

Underline each ***NOUN*** and ***PRONOUN***. There may be multiple!

1. The highest benediction is to always serve Lord Kṛṣṇa!
2. A head bedecked with a beautiful silk turban is a burden if it is not used to bow down at Kṛṣṇa's lotus feet.
3. If the legs aren't used to travel to holy places, then they are as good as tree trunks.

Underline each ***VERB*** in the sentences below. There may be multiple!

1. Life for all is shortened by one day, except for those who spend time discussing and hearing topics of Lord Kṛṣṇa.

2. For one who hasn't heard about Kṛṣṇa, his earholes are like the holes where snakes live.
3. If the nose has not been used to smell tulasi, then the body is as good as dead.

Underline each ***ADJECTIVE*** in the sentence below. There may be multiple!

1. The heart is certainly steel-framed if in spite of one chanting the holy names with attention, it still doesn't melt!"
2. All the great souls approve of this, so who wouldn't be attracted to such a generous offer to hear about Lord Kṛṣṇa?
3. A head that is bedecked with a beautiful silk turban is simply a heavy burden if it's not used to bow down at Kṛṣṇa's lotus feet.

Underline each ***ADVERB*** in the sentence below. There may be multiple!

1. The heart is certainly steel-framed if in spite of one chanting the holy names with attention, it still doesn't melt!"
2. The highest benediction is to always serve Lord Kṛṣṇa selflessly, with love.
3. The sages gathered on the banks of the River Ganges were eagerly listening to the wise answers of the great sage Śukadeva.

KEYWORDS

- Explain the meanings of the following keywords from the summary.
- Use each word in a sentence (either in oral or written form).
- Find at least one synonym and one antonym.
- Identify the word's part of speech (noun, verb, adjective, pronoun, or adverb).

Key Word *(part of speech)*	**Definition**	**Synonym & Antonym**
benediction (________________)		**Syn.** **Ant.**
associate (________________)		**Syn.** **Ant.**

generous (__________________)		**Syn.** **Ant.**
bedecked (__________________)		**Syn.** **Ant.**
generally (__________________)		**Syn.** **Ant.**

WHO WORSHIPS WHOM?

In the table below, the column on the left has various things or qualities a person may desire in this world, whereas the column on the right lists entities who are empowered to fulfill such desires. Match the correct desire with its corresponding deity in the table below. While doing so, always remember that devotees seek to purify all material desires by engaging everything in Kṛṣṇa's service. They also worship only Kṛṣṇa and no one else.

1) Good bank balance	a) Viśvadeva
2) Long life	b) Varuṇa
3) Popularity	c) The Earth
4) Sense gratification	d) Apsarās
5) Fortune	e) Aśvinī-kumāras
6) Power	f) The Demons
7) Good marriage	g) The Supreme Personality of Godhead
8) Good wife	h) The Manus
9) Beauty	i) The Gandharvas
10) Domination over others	j) Lord Brahmā
11) To be very learned	k) Lord Śiva
12) Stability in one's post	l) The Moon
13) A worldly kingdom	m) Durgādevī
14) Victory over an enemy	n) Demigod of Fire
15) Domination over an empire	o) Horizon and earth combined
16) A strong body	p) Sādhya
17) Nothing material	q) Umā, the wife of Lord Śiva

IN SERVICE OF KṚṢṆA

In the box on the right, describe how you can use the item on the left in Kṛṣṇa's service. Also draw a picture illustrating it. Use your imagination!

Item	Describe and Illustrate!
Silk turban	
Saree	
Hands	
Eyes	

Now write a story about you or about someone you know who uses at least three of the four items above to serve Kṛṣṇa. Start the narration with "One Sunday" or "During Janmāṣṭamī" or some day when you or they would be fully engaged in Kṛṣṇa's service. Try to give the readers as much detail as possible. What was he or she wearing? Where were they? What were they doing? How were they feeling?

Resource 1

Days	Sun	Mon	Tue	Wed	Thu	Fri	Sat
Bow down to Kṛṣṇa.							
Discuss topics of the Lord.							
Hear about Kṛṣṇa.							
Chant Hare Kṛṣṇa on *japa-mālā.*							
See the Kṛṣṇa Deity.							
Sing *kīrtana / bhajans.*							
Go to the temple (or other holy place).							
Take the dust of the devotees on your head.							
Smell and taste the *tulasī* leaves offered to the Lord.							

Resource 2

ACT OUT:

The eyes that don't look at the deity form of Kṛṣṇa are like those printed on the plumes of a peacock.

ACT OUT:

One who has not listened to the messages of the Lord possesses earholes like the holes where snakes live.

ACT OUT:

The heart is steel-framed if one does not feel ecstatic when chanting the holy name (tears fill the eyes and the hairs stand on end).

ACT OUT:

One who has not sung or chanted songs about the Lord possesses a tongue like that of a frog.

ACT OUT:

The upper portion of the body, though crowned with a silk turban, is only a heavy burden if not bowed down before the Personality of Godhead.

ACT OUT:

The hands, though decorated with glittering bangles, are like those of a dead man if not engaged in the service of the Lord.

ACT OUT:

The legs which do not move to the holy places are considered to be like tree trunks.

ACT OUT:

The person who has not received the dust of the feet of the Lord's pure devotee upon his head is certainly a dead body.

ACT OUT:

And the person who has never experienced the aroma of the *tulasī* leaves from the lotus feet of the Lord is also a dead body, although breathing.

ACT OUT:

Men who are like dogs, hogs, camels, and asses praise those men who never listen to the transcendental pastimes of Lord Kṛṣṇa.

ACT OUT:

Both by rising and by setting, the sun decreases the duration of life of everyone, except one who utiliz-es the time by discussing topics of the Lord.

ANSWERS

Understanding the Story (pages 66-67)

1) c, 2) c, 3) b, 4) a, 5) b, 6) a, 7) a, 8) c, 9) b, 10) a, 11) b, 12) a, 13) c

Get the Words Right (page 71)

begins, except, asses, heard, tongue, bedecked, turban, beautiful, dead, plumes, trunks, devotee, attention

Sequencing (pages 71-72)

1. Sūta described how the sages gathered on the banks of the River Ganges were eagerly listening to the wise answers of the great sage Śukadeva to King Parīkṣit.
2. If people desire something material, they generally worship the demigod in charge.
3. If they want a strong body, they worship the very strong earth.
4. If they want a lot of money, they worship the very wealthy Varuṇa.
5. But if they prefer to be spiritually happy, and don't desire anything material, they worship the Supreme Personality of Godhead, Lord Kṛṣṇa.
6. The person who is more intelligent worships Lord Kṛṣṇa directly – whether he has no material desires, or is full of material desires
7. The highest benediction – much more than all these material desires – is to always serve Lord Kṛṣṇa selflessly, with love.
8. This means that the only reason you serve Lord Kṛṣṇa is because you love Him – and because you love Him so much, you want to serve Him all day and all night.
9. If one hears about Lord Kṛṣṇa from His pure devotees, they receive transcendental knowledge which has the power to cut away all material desires and attachments of this material world and make the soul completely satisfied.
10. Life for all is shortened by one day, except for those who spend their time discussing and hearing topics of Lord Kṛṣṇa.
11. For one who hasn't heard about Kṛṣṇa, his earholes are described as being like the holes where snakes live.
12. If he hasn't chanted the names of Kṛṣṇa, then his tongue is just like that of a frog.
13. And eyes that don't look at Kṛṣṇa are just like the eyes on the plumes of a peacock.
14. That heart is certainly steel-framed if, in spite of one chanting the holy names with attention, it still doesn't melt!

Younger Kids' Word Search (pages 72-73)

			F					
		K	I	N	D	G		
			X			R	C	
	S		E	Q	U	A	L	E
M	I	L	D			V	E	X
	M					E	A	P
	P	O	E	T	I	C	N	E
	L	S	I	L	E	N	T	R
M	E	E	K					T

Crossword (pages 74-75)

ACROSS
1) Trunk
2) Bangles
4) Sun
6) Frog
7) Snake
8) Camel

DOWN
1) Turban
3) Dust
5) Peacock
7) Steel
9) Ass

Older Kids' Word Search (pages 73-74)

P		C	O	M	P	A	S	S	I	O	N	A	T	E
E		S	H	I	V	A					A		F	
A	S	U	T	A	A						T		A	
C		K			R	E	S	P	E	C	T	F	U	L
E		A			U						A		L	
F	F	R	I	E	N	D	L	Y			C		T	
U				S	A	U	N	A	K	A	H		L	
L											E		E	
											D		S	
				G	A	N	D	H	A	R	V	A	S	
B	E	N	E	V	O	L	E	N	T					
		C	H	A	R	I	T	A	B	L	E			

What do you think? (page 76)

1. Incorrect
2. Correct
3. Incorrect
4. Incorrect
5. Correct
6. Incorrect

Part of speech detective (pages 77-78)

Noun and Pronoun.

1. The highest benediction is to always serve Lord Kṛṣṇa!
2. A head bedecked with a beautiful silk turban is a burden if it is not used to bow down at Kṛṣṇa's lotus feet.
3. If the legs aren't used to travel to holy places, then they are as good as tree trunks.

Verb (excluding 'state of being' verbs such as 'is', 'am', 'was', 'are', 'were', etc.)

1. Life for all is shortened by one day, except for those who spend time discussing and hearing topics of Lord Kṛṣṇa.
2. For one who hasn't heard about Kṛṣṇa, his earholes are like the holes where snakes live.
3. If the nose has not been used to smell tulasi, then the body is as good as dead.

Adjective

1. The heart is certainly steel-framed if in spite of one chanting the holy names with attention, it still doesn't melt!"
2. All the great souls approve of this, so who wouldn't be attracted to such a generous offer to hear about Lord Kṛṣṇa?
3. A head that is bedecked with a beautiful silk turban is simply a heavy burden if it's not used to bow down at Kṛṣṇa's lotus feet.

Adverb

1. The heart is certainly steel-framed if in spite of one chanting the holy names with attention, it still doesn't melt!"
2. The highest benediction is to always serve Lord Kṛṣṇa selflessly, with love.
3. The sages gathered on the banks of the River Ganges were eagerly listening to the wise answers of the great sage Śukadeva.

Keywords (pages 78-79)

Key Word *(part of speech)*	**Definition**	**Synonym & Antonym**
benediction (noun)	a. a blessing. b. something that promotes goodness or well-being.	**Syn.** blessing, benefit, boon **Ant.** curse, disadvantage
associate (verb)	a. to join or connect together b. to bring into relationship in various ways (like in memory)	**Syn.** relate, link, connect **Ant.** avoid, separate, disband
generous (adjective)	a. liberal in giving b. more plentiful than necessary	**Syn.** charitable, bighearted, ample **Ant.** miserly, selfish
bedecked (adjective)	a. decorated with fine things	**Syn.** adorned, garmented **Ant.** uncovered, disrobed, disarrayed
generally (adverb)	a. usually; in most instances; as a rule b. without reference to details	**Syn.** broadly, typically, commonly **Ant.** atypically, irregularly, extraordinary

Who Worships Whom? (page 79)

1b, 2e, 3p, 4l, 5m, 6n, 7q, 8d, 9i, 10j, 11k, 12o, 13a, 14f, 15h, 16c, 17g

4

The Process Of Creation

Story Summary

The sages at Naimiṣāraṇya were very eager to hear the conversation between King Parīkṣit and Śukadeva Gosvāmī. "Please tell us more!" said Śaunaka Ṛṣī to Sūta Gosvāmī. "Yes, please tell us more!" piped up the rest of the sages.

Sūta Gosvāmī said, "Well, remember my dear sages, King Parīkṣit was a very special soul. He saw Lord Kṛṣṇa face to face while he was only a baby in the womb of his mother Uttarā. So when he heard about the truth of the self from the great Śukadeva, he was easily convinced and accepted what his spiritual master had said. Upon hearing, Parīkṣit immediately began to think only of Lord Kṛṣṇa. Oh, how he was attracted to the sweet Lord! He was so attracted that without even trying, the King automatically gave up all his strong affection for his body, his wife, children, palaces, animals, riches, friends, family, and kingdom. He didn't mind at all that he would no longer see these people and possessions.

"King Parīkṣit naturally loved Lord Kṛṣṇa so he was always thinking about Him. He loved Kṛṣṇa so much that he just let go of all his other desires. The King said: 'My dear Śukadeva, because you don't have any material desires, whatever you are saying must be correct. Your words are gradually destroying my dark ignorance because you're talking about Kṛṣṇa!

'I'd really like to know how Lord Kṛṣṇa creates and maintains all these universes and then winds them all up just like a player. The things Lord Kṛṣṇa does are so amazing that even great scholars and demigods are bewildered and can't fully understand Him. Lord Kṛṣṇa is always one person. Whether He alone acts with the material world, or He expands into different forms to deal with the material world, He still remains one person... amazing!

'Can you help me understand this, my dear spiritual master Śukadeva? You are not only very learned and self-realized but you are also a great devotee of Lord Kṛṣṇa. This makes you as good as Kṛṣṇa Himself!'

Śukadeva Gosvāmī paused for a while before responding. He was remembering Lord Kṛṣṇa as Hṛṣikeśa, the master of the senses. Before replying to King Parīkṣit's questions about the creation of this world, the great Śukadeva Gosvāmī offered his obeisances to the Lord . . .

"This world You created
But how? It's much debated!
You stop devotees suffering
And demons advancing!
You enjoy all the worlds with no
consequence – And none is equal to You
because of Your opulence!

"Anyone who glorifies and worships You
Who sees You and prays to You

Who hears You and serves You
Will clear their sins away!

"Surrender to Your lotus feet
Will clear all attachments
Without a bit of difficulty
Enter transcendence!

"Taking shelter of devotees
Will wash our sins away
Thinking of Your lotus feet
Every second of every day!

"Following footsteps of authorities
We can see the Absolute Truth
O Kṛṣṇa be pleased with me!
You're the Supersoul
And Brahmā and Śiva's worshipful goal!

"O Kṛṣṇa be pleased with me
And decorate my statements with your energy
You came as Vyāsadeva
And wrote the scriptures for the world to see!"

Key Messages

- Look them up in your *Śrīmad-Bhāgavatam.*
- Put them in your own words to help you memorize them.
- Discuss each one further.
- Apply them in your life.

Theme	References	Key Messages
The true test of hearing the topics of *Śrīmad-Bhāgavatam*	2.4.5	As Śukadeva Gosvāmī was narrating topics related to Lord Kṛṣṇa, King Parīkṣit felt his ignorance being dissipated. Of course, being a pure devotee, King Parīkṣit was not ignorant, but he is demonstrating that the true test of hearing topics of *Śrīmad-Bhāgavatam* is that one feels enlightened. Also, this is only possible when one hears the *Śrīmad-Bhāgavatam* from a sincere devotee who has conquered all material desires.
Systematic way to read the *Śrīmad-Bhāgavatam*	2.4.6	King Parīkṣit shows by example how we should first inquire about the material creation, which is manifested by the Lord's external energy Durgā-devī, who is fully under His control. Only then should we hear about the activities of His internal energy – which are His transcendental pastimes in Goloka Vṛndāvana. Neophyte devotees must first understand and appreciate the greatness of Lord Kṛṣṇa, which creates strong faith about Him in our minds. Only then should we proceed to hear about His transcendental pastimes. This is the proper, systematic way of reading the *Śrīmad-Bhāgavatam* as demonstrated by King Parīkṣit himself.
How to understand the unlimited Lord	2.4.8	Since the Lord is unlimited, it is not possible to obtain knowledge about Him by using our limited and imperfect material senses. We can obtain such knowledge from Lord Kṛṣṇa's own words like in the Bhagavad-gītā. Another way to obtain such knowledge about the unlimited Supreme Person is from realized souls in the chain of disciplic succession.
Dovetailing good qualities in the service of Kṛṣṇa	2.4.17	Perfection can be achieved only when any good qualities we may have are dedicated to the service of Lord Kṛṣṇa. Examples of such qualities include advanced learning, a charitable disposition, leadership, practice of yoga, etc. If such qualities are not used for the service of Kṛṣṇa, they get utilized for personal sense-gratification and ultimately cause trouble for people in general.

Understanding the Story

Now it's time for you to check how well you understood the story by answering these multiple-choice questions. (Answers at the end of the chapter.)

1. What was the mood of the sages at Naimiṣāraṇya when they were hearing *Śrīmad-Bhāgavatam* from Sūta Gosvāmī?
   a) They wanted to hear more and more of it.
   b) They were feeling tired of sitting and listening and wanted the sermon to stop for some time.
   c) They wanted to hear about topics of someone other than Kṛṣṇa.
2. When did King Parīkṣit first see Kṛṣṇa in his current lifetime?
   a) At the time of his death.
   b) In his dreams when he was King.
   c) While he was in his mother's womb.
3. What was King Parīkṣit's mood when he was hearing *Śrīmad-Bhāgavatam* from his spiritual master, Śukadeva Gosvāmī?
   a) He wondered if the stories in the *Śrīmad-Bhāgavatam* were true or made up.
   b) He was easily convinced that Kṛṣṇa and His pastimes were real and he accepted whatever Śukadeva Gosvāmī told him.
   c) He was distracted as he knew he was about to die soon.
4. What main benefit did King Parīkṣit get as a result of hearing *Śrīmad-Bhāgavatam*?
   a) He felt very attracted to Kṛṣṇa and did not mind that after death he would no longer see his family and possessions.
   b) That Kṛṣṇa would help him take birth in the same family so he could reunite with them.
   c) That Kṛṣṇa would protect his kingdom so his family could continue to rule and enjoy.
5. Why was it important for King Parīkṣit to hear *Śrīmad-Bhāgavatam* from Śukadeva Gosvāmī?
   a) Śukadeva Gosvāmī was the eldest of all the sages and therefore most knowledgeable in *Śrīmad-Bhāgavatam*.
   b) Parīkṣit Mahārāja knew Śukadeva Gosvāmī from childhood and therefore trusted everything he said.
   c) Kṛṣṇa empowers pure devotees like Śukadeva Gosvāmī so when they speak *Śrīmad-Bhāgavatam* we can easily accept that Kṛṣṇa and His pastimes are real.

6. What did King Parīkṣit inquire from Śukadeva Gosvāmī?
   a) He wanted to know about Kṛṣṇa's pastimes in Vṛndāvana.
   b) He wanted to know how Kṛṣṇa creates, maintains, and winds up all the universes.
   c) He wanted to know if there was a way he could prolong his life.
7. What did King Parīkṣit find most fascinating about Kṛṣṇa?
   a) The fact that Lord Kṛṣṇa is always one person, whether He alone acts with the material world, or He expands into different forms to deal with the material world.
   b) That Kṛṣṇa can play His flute so beautifully.
   c) That Kṛṣṇa is so attractive and still many people do not want to know Kṛṣṇa.
8. What did Śukadeva Gosvāmī do after he heard King Parīkṣit's question?
   a) He began to recollect *Śrīmad-Bhāgavatam* in his mind and answered Mahārāja Parīkṣit's questions.
   b) He offered His obeisances to Lord Kṛṣṇa so he could speak *Śrīmad-Bhāgavatam* without any adulteration.
   c) He could not recall the topic of creation and wondered what he was going to tell Parīkṣit Mahārāja.

Higher-Thinking Questions

Now it's time to deepen your understanding of Chapter 4 by delving into Śrīla Prabhupāda's purports for this chapter and reflecting upon the following questions.

1. Does the message of the *Śrīmad-Bhāgavatam* have the proper effect when heard from a professional teacher? Why?
2. How did King Parīkṣit know that hearing about Lord Kṛṣṇa was destroying his ignorance?
3. Why is it difficult to learn about the Supreme Lord by reading the *Vedas* only? Why is it easy by hearing from devotees?
4. If you become a great scholar or a demigod in your next life, will it be easy for you to understand Kṛṣṇa in this way?
5. Is birth in a Kṛṣṇa conscious family more important than following Vedic principles?
6. What is the most important qualification to become Kṛṣṇa conscious?
7. Do we have to give up attraction for family, friends, possessions, etc., to become a devotee?

8. Why did Śukadeva Gosvāmī stop to remember the Lord before speaking? What do we learn from this?
9. Why should we worship according to the rules of the scriptures and not make up our own ways of worshiping the Lord?
10. Śukadeva Gosvāmī mentions how the devotee can see the Lord at every moment, while even great yogīs can only have a glimpse of Him after severe austerities. Explain why the process of *bhakti* is so easy, yet so powerful?
11. We cannot see the Lord simply by our own efforts, even in *bhakti-yoga*. The Lord has to reveal Himself to us. When and how might the Lord do this?
12. What did King Parīkṣit do immediately after hearing the instructions of Śukadeva Gosvāmī?
13. Why did King Parīkṣit believe everything Śukadeva Gosvāmī was saying as the truth?

ACTIVITIES

In this section you will find many exciting things to do! They will get you thinking, moving, drawing, acting, and most importantly, having loads of fun!

Action Activities . . . to get you moving!

LORD MUKUNDA'S LOTUS FEET

Description: Learn the auspicious markings on the Lord's lotus feet. This game can be played between an adult and a child or between two children. The picture of the Lord's lotus feet is provided in **Resource 1**.

How to play:

1. Both players memorize all 19 auspicious markings – 11 on the left foot, and 8 on the right foot.
2. Two copies of the outline of the Lord's lotus feet are needed, one for each player. You can either draw or trace them. The marks are not required, just the basic shape of both the feet is needed for the game.
3. Now the players have 3 minutes to draw all 19 marks on their set of lotus feet before the timer goes off.
4. Whoever finishes first, with the most correct markings, wins the game. If both players finish together then the one with the neatest drawing wins.

Variation:

1. The following *śloka* can be memorized:

candrārdhaṁ kalaśaṁ tri-koṇa-dhanuṣī khaṁ goṣpadaṁ proṣṭhikaṁ
śaṅkhaṁ savya-pade 'tha dakṣiṇa-pade koṇāṣṭakaṁ svāstikam
cakraṁ chatra-yavaṅkuśaṁ dhvaja-pavī jambūrdhva-rekhāmbujaṁ
bibhrāṇaṁ harim ūnaviṁśati-mahā-lakṣmy-arcitāṅghriṁ bhaje

I worship Lord Hari (Kṛṣṇa), whose feet are endowed with the 19 great opulences, on the left foot, the half-moon, water-pot, triangle, bow, sky, cow's hoofprint, fish, conch, and on the right foot, the eight-pointed star, swastika, wheel, parasol, barley corn, elephant-goad, flag, thunderbolt, *jambu* fruit, *ūrdhva-rekhā*, and lotus.

2. The players can give clues to a particular mark and then the opponent has to draw them.
3. Similarly, one can study the lotus footprints of Śrīmati Rādhārāṇī, Lord Caitanya, and Lord Nityānanda.

Critical Thinking Activities
. . . to bring out the spiritual investigator in you!

THE MIND OF PURE DEVOTEES

Description: Let us learn some lessons from the way Parīkṣit Mahārāja gave up his family and all possessions when he knew he had only one week to live. Divide the participants into two groups. Discuss the following questions, with the two groups presenting opposing viewpoints.

1. Did Parīkṣit Mahārāja make a good decision when he left his kingdom and his family, who was dependent on him?

2. If a common person has a near-death experience and realizes that life is temporary, should he follow Parīkṣit Mahārāja's example and suddenly give up all family responsibilities?

Finally, discuss how Parīkṣit Mahārāja's thinking differed from others and how we should train ourselves to think and act in our lives. Also, talk about the wonderful qualities of Parīkṣit Mahārāja and the spiritual strength that enabled him to make this difficult decision.

THE INCONCEIVABLE LORD

Description: Verse 8 of this chapter makes it clear that we can understand God only when He reveals Himself to us, and not through our own efforts.

- So many people nowadays – scientists, atheists, scholars – are trying to understand creation in their own way. Read the purport to verse 8 and find out why they cannot succeed in finding out the truth.
- Find quotes by those famous people who have realized that their own efforts cannot

lead them to the truth! For example, Sir Isaac Newton said, "I do not know what I may appear to the world, but to myself I seem to have been only like a boy playing on the seashore, and diverting myself in now and then finding a smoother pebble or a prettier shell than ordinary, whilst the great ocean of truth lay all undiscovered before me."

- Discuss the role of *Śrīmad-Bhāgavatam* in helping us understand the Lord's creation.

WALKING UP THE DISCIPLIC SUCCESSION

"Disciplic succession" (guru-śiṣya paramparā) refers to a line of spiritual teachers that has transmitted transcendental knowledge until the present day in an unaltered form starting from Lord Kṛṣṇa Himself. A spiritual master (guru) must be in an authorized disciplic succession to be bonafide. It is not possible for someone to be a bonafide spiritual master in a line of spiritual authority that does not come from Kṛṣṇa. In the disciplic succession, Vaiṣṇava teachings are passed on unchanged from guru to disciple.

Directions: Your mission is to investigate and complete the chain of disciplic succession starting from the sages of Naimiṣāraṇya all the way up to Kṛṣṇa.

- Start by asking yourself, "Who instructed the sages at Naimiṣāraṇya about the transcendental topics of the Śrīmad Bhāgavatam?" That person is the spiritual master for the sages.
- Then find out who instructed that person in transcendental knowledge, and so on.
- Consult other devotees if you have trouble identifying the next link in the chain.

Use the squares below to write each successive teacher's name. If you wish, also draw a little sketch of the person in the same square! Then cut the squares and paste them onto the drawing on the following page, starting with the sages at the bottom left and proceeding in ascending order towards Kṛṣṇa in Goloka Vṛndāvana on the top right.

Sages at Naimiṣāraṇya		
	Śrī Kṛṣṇa	

Analogy Activities . . . to bring out the scholar in you!

ABOUT THE PĀṆḌAVAS

(See Resource 2)

Description: Śrīla Prabhupāda says in the purport (2.4.2), "An expert devotee can turn everything to the path of light by an attitude of service to the Lord, and the best example here is the Pāṇḍavas."

First, research specific parts of the *Mahābhārata* and see what descriptions you can find about the Pāṇḍavas. You can ask an adult to help you with this. Next, attempt to complete the character chart, focusing on which qualities are most prominent in each personality. To conclude your activity, cite and discuss examples of how each character displayed the relevant quality in the *Mahābhārata*.

Prompt Questions (a challenge for older children):

- Discuss why Yudhiṣṭhira was considered a just and fair king? Can you think of a time when he acted on moral grounds?

- Why was Bhīma known for his strength?
- Why was Arjuna considered to be unrivaled in his sense control and the finest of archers? Could his sense control have anything to do with the fact that he would never be cruel to anybody? Can you think of an example?
- Why was Nakula so loyal to his brothers? And in return how did his brothers treat him?
- How would you describe Sahadeva?
- Most importantly, how did the Pāṇḍavas use their strengths and good qualities in devotional service to Kṛṣṇa?

Artistic Activities

. . . to reveal your creativity!

UNIVERSE POP-UP CARD

Description: Śukadeva Gosvāmī was asked to describe how Lord Kṛṣṇa creates and maintains all these universes and then winds them all up just like a player. Make a 3D card that springs to life.

You will need: Three pieces of stiff paper, glue, scissors, double-sided tape.

1. Fold one piece of paper in half and draw a picture of Kṛṣṇa on the front.
2. Get another piece of paper and cut lengthwise into long strips, about 1 inch wide. Lay two strips in a V shape on the table, tape them together.
3. Fold one strip across the other end, creasing and folding across each other to form a concertina method forming a spring. Continue folding across each other until your two strips of paper are finished. Tape down the last flap to secure. Repeat with your other strips to create more "springs."
4. Use your last piece of stiff paper to draw things within the universe such as planets, animals, trees, and cut them out.
5. Use double-sided tape to secure your picture onto a spring and then secure with more tape into the inside of your folded card.
6. When all your pictures are secured on springs inside the card carefully close your card so it shows the picture of Kṛṣṇa on the front. When you open it, watch how the universe springs out!

UNIVERSE ART

You will need: White thick paper, wax crayons (check that they can't be painted over before starting this activity), black/blue watercolor paints, large brushes.

Steps:

1. On your sheet of card, draw galaxies, large and small planets, trails of stars, moons, etc. Draw and color them in light-colored thick wax crayon. Make sure you apply the crayon as thick as you can so it will show up boldly as you will be painting over it.
2. Add some water to your black/dark blue paints, and using a large brush sweep it over your drawing. Your background should now absorb your paint to create an outer space, while your universe picture in wax will stand out, waterproof, remaining light-colored.

Introspective Activities

. . . to bring out the reflective devotee in you!

CAN YOU GIVE IT UP?

Description: Parīkṣit Mahārāja was easily able to give up affection for his body, wife, children, palace, animals, riches, friends, family and kingdom. Let's see how easily you can do that!

Steps:

- Pretend you are Parīkṣit Mahārāja and gather all your favorite things: First of all, your body!
- Next, pretend your favorite teddy bears/dolls are your wife and children. If you have any pets, they can be your animals. All your favorite jewelry and gadgets can be your riches, and your bedroom or garden can be your kingdom.
- Now bring in your parents and pretend to be the King, enjoying all kinds of things in your kingdom with your family and friends. Because you are the King, you can do whatever you want and everyone has to do what you say!
- After some time you receive a message that you are to die soon and so you have to give everything up.

- Start by giving away all your toys and gadgets, then your pets/animals, your parents and your friends.
- Now walk away to a quiet spot and sit on your own and think about what it would be like to have to leave your kingdom and home.
- How do you feel when you think like that? Do you think it would be easy for you to walk away from everything you love?
- Why do you think it was easy for King Parīkṣit to do it?

Writing Activities . . . to bring out the writer in you!

DEAR DIARY

Description: Imagine that you are Śukadeva Gosvāmī and King Parīkṣit has asked you to describe the process of creation. Before you begin, you want to first invoke Lord Kṛṣṇa's blessings and auspiciousness and also praise Him. Write a diary entry about your feelings for Lord Kṛṣṇa and describe all the different ways in which you know Lord Kṛṣṇa is the greatest.

GET THE WORDS RIGHT

Description: Look at the following passages selected from the Story Summary. Some words in the sentences are scrambled. Try to unscramble the words.

Sūta Gosvāmī said, "Well remember my dear gessa ________, King Parīkṣit was a very special losu ________. He saw Lord Kṛṣṇa face to face while he was only a baby in the womb of his themor__________ Uttarā; so when he heard about this truth from the great Śukadeva, he was very easily vincednoc _______________ and accepted what his spiritual master had said. Upon hearing, Parīkṣit immediately began to think only of Lord Kṛṣṇa. Oh how tradcttea ____________ he was to the sweet Lord. He was so attracted that without even trying, the king automatically gave up all his strong affection for his body, his fiew ________, children, palace, animals, riches, friends, family and modnikg _____________ He didn't mind at all that he would no longer see these people and possessions anymore.

King Risīktap _____________naturally loved Lord Kṛṣṇa so he was always thinking about Him. He loved Kṛṣṇa so much that he just let go of all his other direess __________. The King said: "My dear Śukadeva, because you don't have any alamteri ____________ desires, whatever you are saying must be correct.

PUNCTUATION PRACTICE

Description: The following passage is from the Story Summary, but someone forgot to punctuate it! Edit the passage using punctuation marks: periods, commas, apostrophes and quotation marks. Add capital letters. Check your answer against the edited version in the answer section.

my dear Śukadeva because you dont have any material desires whatever you are saying must be correct your words are gradually destroying my dark ignorance because youre talking about Kṛṣṇa

id really like to know how lord Kṛṣṇa creates and maintains all these universes and then winds them all up just like a player the things lord Kṛṣṇa does are so amazing that even great scholars and demigods are bewildered and cant fully understand him the fact that lord Kṛṣṇa is always one person whether he alone acts with the material world or whether he expands into different forms to deal with the material world and still remains one person amazing

can you help me understand this my dear spiritual master Śukadeva youre not only very learned and self realized but youre also a great devotee of lord Kṛṣṇa and this makes you as good as Kṛṣṇa himself

READING AND COMPREHENSION 3-2-1

Description: After reading this chapter, use this reading strategy to summarize key events to focus on important points of interest, and to clarify areas that you may be unsure about.

3 things you found out
2 interesting things, and why
1 question you still have

SENTENCE WRITING EXERCISE

Connective words ("connecting words")

Connectives are words that link sentences together or make a sentence longer.

Learning Objective: To extend sentences and use connective words.

Task: For each sentence, select a joining word from the box below, and then finish the sentence in your own words. The first one is done for you as an example (the added part is underlined).

and	so	but	when	because

Parīkṣit told Śukadeva Gosvāmī that whatever he had spoken was perfectly right because Śukadeva Gosvāmī was without material contamination.

1. Śukadeva Gosvāmī was considered as good as the Supreme Personality of Godhead ____.
2. __________________________________ He simultaneously enjoys His own abode in the spiritual sky.
3. ______________________________________the devotees (*bhaktas*) can see the Absolute Truth by thinking always of His lotus feet.

Whatever good qualities we have yield a fruitful result ____.

SEQUENCING

Given below are a few of the events that happened in Chapter 4. They are all mixed up. Arrange them in the order mentioned in the summary of the chapter.

1. The King said: "My dear Śukadeva, because you don't have any material desires, whatever you are saying must be correct.
2. Sūta Gosvāmī said, "Well remember my dear sages, that King Parīkṣit was a very special soul.
3. *Surender to your lotus feet*
Will clear all attachments
Without a bit of difficulty
Enter transcendence!
4. He loved Kṛṣṇa so much that he just let go of all his other desires.
5. The sages at Naimiṣāraṇya were so eager to hear the conversation between King Parīkṣit and Śukadeva Gosvāmī.

6. "I'd really like to know how Lord Kṛṣṇa creates and maintains all these universes and then winds them all up just like a player."
7. *O Kṛṣṇa be pleased with me*
   And decorate my statements with your energy
   You came as Vyāsadeva
   And wrote the scriptures for the world to see!
8. Śukadeva Gosvāmī paused for a while before responding. He was remembering Lord Kṛṣṇa as Hṛṣīkeśa, the master of the senses.

WHAT DO YOU THINK?

Set 1: Tick the statements that you think are correct.

1. Taking shelter of pure devotees will wash our sins away.
2. King Parīkṣit saw Lord Kṛṣṇa face to face while he was only a baby in the womb of his mother Subhadrā.
3. King Parīkṣit loved Kṛṣṇa so much that he just let go of all his other desires.
4. Lord Kṛṣṇa removes non-devotees/demons from all distresses and helps them advance further in atheistic temperament.
5. Lord Brahmā, Śiva, and all self-realized souls worship the Supreme Lord Kṛṣṇa.
6. It is only because Lord Kṛṣṇa enters the material universe that everything becomes enlivened.

Set 2: Inferring questions. Which questions do you agree with and disagree with, using what the author says and what you know. Back up your argument with reasons.

1. Due to insufficient advancement in material science, we cannot yet fully understand all the wonderful activities and qualities of the Supreme Lord.
2. A serious devotee must approach a spiritual master who is not only well versed in Vedic literatures but is also a great devotee of Lord Kṛṣṇa.
3. When the Supreme Lord is acting as the enjoyer of the material universe and the various spiritual planets, He is temporarily absent from His own personal abode.
4. A devotee always prays to the Lord before activities such as eating or speaking because he knows that the Lord is the controller of all senses and no one is free to act freely and independently.

YOUNGER KIDS' WORD SEARCH

C	S	O	A	D	G	O	L	D	T	U	H
A	E	S	U	F	F	R	E	L	H	P	L
D	E	A	L	E	A	N	Y	A	T	A	U
E	A	G	G	E	R	G	S	O	U	L	R
S	O	F	F	E	R	B	U	G	R	A	T
T	E	N	E	E	R	G	P	R	T	C	D
I	G	N	N	R	G	R	R	E	T	E	I
R	D	E	S	I	R	E	A	A	E	O	S
E	E	I	Y	E	S	A	E	L	P	G	R
W	S	W	O	M	B	T	M	E	L	A	E
O	R	T	R	R	O	N	X	A	E	Y	F
M	O	A	T	A	U	P	E	R	D	R	F
P	Y	B	S	U	A	F	E	N	E	E	U
E	A	E	E	N	L	S	E	S	N	E	S
D	N	A	D	E	B	A	T	E	F	F	O

EAGER	
EXPAND	
ENERGY	
TRUTH	
LEARN	
WOMB	

PALACE	
SENSES	
DESTROY	
DESIRE	
DEBATE	
SOUL	

DEAL	
SUFFER	
PLEASE	
GREAT	
GOAL	
OFFER	

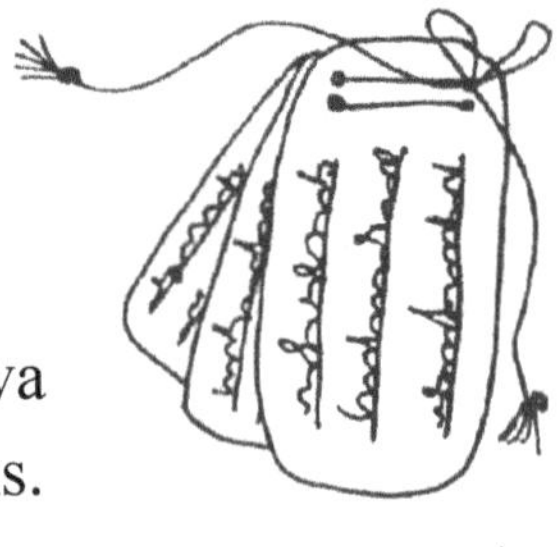

GLORIFYING KṚṢṆA - IN YOUR OWN WORDS

Part I: Read the poem at the end of the chapter summary wherein Śukadeva Gosvāmī glorifies the Lord before he answers Mahārāja Parīkṣit's questions. Choose one stanza from the middle four stanzas of the poem that describe ways in which we take shelter of the Lord. Then write a brief prayer of your own by using the selected stanza as an example. Glorify Kṛṣṇa and explain how and why your chosen way of taking shelter of Him helps devotees advance spiritually.

Part II: Looking at the structure of Śrīla Śukadeva Gosvāmī's prayer, you will follow in his footsteps by writing our own similar prayer. Below is a brief structure of the prayer, which you can use as a guide for your own composition. You can copy and fill in the blanks with your own words - remembering who Kṛṣṇa is, what He ultimately does in the material world/spiritual world, and His different qualities. You can consult the translations of Verses 12 thru 24 for further examples.

Let me offer my respectful obeisances to the Supreme Personality of Godhead, who is ________________ *(give another name for Lord Kṛṣṇa)* _____________.

Again, let me offer my respectful obeisances unto the form of complete existence who __________ *(what does Kṛṣṇa do when He comes to this world?)*__________.

I offer my obeisances unto He who _________ *(who is He? Whose friend is He, whose child is He, whose King is He? Choose a name.)* ________ There is no one equal to You!

I offer my respectful obeisances to the all-auspicious Lord Sri Kṛṣṇa whose glorification, hearing, and worship can at once cleanse the heart of the performer.

Let me offer my obeisances to Lord Sri Kṛṣṇa again and again because __________ *(any type of person; philosopher, mystic)* ___________ would be unable to reap results of their actions without dedication or service unto You.

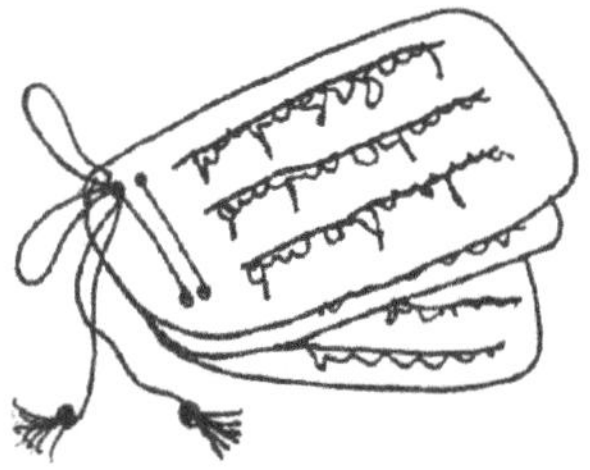

Personalities addicted to sinful activities such as _____________ can be purified just by taking shelter of Your devotees.

He is worshiped by saintly people such as ______________ *(choose any sages, demigods or saintly person(s) you may know)* _______________ without pretension. By following in their footsteps, may He be pleased by me.

May Lord Kṛṣṇa, who is ____________ *(give some quality or opulence of the Lord)* ______________, be merciful upon me. May He who ______________ *(describe an activity of the Lord)* ______________, be pleased with me.

PUNCTUATION PRACTICE

Description: The following passage is from the Story Summary, but someone forgot to punctuate it! Edit it, using punctuation marks: periods, commas, apostrophes, and quotation marks. Add capital letters. Check your answer against the edited version in the answer section.

the sages at naimiṣāraṇya were very eager to hear the conversation between king parīkṣit and śukadeva Gosvāmī please tell us more said śaunaka ṛṣi to sūta Gosvāmī yes please tell us more piped up the rest of the sages

sūta Gosvāmī said well remember my dear sages king parīkṣit was a very special soul he saw lord kṛṣṇa face to face while he was only a baby in the womb of his mother uttarā so when he heard about the truth of the self from the great śukadeva he was easily convinced and accepted what his spiritual master had said upon hearing parīkṣit immediately began to think only of lord kṛṣṇa oh how he was attracted to the sweet lord he was so attracted that without even trying the king automatically gave up all his strong affection for his body his wife children palaces animals riches friends family and kingdom he didnt mind at all that he would no longer see these people and possessions

JUMBLED WORDS

Description: The following words are from the story summary, but they are all jumbled up. Unscramble them. (The answers can be found in the Answers section).

1. nroignaec
2. gnmodik
3. zgniaam
4. yaisanariamN
5. dnsndureta

6. ieshcr
7. gniklat
8. lsarshco
9. alrezdei
10. otuihwt

ONE PERSON, MANY FORMS

Directions: In the chapter summary, Mahārāja Parīkṣit exclaims, "Whether He alone acts with the material world, or He expands into different forms to deal with the material world, the Lord always remains one person!" Think of all the different ways Lord Kṛṣṇa expands Himself within the material world and then list at least SIX forms on the lines around His original form in Resource 3. You could also draw or sketch a picture of these different forms, writing a brief explanation of His appearance. Then on a separate sheet of paper, choose any one of the Lord's forms and and write a brief explanation about His purpose for appearing in that form, and the lessons we can derive from His pastimes. Include the following:

- What is His name?
- What is/was His role and purpose of appearing in the material world in that form?
- What can you learn from Him and apply in your life?

Remember that the Lord also expands as inanimate objects such as Mount Meru, the Himalayas and the Vedic syllable Om as mentioned in Chapter 10 of the Śrīmad Bhagavad-gītā.

KEYWORDS

- Explain the meanings of the following keywords from the summary.
- Use each word in a sentence (either in oral or written form).
- Find at least one synonym and one antonym.
- Identify the word's part of speech (noun, verb, adjective, pronoun, or adverb).

Key Word *(part of speech)*	**Definition**	**Synonym & Antonym**
immediately (________________)		**Syn.** **Ant.**
ignorance (________________)		**Syn.** **Ant.**
reply (________________)		**Syn.** **Ant.**
consequence (________________)		**Syn.** **Ant.**
worshipful (________________)		**Syn.** **Ant.**

OLDER KIDS' WORD SEARCH

S	U	R	E	D	N	E	R	R	U	S	P
T	R	E	E	A	B	T	S	L	O	O	E
E	D	C	C	E	S	U	A	P	S	B	A
C	B	N	N	A	U	L	B	S	U	E	U
N	E	E	E	C	H	O	E	D	E	I	S
E	W	U	L	B	R	S	W	N	C	S	E
D	I	Q	U	R	S	B	I	O	N	A	O
N	L	E	P	I	D	A	L	I	A	N	E
E	R	S	O	G	N	S	D	S	R	C	C
C	E	N	A	R	E	U	E	S	O	E	N
S	D	O	C	A	R	A	R	N	N	S	E
N	S	C	P	L	T	P	V	O	G	L	L
A	U	T	H	O	R	I	T	Y	I	O	N
R	E	C	H	H	N	E	D	P	A	B	U
T	A	R	N	C	R	E	A	T	I	O	N
C	R	E	E	S	R	E	V	N	O	C	O

ECHOED	
IGNORANCE	
OPULENCE	
ABSOLUTE	
CONVERSE	
PAUSE	

SCHOLAR	
BEWILDER	
CREATION	
POSSESSION	
SURRENDER	
OBEISANCES	

CONVINCE	
CONSEQUENCE	
AUTHORITY	
TRANSCENDENCE	

Resource 1

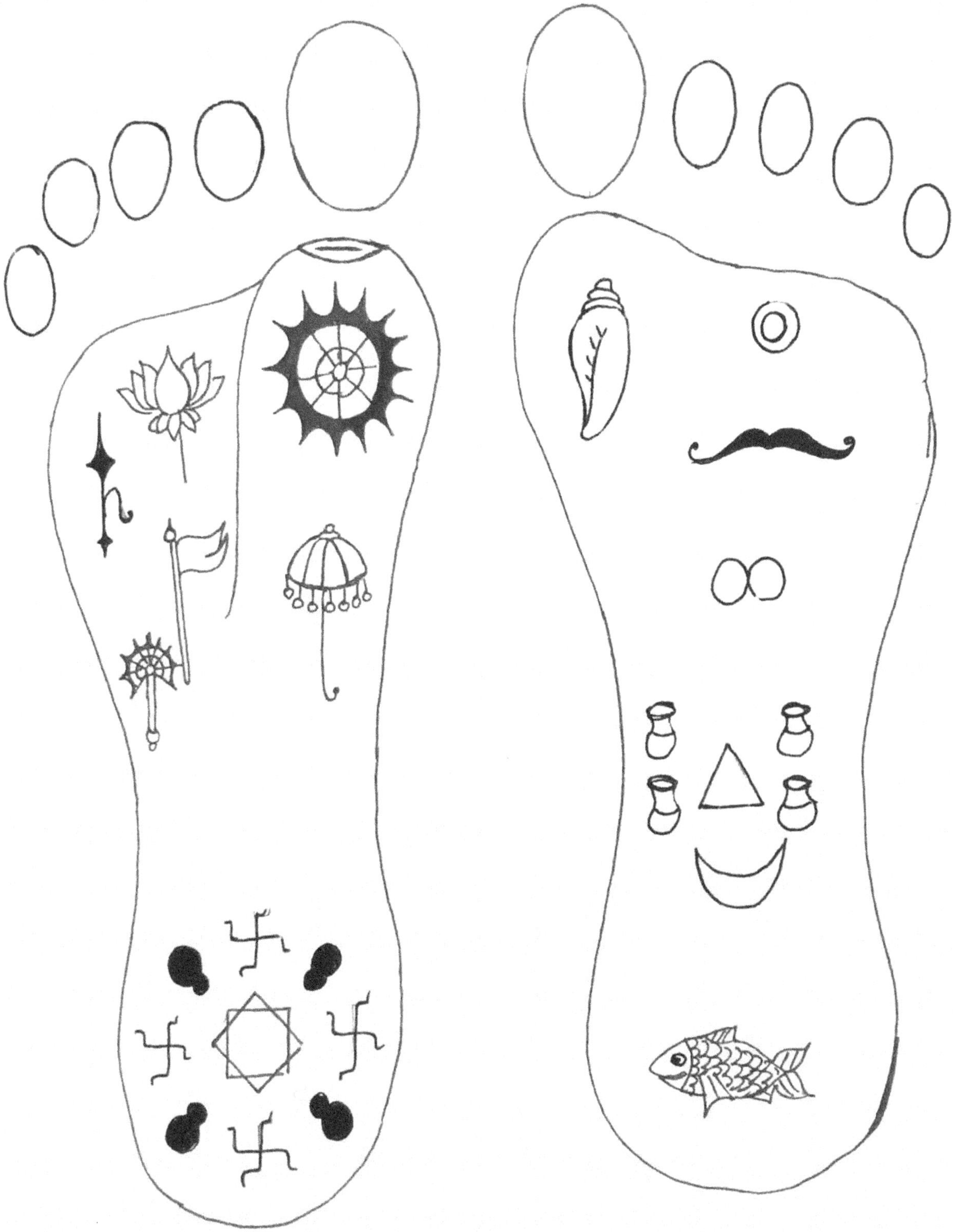

Resource 2

	Morality	Strength	Sense Control	Intelligence	Devotion to the Pāṇḍavas
Arjuna was most famous for . . .					
Yudhiṣṭhira was most famous for . . .					
Bhīma was most famous for . . .					
Nakula was most famous for . . .					
Sahadeva was most famous for . . .					

Each Character's Expertise Is:

Resource 3

ANSWERS

Understanding the Story (pages 93-94)
1) a, 2) c, 3) b, 4) a, 5) c, 6) b, 7) a, 8) b

Analogy Activity (pages 100-101)

	Morality	Strength	Sense Control	Intelligence	Devotion to the Pāṇḍavas	Each Character's Expertise Is:
Arjuna was most famous for . . .			☐			Archery
Yudhiṣṭhira was most famous for . . .	☐					Spear
Bhīma was most famous for . . .		☐				Mace
Nakula was most famous for . . .					☐	Sword
Sahādeva was most famous for . . .				☐		Sword

Get the Words Right (pages 103-104)
sages, soul, mother, convinced, attracted, wife, kingdom, Parīkṣit, desires, material

Punctuation Practice (pages 104)
"My dear Śukadeva, because you don't have any material desires, whatever you are saying must be correct. Your words are gradually destroying my dark ignorance because you're talking about Kṛṣṇa!

"I'd really like to know how Lord Kṛṣṇa creates and maintains all these universes and then winds them all up just like a player. The things Lord Kṛṣṇa does are so amazing that even great scholars and demigods are bewildered and can't fully understand Him. Lord Kṛṣṇa is always one person. Whether He alone acts with the material world or whether He expands into different forms to deal with the material world, He still remains one person . . . amazing!

"Can you help me understand this, my dear spiritual master Śukadeva? You're not only very learned and self-realized, but you're also a great devotee of Lord Kṛṣṇa and this makes you as good as Kṛṣṇa Himself!"

Sequencing (pages 105-106)

1. The sages at Naimiṣāraṇya were so eager to hear the conversation between King Parīkṣit and Śukadeva Gosvāmī.
2. Sūta Gosvāmī said, "Well remember my dear sages, that King Parīkṣit was a very special soul.
3. He loved Kṛṣṇa so much that he just let go of all his other desires.
4. The King said: "My dear Śukadeva, because you don't have any material desires, whatever you are saying must be correct.
5. "I'd really like to know how Lord Kṛṣṇa creates and maintains all these universes and then winds them all up just like a player.
6. Śukadeva Gosvāmī paused for a while before responding. He was remembering Lord Kṛṣṇa as Hṛṣīkeśa, the master of the senses.
7. *Surrender to your lotus feet*
   Will clear all attachments
   Without a bit of difficulty
   Enter transcendence!
8. *O Kṛṣṇa be pleased with me*
   And decorate my statements
   with your energy
   You came as Vyāsadeva
   And wrote the scriptures
   for the world to see!

What Do You Think? (page 106)

Set 1	**Set 2**
1. Correct	1. False
1. Incorrect	2. True
2. Correct	3. False
3. Incorrect	4. True
4. Correct	
5. Correct	

Younger Kids' Word Search (page 107)

	E							L	H	P	
D	E	A	L				Y	A	T	A	
			G			G	S	O	U	L	
	O	F	F	E	R			G	R	A	
				E	R	G			T	C	
			N			R				E	
	D	E	S	I	R	E					
			Y	E	S	A	E	L	P		R
		W	O	M	B	T		E			E
			R				X	A			F
			T			P		R			F
			S		A			N			U
			E	N		S	E	S	N	E	S
			D	E	B	A	T	E			

Older Kids' Word Search (page 112)

		R	E	D	N	E	R	R	U	S	P
		E	E			T				O	
E		C	C	E	S	U	A	P	S	B	
C		N	N			L	B	S		E	
N		E	E	C	H	O	E	D	E	I	
E		U	L			S	W		C	S	
D		Q	U		S	B	I		N	A	
N		E	P	I		A	L		A	N	
E		S	O				D		R	C	
C		N		R			E		O	E	
S		O		A			R	N	N	S	
N		C		L			V		G		
A	U	T	H	O	R	I	T	Y	I		
R				H	N						
T				C	R	E	A	T	I	O	N
			E	S	R	E	V	N	O	C	

Punctuation Practice (page 109)
The sages at Naimiṣāraṇya were very eager to hear the conversation between King Parīkṣit and Śukadeva Gosvāmī. "Please tell us more!" said Śaunaka Ṛṣi to Sūta Gosvāmī. "Yes please tell us more!" piped up the rest of the sages.

Sūta Gosvāmī said, "Well, remember my dear sages, King Parīkṣit was a very special soul. He saw Lord Kṛṣṇa face to face while he was only a baby in the womb of his mother Uttarā. So when he heard about the truth of the self from the great Śukadeva, he was easily convinced and accepted what his spiritual master had said. Upon hearing, Parīkṣit immediately began to think only of Lord Kṛṣṇa. Oh, how he was attracted to the sweet Lord! He was so attracted that without even trying, the King automatically gave up all his strong affection for his body, his wife, children, palaces, animals, riches, friends, family and kingdom. He didn't mind at all that he would no longer see these people and possessions."

Jumbled Words (pages 109-110)
1. ignorance
2. kingdom
3. amazing
4. Naimiṣāraṇya
5. understand
6. riches
7. talking
8. scholars
9. realized
10. without

Keywords (page 111)

Key Word *(part of speech)*	**Definition**	**Synonym & Antonym**
immediately (adverb)	a. at once; instantly b. without any intervening time or space	**Syn.** directly, promptly **Ant.** later, never, eventually
ignorance (noun)	a. lack of knowledge, information, or language b. State of being ignorant	**Syn.** bewilderment, darkness, blindness **Ant.** intelligence, wisdom
reply (verb)	a. to respond in words or writing b. to say something in response to something someone said	**Syn.** acknowledge, respond, reciprocate **Ant.** question
consequence (noun)	a. a result or effect of an action or condition b. importance or relevance	**Syn.** effect, aftermath, importance **Ant.** cause, source, origin
worshipful (adjective)	a. giving and or expressing worship or veneration b. Feeling or showing reverence or adoration	**Syn.** adoring, reverential **Ant.** contemptuous, scornful, disrespectful

5

The Cause of All Causes

Story Summary

One day, Nārada Muni approached Lord Brahmā and asked him some questions.

"My dear father Brahmā," began Nārada, "can you tell me about the soul and the Supersoul? And this world – how is it created and maintained? Who is in control?" He paused for a moment before continuing, "I'm asking you because you know everything – past, present and future. Like a spider who creates a web all by himself, everything we know is created by you. But where do you come from? Do you really do this all by yourself, or is there someone higher than you?"

Happy to hear such a question, Lord Brahmā smiled. Then, hastily, Nārada Muni added, "I'm just asking because I see that you perform austerities and meditate. I wonder who you are meditating upon. Is there someone higher than you? My dear father, you know everything, so please instruct me as your student."

Oh, Lord Brahmā was so excited! He loved any opportunity to talk about Kṛṣṇa.

"Nārada!" beamed Lord Brahmā, "I'm really happy to answer your question. You are right. People who don't know Lord Kṛṣṇa might think I am the Supreme Personality of Godhead because I am so powerful, but you see there's this light that comes from Lord Kṛṣṇa . . .

"The brahmajyoti?" asked Nārada.

"Yes," said Lord Brahmā. "I create everything from this light, so actually everything I create really comes from Lord Kṛṣṇa. He is so powerful that through His external energy, He makes foolish people think I am in control."

"Oh, I know her – the illusory lady," said Nārada Muni, "She is a devotee of Kṛṣṇa and feels ashamed that her job is to stop people seeing Kṛṣṇa. She makes them think that they're actually God, or someone else is actually God."

"Yes" confirmed Lord Brahmā, "but luckily she has no power to cover the devotees of Kṛṣṇa or Kṛṣṇa Himself. She only covers people who have a false ego who think, 'I am this body,' and 'that belongs to me.' But they are bewildered my dear Nārada, because the truth is that everything we know of in this world – like the ingredients of this creation, the ropes that bind the soul here, and the way they work together – are all part of Kṛṣṇa. Nothing is separate from Him," said Lord Brahmā.

"I only knew how to create this world because Kṛṣṇa showed me in my heart. He even showed me that I'm created by Him too. Kṛṣṇa's energy – the illusory lady – ties the souls to this world with three ropes called goodness, passion, and ignorance, and because of these they can't see Kṛṣṇa or understand that He controls everything.

He makes time, their bodies, their nature, the fate they desire after playing in a particular way . . . and then He merges it all again. Let me explain how. Nārada you are quite competent to understand this."

Lord Brahmā explained how Lord Kṛṣṇa expands Himself into Mahā-Viṣṇu and lies down in the Causal Ocean. He glances over at Mother Nature and then expands into Lord Śiva. Lord Śiva passes those spirit souls who would like to try and enjoy separate from Lord Kṛṣṇa to his dear wife Mother Nature.

Together, Mother Nature and the spirit souls are called *mahat-tattva*. Lord Kṛṣṇa then starts to make a material world where the spirit souls can try to enjoy without Him.

First He makes time – past, present and future, beginning, middle and end, as these don't exist in the spiritual world. Then He makes false ego, an important ingredient which helps the spirit soul to think, 'I am the most important,' 'this is mine,' and 'this body is me.' This false ego transforms into three ropes – goodness, passion and ignorance – that bind the soul to Mother Nature.

Lord Brahmā said: "Now you see Nārada, all of this needs to be made and put together by the Lord before Mother Nature can make suitable bodies for the spirit souls. So once this was all assembled, the universes came into being. These universes remained in the Causal Ocean for a long time until Mahā-Viṣṇu expanded and entered into each of them as Garbhodakaśāyī Viṣṇu and got them working as the virāṭ-rūpa – the universal form."

Key Messages

- Look them up in your *Śrīmad-Bhāgavatam.*
- Put them in your own words to help you memorize them.
- Discuss each one further.
- Apply them in your life.

Theme	References	Key Messages
Position of the spiritual master	2.5.7	Nārada Muni accepted Lord Brahmā as a superior being but realized that even Lord Brahmā was not the Supreme Personality of Godhead. Similarly, one should respect the spiritual master who is on par with God, but the spiritual master is not God Himself. Any guru who claims to be God must be rejected.
The spirit of preaching	2.5.9	A sign of a pure devotee of Kṛṣṇa is that he/she is always very eager to discuss topics related to Kṛṣṇa, His associates, and His devotees. Such discussions purify the place where they take place, and energize those who speak or hear such topics. Also, pure devotees have the spirit of preaching – they are not satisfied by simply knowing the glories of Kṛṣṇa. They also want to tell everyone about the Lord whenever the opportunity arises.
How to understand the unlimited Lord	2.4.8	Since the Lord is unlimited, it is not possible to obtain knowledge about Him by using our limited and imperfect material senses. We can obtain such knowledge from Lord Kṛṣṇa's own words like in the *Bhagavad-gītā*. Another way to obtain such knowledge about the unlimited Supreme Person is from realized souls in the chain of disciplic succession.
The influence of false ego	2.5.12–13	The misconceptions such as "It is I" or "It is mine" arise because of the influence of false ego, which acts on those who are not surrendered to the Lord. Persons who are thus influenced take pleasure in being addressed as God by others. Pure devotees, on the other hand, are surrendered to Kṛṣṇa and the deluding energy cannot act on them. Therefore, a bona fide spiritual master refuses to be addressed as the Supreme Lord by his disciples or subordinates.
Lord Brahmā is a secondary creator	2.5.17	Lord Brahmā admits that he is not the actual creator of the universe. He creates under the inspiration and supervision of Lord Kṛṣṇa. The more we surrender to Kṛṣṇa, the more He empowers us to do wonderful things. Lord Brahmā is such a great devotee of the Lord that he has been empowered by Kṛṣṇa to create all the different objects and species in our material universe.

Understanding the Story

Now it's time for you to check how well you understood the story by answering these multiple-choice questions. (Answers at the end of the chapter.)

1. What did Śukadeva think was the best way to answer King Parīkṣit's question?
   a) Tell a story. It is fun to hear Kṛṣṇa's stories and they make it easier to understand Him.
   b) Refer the question to a more senior sage as Śukadeva did not feel qualified to answer the question.
   c) He asked the king to perform yoga exercises as that will reveal the answer to his question.
2. The story is a conversation between which two people?
   a) Śiva and Sati.
   b) Sūta Gosvāmī and sages of Naimiṣāraṇya.
   c) Brahmā and Nārada.
3. What did Nārada Muni inquire from Lord Brahmā?
   a) He inquired about Kṛṣṇa's pastimes with the gopīs of Vṛndāvana.
   b) He inquired about the soul and the Supersoul, how this world is created and maintained and who controls it.
   c) He inquired about King Parīkṣit's history.
4. Why did Nārada Muni ask Brahmā these questions?
   a) Because Nārada Muni knew that Brahmā had created everything. However, as Nārada had seen Brahmā meditate on someone, he concluded that there must be someone higher than Brahmā.
   b) Śiva asked Nārada Muni to raise these questions as he wanted the answers but did not feel qualified to approach Brahmā directly.
   c) Nārada Muni knew that by knowing answers to these questions he can go back to Godhead.
5. What energy does Brahmā use for creation and where does it come from?
   a) Brahmā uses solar energy for creation and it comes from the Sun god.
   b) Brahmā uses a light call brahmajyoti for creation and this light comes from Kṛṣṇa.
   c) Brahmā uses electricity for creation and it comes from Indra.
6. Why do people think that Brahmā is the source of everything and not Kṛṣṇa?
   a) With his mystical powers Brahmā keeps people under the spell that he is the original creator.

   b) Śiva's illusory energy makes people think that Brahmā is the source of everything and there is no one greater than Brahmā.
   c) Kṛṣṇa's illusory energy makes people think that since Brahmā created everything, there is no one greater than him.
7. How does the goddess of illusory energy feel about her service to Kṛṣṇa?
   a) She is a devotee of Kṛṣṇa and would love to glorify Him. However, Kṛṣṇa has given her the service of distract people away from Him, so she feels embarrassed of her service.
   b) She loves her service to keep people away from Kṛṣṇa because this way she does not have to share Him with many people.
   c) She loves her service because this way she gets people to worship her with their wealth.
8. What kinds of people get tricked by Kṛṣṇa's illusory energy?
   a) Devotees of Kṛṣṇa.
   b) People who think, "I am this body, and I am the controller and enjoyer of everything I do."
   c) Devotees of Lord Śiva.
9. According to Brahmā, what is the truth about who the original creator is?
   a) Everything that we know of in this world, including Brahmā, is a part of Śiva.
   b) Brahmā is the original creator, and hence the source of everything.
   c) Everything that we know of in this world, including Brahmā, is a part of Kṛṣṇa, who instructed Brahmā in his heart on how to create.
10. What is the first thing Kṛṣṇa does when He starts the process of creation?
   a) Lord Kṛṣṇa expands Himself into Mahā-Viṣṇu and lies down in the Causal Ocean.
   b) Lord Kṛṣṇa creates brahmajyoti out of which he creates Brahmā.
   c) Lord Kṛṣṇa creates Śiva and instructs him on the process of creation.
11. Who does Mahā-Viṣṇu glance over while lying in the Causal Ocean?
   a) He glances over the Causal Ocean in which He is lying.
   b) He glances over Brahmā.
   c) He glances over at Mother Nature.
12. What are the spirit souls and Mother Nature together known as?
   a) Viṣṇu-tattva
   b) Mahat-tattva
   c) Śiva-tattva
13. What does Mother Nature do for the spirit souls?
   a) She starts to create a material world where the spirit souls can try to enjoy without Lord Kṛṣṇa.
   b) She creates Brahmā to help her with creation.
   c) She creates Śiva so he can help her destroy creation when such a need arises.

14. Who enters these universes to get them working?
    a) Śiva enters these universes and gets them working with the fire emanating from his body.
    b) Brahmā enters these universes and gets them working with his mystical powers.
    c) Mahā-Viṣṇu expands and enters them as Garbhadakśāyī Viṣṇu and gets them working as the virāṭ-rūpa – the universal form.

Higher-Thinking Questions

Now it's time to deepen your understanding of Chapter 5 by delving into Śrīla Prabhupāda's purports for this chapter and reflecting upon the following questions.

1. Why did Nārada Muni ask Lord Brahmā all about creation, and why was Lord Brahmā happy that Nārada asked him those questions?
2. How did Nārada come to wonder about another creator greater than Lord Brahmā, although there was no such creator visible? Why was Lord Brahmā the right person to inquire from?
3. Nārada is a pure devotee. Why then did he not know of the Supreme Lord, as it seems from these verses?
4. What could you say to people who accept that any powerful person with magical powers is God?
5. Why can't we see Kṛṣṇa? Why is He not visible to the conditioned living entity?
6. What does Lord Brahmā refer to as the imaginary form of the Lord? In what sense is that form imaginary?
7. Fill in the blanks: The *brāhmaṇas* represent His __________, the *kṣatriyas* His __________, the *vaiśyas* His __________, and the *śūdras* are born of His __________. What does this imply about the duty of each of the *varṇas*?
8. In the first purport in this chapter, Prabhupāda says: "Asking for transcendental knowledge from the right person and receiving it properly is the regulation of the disciplic succession."
    a) Cite the *Bhagavad-gītā* verse where this is mentioned.
    b) How does one approach a spiritual master? Cite the *Bhagavad-gītā* verse.
    c) Provide some examples of disciples who approached their spiritual master this way.
9. Arrange each of the following series in systematic order:
    a) time, activities, *mahat-tattva*, three qualities
    b) fire, air, water, ether, earth
    c) *talātala, mahātala, rasātala, pātāla, sutala, atala, vitala, maharloka, satyaloka, bhurloka, bhuvarloka, svarloka, tapoloka, janaloka*

10. Organize the following in the order of their creation. What comes after what?
    - Different activities of the modes
    - Goodness and Passion
    - Sky and sound
    - Kāraṇodakaśāyī Viṣṇu
    - Fire and shape
    - *Mahat-tattva*
    - Ear, skin, nose, eyes, tongue, mouth, hands, genitals, and the outlet for evacuating
    - Water and taste
    - Three qualities
    - Earth and smell
    - Mind
    - Ignorance
    - Air and touch
    - Ten demigods controlling the bodily movements

ACTIVITIES

In this section you will find many exciting things to do! They will get you thinking, moving, drawing, acting, and most importantly, having loads of fun!

Action Activities . . . to get you moving!

SECONDARY CREATORS:
PLANTING AN HERB GARDEN

Description: Lord Brahmā says in this chapter that he is not the primary creator. He explains to Nārada Muni that Lord Kṛṣṇa is source of all creation and is also the cause of all causes of maintenance and destruction. Similarly, we are also secondary creators.

Steps:

If the weather permits this can be done outdoors, but can be done inside too.

1. Prepare the selected area of the garden by clearing it and adding potting soil.
2. Choose the seeds and plant according to the directions on the packets.
3. Make sure there is enough sunlight and water the plants.
4. As the saplings start to appear, try to keep the area clean by removing the weeds.
5. Carefully harvest the leaves and flowers and offer them to Kṛṣṇa.
6. When the plants dry out, you can then clear the area.

Reflections:

The goal of this activity is to become aware that the humans cannot create the seeds but can facilitate their germination and growth. Similarly, sunlight, water, and air are already provided, and nature and time control the life cycle of the plants. But we can use these resources intelligently to produce the best possible *bhoga* for Kṛṣṇa to ensure variety and quality. In our own way, we also play the roles of creators, maintainers, and destroyers.

Artistic Activities

. . . to reveal your creativity!

SPIDER'S WEB

Description: Create your own spider's web with a spider as described in the story summary. "I'm asking you because you know everything past, present, and future and you are like a spider who creates a web all by himself – everything we know is created by you!

You will need: Two pieces of black paper, scissors

Steps (see **Resource 1**):

1. Take a square piece of paper. Fold it in half to a right-angle triangle.
2. Repeat Step 1 another three times.
3. Fold one last time to form a thinner triangle.
4. Cut a slight curve shape along your smallest triangle side.
5. Draw and cut out curved rectangles as shown in image.
6. Unfold your paper carefully to show your spider's web!
7. Using some more black paper, draw and cut out a silhouette of a spider.
8. Cut out shapes for its eyes and fangs.
9. Using string, hang the spider from the web, or attach it to a window.

SCULPTURE

Description: Make a sculpture to signify how the false ego transforms into three ropes – goodness, passion, and ignorance – that bind the soul to Mother Nature.

Steps: For example, you can use a marble for the soul and make a cage for the soul representing false ego from wire or twigs. From the cage, weave in string or pieces of paper representing the soul being further bound by the modes of nature. Let the child explore with their chosen materials. Be as creative as possible. You could use clay, play dough, or a painted stone in a jar wrapped in wool. Once the sculpture is complete, take close-up photographs of the various sections.

Introspective Activities
. . . to bring out the reflective devotee in you!

WHO ARE YOU?

Description: In the purport of verse 5, Śrīla Prabhupāda gives the analogy of the sun as self-illuminating – you don't need to shine another light at the sun in order to see it. In the same way, you don't need the help of any other instruments to perceive yourself as an individual soul.

Think about this a little bit:

- How do you know that other things besides yourself exist? You need to use your senses – seeing, hearing, touching, tasting and smelling – to know if other things are there. Try it out! Close your eyes and listen to loud music on headphones. How will you know if someone comes into the room?
- But even without using any of your senses you can tell that YOU are there. Why? Because you are the soul and the soul doesn't need to be seen or heard to be experienced – just like the sun doesn't need any other light to show that it exists.
- In this chapter, Nārada Muni begins to explain that there is a difference between the world that we experience through our senses, and we ourselves.
- Take some time to think about who you are and see if you can explain who you are without using any information that comes from the senses. Can you do it?
- If you can't do it then what does that say about us? If we try to describe ourselves are we only describing our body? Do we actually know who we are, spiritually?

Writing Activities . . . to bring out the writer in you!

DEAR DIARY

Description: Imagine that you are Nārada Muni. For a long time, you have considered your father Lord Brahmā to be the Supreme Creator but now you believe that there may be someone greater than him. Write a diary entry about why you started having the doubts and what questions you are going to ask

Lord Brahmā when you approach him for transcendental knowledge.

CREATION IN YOUR OWN WORDS

Description: In this chapter, Lord Brahmā has provided a lot of information about how creation takes place. Write a summary of the process in your own words in no more than 500 words.

PUNCTUATION PRACTICE

Description: The following passage is from the Story Summary, but someone forgot to punctuate it! Edit it, using punctuation marks: periods, commas, apostrophes, and quotation marks. Add capital letters. Check your answer against the edited version in the answer section.

lord Brahmā explained how lord Kṛṣṇa expands himself into mahā Viṣṇu and lies down in the causal ocean he glances over at mother nature and then expands into lord Śiva lord Śiva passes those spirit souls who would like to try and enjoy separate from lord Kṛṣṇa to his dear wife mother nature together mother nature and the spirit souls are called mahat tattva she then starts to make a material world where the spirit souls can try to enjoy without lord Kṛṣṇa first she makes time past present and future beginning middle and end as these dont exist in the spiritual world she makes false ego an important ingredient which helps the spirit soul to think im the most important this is mine and this body is me this false ego transforms into three ropes goodness passion and ignorance that bind the soul to mother nature

WHAT DO YOU THINK?

Set 1: Tick the statements that you think are correct.

1. This false ego is a very important ingredient. It helps the spirit soul to think, "I'm the most important," "this is mine," and "this body is me."
2. One day, Lord Brahmā approached Nārada Muni and asked him some questions.
3. Lord Brahmā was not happy to hear such a question.
4. People who don't know Lord Kṛṣṇa might think I'm the Supreme Personality of Godhead because I'm so powerful, but you see there's this light that comes from Lord Kṛṣṇa . . .
5. The illusory lady is really proud of her service because she loves Kṛṣṇa.
6. Everything that we know of in this world – like the ingredients of this creation, the ropes that bind the soul here, and the way they work together – are all part of Kṛṣṇa.
7. Mahā-Viṣṇu expands Himself into Lord Kṛṣṇa and lies down in the Causal Ocean.

8. There are some spirit souls that would like to try and enjoy separate from Lord Kṛṣṇa, so Lord Śiva gives these spirit souls to his dear wife, Mother Nature.
9. The universes remained in the Causal Ocean for long time until Mahā-Viṣṇu expanded and entered into each of them as Garbhodakaśāyī Viṣṇu and got them working as the virāṭ-rūpa – the universal form.

Set 2: *Inferring Questions.* Which questions do you agree with and disagree with, using what the author says and what you know. Back up your argument with reasons.

1. Nārada Muni suspected that Lord Brahmā was not the Supreme Lord because Lord Brahmā was worshipping someone else.
2. The purpose of the Vedic literatures is to help us properly speculate about the impersonal nature of the Supreme Lord.
3. After Mahā-Viṣṇu creates the innumerable universes, Lord Brahmā enters into each and every one of them and performs the secondary creation.

ACTION ACTIVITY SHEET

a) Action words (verbs) are doing words. They describe the "action." For example: "I will quickly run to the temple," and, "We will jump into the Ganges." Can you think of your own examples? How do you determine if a word can be a verb? (You can precede it with either "to," a noun, or one of the personal pronouns: he, she, it, I, you, we, or they.)

b) Circle the action words in the box below. Now fill in the blank spaces with action words from the box.

perform	chanting	fortunate	transforms	lies	covers
create	expands	approached	Creator	disciple	showed

1. One day, Nārada Muni ________________ Lord Brahmā and asked him some questions.
2. She only _____________ people who have a false ego thinking, "I am this body," and, "that belongs to me."
3. I see that you _____________ austerities and meditate. I wonder who you are meditating upon.
4. "I ____________ everything from this light, so actually everything I create really comes from Lord Kṛṣṇa.
5. Kṛṣṇa even _____________ me that I'm created by Him too.

6. Lord Brahmā explained how Lord Kṛṣṇa ___________ Himself into Mahā-Viṣṇu and _________down in the Causal Ocean.
7. This false ego __________________ into three ropes – goodness, passion and ignorance – that bind the soul to Mother Nature.

SEQUENCING

Given below are a few of the events that have happened in *Chapter 5: The Cause of All Causes.* They are all mixed up. Arrange them in the order mentioned in the summary of the chapter.

- Lord Brahmā explained how Lord Kṛṣṇa expands Himself into Mahā-Viṣṇu and lies down in the Causal Ocean.
- One day, Nārada Muni approached Lord Brahmā and asked him some questions.
- Happy to hear such a question, Lord Brahmā smiled.
- "My dear father Brahmā," began Nārada, "can you tell me about the soul and the Supersoul? And this world . . . how is it created and maintained? Who is in control?"
- "Yes," said Lord Brahmā, "I create everything from this light, so actually everything I create really comes from Lord Kṛṣṇa."
- First, she makes time – past, present and future, beginning, middle and end.

- Lord Śiva passes those spirit souls who would like to try and enjoy separate from Lord Kṛṣṇa his dear wife, Mother Nature.
- Now you see, Nārada, all of this needs to be made and put together before Mother Nature can make suitable bodies for the spirit souls. So once this was all assembled, the universes came into being.

- This false ego transforms into three ropes – goodness, passion and ignorance – that bind the soul to Mother Nature.
- She makes false ego, an important ingredient which helps the spirit soul to think, "I'm the most important," "this is mine," and, "this body is me."

YOUNGER KIDS' WORD SEARCH

C	A	U	E	S	R	E	D	N	O	W	W
M	E	R	G	E	R	N	A	T	R	E	A
E	S	A	R	U	A	E	R	A	B	D	T
M	L	E	T	T	E	R	I	N	T	G	T
B	A	U	S	A	C	G	R	A	T	E	E
R	F	A	T	R	A	Y	E	L	L	E	M
A	I	A	R	R	A	L	I	G	H	M	T
T	I	K	L	E	A	R	A	R	S	Y	E
U	E	S	U	A	C	N	I	S	Q	T	E
L	F	A	E	D	N	I	B	I	U	E	T
O	B	A	R	A	B	O	V	A	I	A	I
L	S	U	T	A	I	B	L	R	T	D	C
I	B	U	S	E	A	M	A	Z	E	A	X
S	R	I	A	S	S	R	E	M	E	S	E
E	A	D	H	A	P	O	W	E	R	I	A

WEB	
EDGE	
MERGE	
FUTURE	
AMAZE	
CAUSAL	

ENERGY	
BIND	
POWER	
SERVICE	
NATURE	
WONDER	

CAUSE	
FATE	
EXCITE	
FALSE	
QUITE	

OLDER KIDS' WORD SEARCH

A	N	T	I	C	I	P	A	T	E	A	G
V	E	R	N	O	G	E	N	E	C	E	L
H	K	A	T	N	E	M	E	V	O	M	A
C	O	N	T	R	O	L	P	A	M	A	N
A	S	S	E	N	B	L	M	A	P	H	C
O	U	A	S	M	B	A	R	T	E	S	E
R	I	N	E	S	I	T	O	U	T	A	A
P	A	S	N	N	E	A	F	T	E	S	T
P	S	I	T	T	P	A	S	S	I	O	N
A	U	A	H	R	C	B	N	E	E	D	E
O	I	N	U	S	T	U	A	M	A	H	S
N	E	A	S	S	A	R	R	A	B	M	E
H	T	N	E	T	R	A	T	T	F	O	R
T	S	E	L	B	A	T	I	U	S	D	P
I	N	G	R	E	D	I	E	N	T	N	N
S	I	N	G	Y	R	O	S	U	L	L	I

APPROACH	
ILLUSORY	
GLANCE	
CONTROL	
TRANSFORM	
SHAME	

MOVEMENT	
PASSION	
PRESENT	
INSTRUCT	
COMPETE	
ANTICIPATE	

ENTHUSE	
SUITABLE	
EMBARRASS	
ASSEMBLE	
INGREDIENT	
MAINTAIN	

STEPS OF MATERIAL CREATION

Directions: In the box below are the different steps of material creation as presented by Lord Brahmā in this chapter. Your task is to order them in the correct sequence. To do so, you will need to consult the chapter summary as well as refer to Śrīla Prabhupāda's translations and purports to Verses 25 through 30 for those steps that are not in the summary.

Mahā-Viṣṇu glances at Mother nature
Universes come into being
The Lord creates time, or kāla
The Lord creates the false ego
Lord Kṛṣṇa expands into Mahā-Viṣṇu
Air, with the subtle form of touch, is created.
Sky, with the subtle form of sound, is created
The Lord creates the three modes of material nature
Earth with the subtle form of smell is created
Mind is created from the mode of goodness
Water with the subtle form of taste is created
Fire with the subtle form of shape is created
The mahat-tattva is created, comprised of Mother Nature and the living entities
Mahā-Viṣṇu expands into each universe as Garbhodakaśāyī Viṣṇu

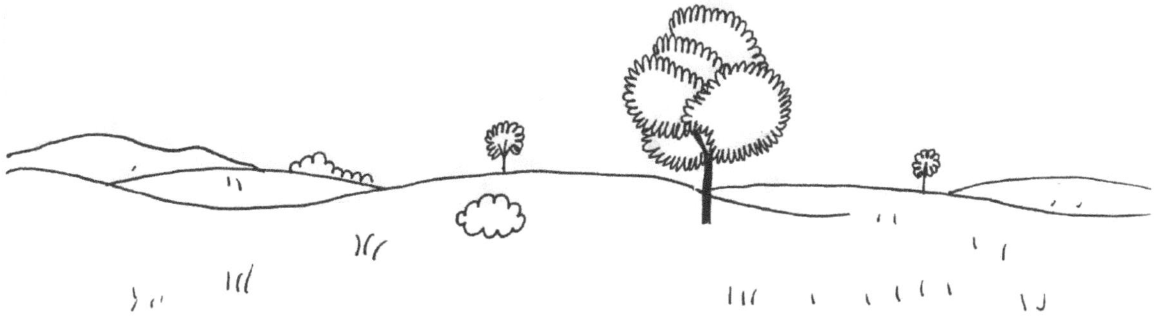

KṚṢṆA – THE SOURCE OF CREATION

Directions: Imagine your mother is preparing to cook your favorite cookies. She puts all the ingredients on the kitchen table and then leaves the room. What happens while she is gone? Do you think the ingredients on the table will magically mix themselves, roll into balls and get baked with no intervention? Probably not.

Just as it is not possible for dead matter to arrange, prepare and bake itself into perfect round cookies, same is the case with the material creation. Someone has to be in charge! Even though He distributes the responsibilities unto others, such as Lord Brahmā, it is Lord Kṛṣṇa who oversees the whole universal creation process.

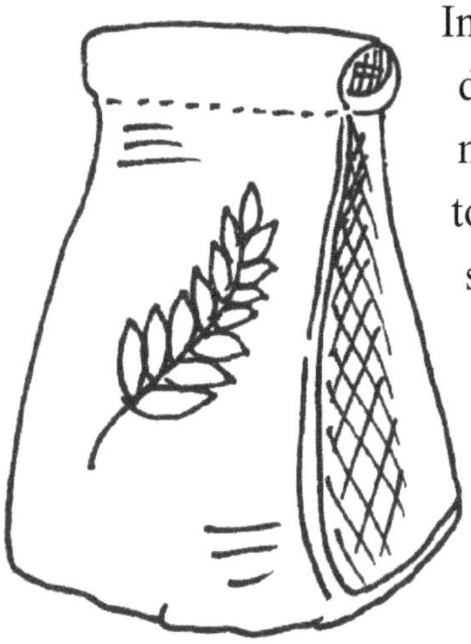

In this activity, you will be thinking about the different creations in the world. What are they made of? What is the purpose? Who puts it together? Where do the creative abilities and skills come from? Where do the raw materials come from? Take this opportunity to really contemplate the process of creation.

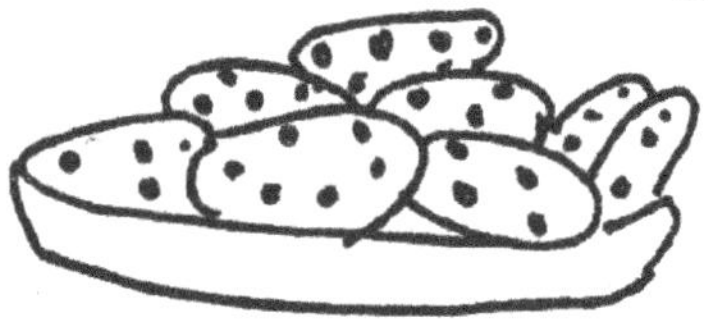

Here is an example.

Object	Purpose	Parts/Material	Secondary Creator
Bicycle	Transportation	Wheels, metal, spokes, seat, frame, wires, handlebars, connecting knobs.	Bicycle Designer and Manufacturer.
Primary Creator			
The Supreme Personality of Godhead, Lord Kṛṣṇa			

Now, think of four of your own examples and capture them in the charts below.

Object	**Purpose**	**Parts/Material**	**Secondary Creator**
Primary Creator			

Object	**Purpose**	**Parts/Material**	**Secondary Creator**
Primary Creator			

Object	**Purpose**	**Parts/Material**	**Secondary Creator**
Primary Creator			

Object	Purpose	Parts/Material	Secondary Creator
Primary Creator			

Reflection: What did you learn from this activity? In a written paragraph or two, share with your peers and family members what you learned and anything else you realized while completing this activity.

MISSING WORDS ACTIVITY SHEET

Directions: After reading the story summary, choose the correct word from the box below to complete the sentences.

Lord Brahmā	meditate	
brahmajyoti	Mother Nature	
Lord Kṛṣṇa	spider	ashamed
higher	the illusory lady	God

- Lord Brahmā said: "Now you see Nārada, all of this needs to be made and put together by the Lord before ________________can make suitable bodies for the spirit souls.
- Happy to hear such a question, ____________________smiled. Then hastily Nārada Muni added, "I'm just asking because I see that you perform austerities and __________________.
- "The__________________?" asked Nārada. "Yes," said Lord Brahmā. "I create everything from this light, so actually everything I create really comes from__________________.
- Like a _____________who creates a web all by himself, everything we know is created by you. But where do you come from? Do you really do this all by

yourself, or is there someone __________ than you?"

- "Oh I know her — ____________________," said Nārada Muni, "She is a devotee of Kṛṣṇa and feels _______________ that her job is to stop people seeing Kṛṣṇa. She makes them think that they're actually God or someone else is actually______."

THE MATERIAL PLANETARY SYSTEMS

Directions: In this activity, you will be researching the fourteen different planetary systems in our material universe – from the topmost Satyaloka to the lowest Pātālaloka. You can consult Vedabase.com or other resources to find information about these planetary systems. Remember to provide the reference for each bit of information you add to the table below. Feel free to do this on a separate sheet of paper or even a poster!

Planetary System	Description (with references)
Satyaloka	E.g.: Lord Brahmā's celestial abode where there is no birth, death, old age, and disease and is beyond the imagination of our minds (SB 5.1.21)
Tapoloka	
Janaloka	
Maharloka	
Svarloka	

Bhuvarloka	
Bhūrloka	
Atala	
Vitala	
Sutala	
Talātala	
Mahātala	
Rasātala	
Pātāla	

KEYWORDS

- Explain the meanings of the following keywords from the summary.
- Use each word in a sentence (either in oral or written form).
- Find at least one synonym and one antonym.
- Identify the word's part of speech (noun, verb, adjective, pronoun, or adverb).

Key Word *(part of speech)*	**Definition**	**Synonym & Antonym**
perform (______________)		**Syn.** **Ant.**
opportunity (______________)		**Syn.** **Ant.**
brahmajyoti (______________)		**Syn.** **Ant.**
quite (______________)		**Syn.** **Ant.**
merge (______________)		**Syn.** **Ant.**
competent (______________)		**Syn.** **Ant.**

Resource 1

Critical Thinking Activities
. . . to bring out the spiritual investigator in you!

CREATION OF THE ELEMENTS

Directions: Lord Brahma creates the entire universe and all its elements, beginning with False Ego. Read the chapter summary and identify the order in which elements are created. Now, record each element in the boxes on the right. In the corresponding box on the left, name the sense that was created at the same time. The first answer is already provided for you.

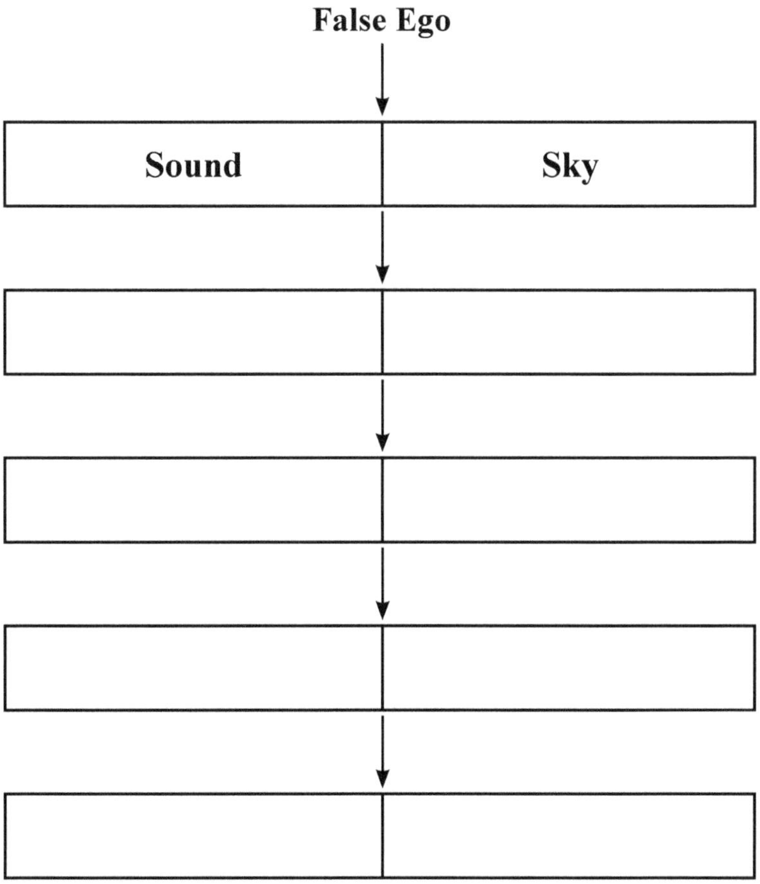

Bonus question: Can you list which body part was created for each element and sense above? As before, the first answer is provided below!

1. Sound / Sky : Ear
2. ______________________________
3. ______________________________
4. ______________________________
5. ______________________________

PLANETARY SYSTEMS AND LORD VIṢṆU'S FORM

Directions: According to verses 38 and 39 in this chapter, the upper, middle, and lower planetary systems are said to be situated on the universal form (virāṭ-rūpa) of Lord Viṣṇu. The diagram below is an artist's conception of the transcendental form of Lord Viṣṇu. Your task is to review the verses and purports in this chapter (especially verse 38 onwards) and annotate the diagram below with the names of the planetary systems from the topmost to the lowest. You may have to locate other resources or consult other devotees to complete the full list of the upper planetary systems.

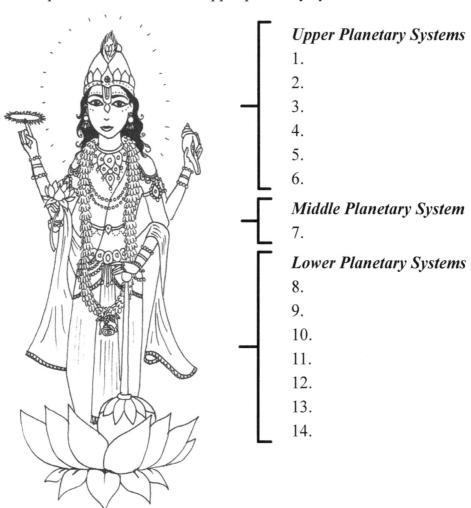

Upper Planetary Systems
1.
2.
3.
4.
5.
6.

Middle Planetary System
7.

Lower Planetary Systems
8.
9.
10.
11.
12.
13.
14.

THE VARṆAS AND LORD VIṢṆU'S FORM

Directions: As described in this chapter, the varṇa system is also represented within Lord Viṣṇu's universal form. Review the chapter and fill in the blanks showing the correct varṇa represented on the specific body part of Lord Viṣṇu.

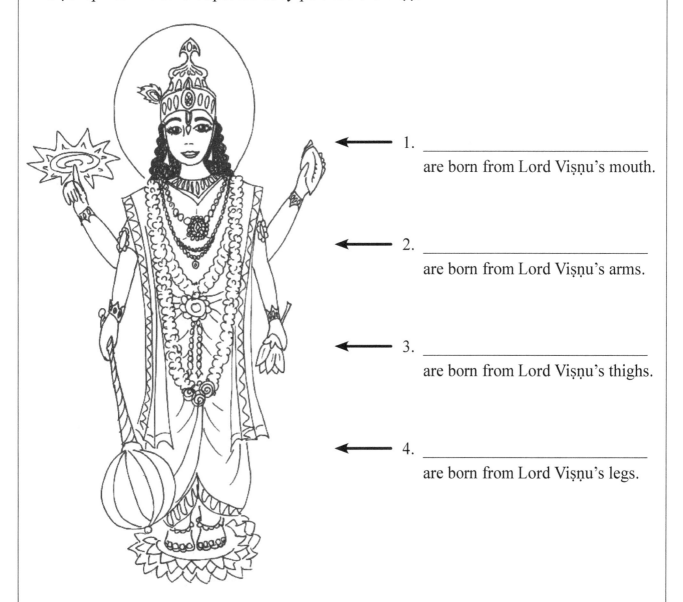

1. ______________________ are born from Lord Viṣṇu's mouth.

2. ______________________ are born from Lord Viṣṇu's arms.

3. ______________________ are born from Lord Viṣṇu's thighs.

4. ______________________ are born from Lord Viṣṇu's legs.

IN SEARCH OF EXTRATERRESTRIAL LIFE

Scientists send probes into outer space hoping to find life in other parts of our universe but they have not been successful. The Bhāgavatam, on the other hand, is full of descriptions of life existing all over the creation of the Lord.

Imagine you are going to meet a scientist who is studying extra-terrestrial life. Prepare notes to speak convincingly to him or her about extra-terrestrial life as mentioned in the Śrīmad Bhāgavatam. Use the following prompts as a guideline to prepare your notes:

- Scientists have sent probes to other planets to search for life. According to the Bhāgavatam, why have they not been successful?
- Scientists assume that life elsewhere in the universe will exist in the same manner as it does on earth (organic compounds), while the Bhāgavatam gives information that this is not always the case. Refer to SB 2.4.8 purport for a better understanding. You can also consult the first chapter of Śrīla Prabhupāda's book "Life Comes from Life".
- Explain an alternate way to understand things through the Śrīmad Bhāgavatam - hearing from authority, and why knowledge obtained this way can be trusted.

FAMOUS DISCOVERIES

In his purport to verse 17 of this chapter, Śrīla Prabhupāda says: "The Lord inspires the individual soul to create what is already created by the Lord, and by the good will of the Lord a discoverer of something in the world is accredited as the discoverer."
List a few famous discoveries in the table below.

Discovery	Discoverer

In your opinion, what factors determine who makes a discovery or invention and becomes famous for it? Is it purely a matter of chance?
Write an essay on a few of the discoveries you listed in the table above in light of the concept of primary and secondary creator that you learnt in this chapter.

THE MYSTICAL CREATOR

Śrīla Prabhupāda says in the purport to verse 11 that the Lord doesn't create like a blacksmith with hammer and instruments. In other words, He does not need to work personally to create the universe. Instead, He creates by His potencies or different energies.
Read that purport and understand the two examples Śrīla Prabhupāda gives to explain

this. Then fill in the table below with more such examples of a primary and secondary creator. Finally, fill in the last row with regard to the universal creation of the Lord.

Example	Primary source	Secondary creator	How the potency acts
Banyan tree	Seed created by the Lord.	Gardener who tends to the seed and plant.	Potency in the seed (a big tree, which is the Lord's creation) manifested by the efforts of the gardener.
Sun			
Your example 1			
Your example 2			
Lord's creation			

ANSWERS

Understanding the Story (pages 125-127)
1) a, 2) c, 3) b, 4) a, 5) b, 6) c, 7) a, 8) b, 9) c, 10) a, 11) a, 12) c, 12) a, 14) b, 15) a, 16) a, 17) c

Higher-Thinking Questions (pages 127-128)
Answer 9:

a) *mahat-tattva*, time, three qualities, activities
b) ether, air, fire, water, earth
c) *satyaloka, tapoloka, janaloka, maharloka, svarloka,bhuvārloka, bhuvarloka, atala, vitala, sutala, talātala, mahātala, rasātala, pātāla*

Answer 10:

a) Kāraṇodakaśāyī Viṣṇu
b) *Mahat-tattva*
c) Three qualities
d) Goodness and passion
e) Ignorance
f) Different activities of the modes
g) Sky and sound
h) Air and touch
i) Fire and shape
j) Water and taste
k) Earth and smell
l) Mind
m) Ten demigods controlling the bodily movements
n) Ear, skin, nose, eyes, tongue, mouth, hands, genitals, and the outlet for evacuating

Punctuation Practice (page 132)
Lord Brahmā explained how Lord Kṛṣṇa expands Himself into Mahā-Viṣṇu and lies down in the Causal Ocean. He glances over at Mother Nature and then expands into Lord Śiva. Lord Śiva passes those spirit souls who would like to try and enjoy separate from Lord Kṛṣṇa to his dear wife Mother Nature.

Together, Mother Nature and the spirit souls are called *mahat-tattva*. She then starts to make a material world where the spirit souls can try to enjoy without Lord Kṛṣṇa.

First she makes time – past, present and future, beginning, middle and end – as these don't exist in the spiritual world. She makes false ego, an important ingredient which helps the spirit soul to think, "I'm the most important," "this is mine," and, "this body is me." This false ego transforms into three ropes – goodness, passion and ignorance – that bind the soul to Mother Nature.

What do you think? (pages 132-133)

Set 1	Set 2
1. Correct	1. True
2. Incorrect	2. False
3. Incorrect	3. False
4. Correct	
5. Incorrect	
6. Correct	
7. Incorrect	
8. Correct	
9. Correct	

Action Activity Sheet (pages 133-134)

1. approached
2. covers
3. perform
4. create
5. showed
6. expands, lies
7. transforms

Sequencing (page 134)

- One day, Nārada Muni approached Lord Brahmā and asked him some questions.
- "My dear father Brahmā," began Nārada, "can you tell me about the soul and the Supersoul? And this world . . . how is it created and maintained? Who is in control?"
- Happy to hear such a question, Lord Brahmā smiled.
- "Yes," said Lord Brahmā, "I create everything from this light, so actually everything I create really comes from Lord Kṛṣṇa."
- Lord Brahmā explained how Lord Kṛṣṇa expands Himself into Mahā-Viṣṇu and lies down in the Causal Ocean.
- Lord Śiva passes those spirit souls who would like to try and enjoy separate from Lord Kṛṣṇa to his dear wife, Mother Nature.
- First, she makes time – past, present and future, beginning, middle and end,

- She makes false ego, an important ingredient which helps the spirit soul to think, "I'm the most important," "this is mine," and, "this body is me."
- This false ego transforms into three ropes – goodness, passion and ignorance – that bind the soul to Mother Nature.
- Now you see, Nārada, all of this needs to be made and put together before Mother Nature can make suitable bodies for the spirit souls. So once this was all assembled, the universes came into being.

Younger Kids' Word Search (page 135)

					R	E	D	N	O	W	W
M	E	R	G	E	R	N				E	
	S			U		E			B	D	
	L		T			R				G	
	A	U				G				E	
	F					Y				C	
						L				E	
				E			A				
	E	S	U	A	C			S	Q		E
	F			D	N	I	B		U		T
		A		A			V		I	A	I
			T					R	T		C
		U	S	E	A	M	A	Z	E		X
	R									S	E
E					P	O	W	E	R		

Older Kids' Word Search (page 136)

A	N	T	I	C	I	P	A	T	E		G
									C	E	L
H			T	N	E	M	E	V	O	M	A
C	O	N	T	R	O	L			M	A	N
A					B		M		P	H	C
O				M		A	R		E	S	E
R			E		I		O		T		
P		S	N	N			F		E		T
P	S		T	T	P	A	S	S	I	O	N
A		A	H		C		N				E
	I		U			U	A				S
N			S	S	A	R	R	A	B	M	E
			E				T	T			R
		E	L	B	A	T	I	U	S		P
I	N	G	R	E	D	I	E	N	T	N	
				Y	R	O	S	U	L	L	I

Steps of Material Creation (page 137)

1. Lord Kṛṣṇa expands into Mahā-Viṣṇu
2. Mahā-Viṣṇu glances at Mother nature
3. The mahat-tattva is created, which is comprised of Mother Nature and the living entities.
4. The Lord creates time, or kalā.
5. The Lord creates the false ego.
6. The Lord creates the three modes of material nature.
7. Universes come into being.
8. Mahā-Viṣṇu expands into each universe as Garbhodakaśāyī Viṣṇu.
9. Sky, with the subtle form of sound, is created.
10. Air, with the subtle form of touch, is created.
11. Fire, with the subtle form of shape, is created.
12. Water, with the subtle form of taste, is created.
13. Earth, with the subtle form of smell, is created.
14. Mind is created from the mode of goodness.

Missing Words Activity Sheet (pages 140-141)

- Lord Brahmā said: "Now you see Nārada, all of this needs to be made and put together by the Lord before Mother Nature can make suitable bodies for the spirit souls.
- Happy to hear such a question, Lord Brahmā smiled. Then hastily Nārada Muni added, "I'm just asking because I see that you perform austerities and meditate
- "The brahmajyoti?" asked Nārada. "Yes," said Lord Brahmā. "I create everything from this light, so actually everything I create really comes from Lord Kṛṣṇa
- Like a spider who creates a web all by himself, everything we know is created by you. But where do you come from? Do you really do this all by yourself, or is there someone higher than you?"
- "Oh I know her — the illusory lady," said Nārada Muni, "She is a devotee of Kṛṣṇa and feels ashamed that her job is to stop people seeing Kṛṣṇa. She makes them think that they're actually God or someone else is actually God."

Keywords (page 143)

Key Word *(part of speech)*	**Definition**	**Synonym & Antonym**
perform (verb)	a. to carry out, accomplish, or fulfill (an action, task, or function). b. to present to an audience.	**Syn.** execute, operate, implement. **Ant.** abstain, destroy, discontinue
opportunity (noun)	a. a set of circumstances that makes it possible to do something. b. a good chance for advancement or progress.	**Syn.** event, connection, contingency. **Ant.** closing, misfortune, bad luck.
brahmajyoti (noun)	a. the spiritual sky. b. the Supreme Lord's personal bodily effulgence.	**Syn.** divine effulgence, divine light **Ant.** darkness, ignorance
quite (adverb)	a. to a certain or fairly significant extent or degree. b. to an extreme.	**Syn.** fairly, absolutely, truly. **Ant.** doubtfully, incompletely.
merge (verb)	a. to blend gradually by stages that blur distinctions. b. to become combined into.	**Syn.** blend, combine, incorporate. **Ant.** disconnect, disjoin, divide.
competent (adjective)	a. having requisite or adequate ability or qualities. b. having the capacity to function or develop in a particular way; specifically.	**Syn.** adequate, capable, proficient. **Ant.** impotent, incapable, unqualified.

Creation of the Elements (page 145)

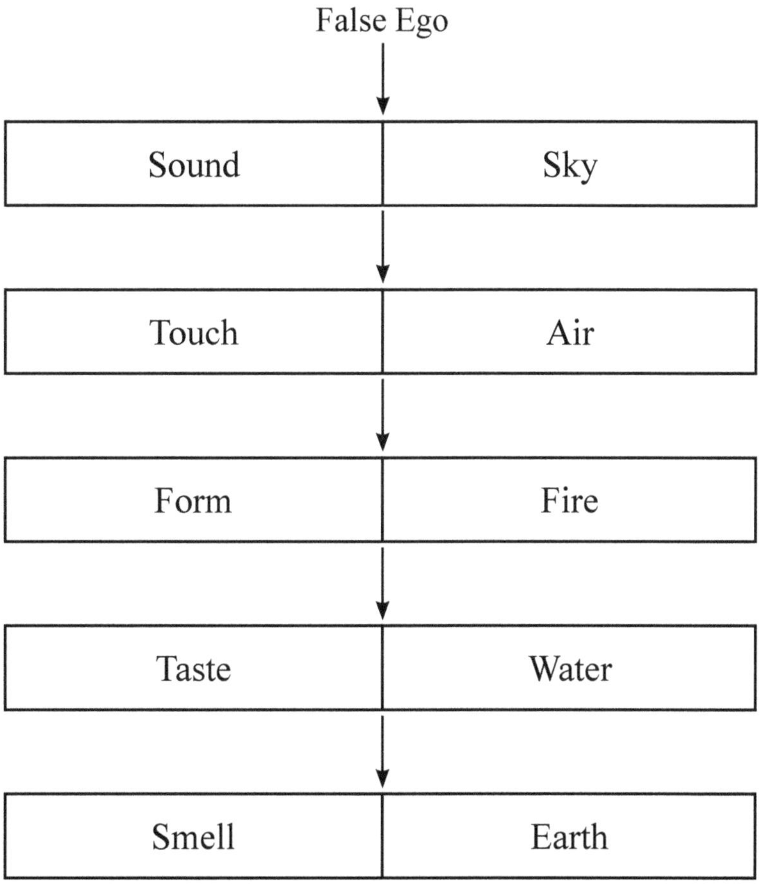

1. Sound / Sky : **Ear**
2. Touch / Air : **Skin**
3. Form / Fire : **Eyes**
4. Taste / Water : **Tongue**
5. Smell / Earth : **Nose**

Planetary Systems and Lord Viṣṇu's form (page 146)

Upper Planetary Systems
1. Satyaloka (Brahmaloka)
2. Tapoloka
3. Janaloka
4. Maharloka
5. Svarloka
6. Bhuvarloka

Middle Planetary System
7. Bhūrloka (Earth)

Lower Planetary Systems
8. Atala
9. Vitala
10. Sutala
11. Talātala
12. Mahātala
13. Rasātala
14. Pātāla

6

Puruṣa-sūkta Confirmed

Story Summary

Nārada Muni's eyes widened in excitement. He felt like a curious explorer unexpectedly finding hidden treasure. Until now, his father was the Supreme. Or so he thought. But his nagging sentiment that something – or someone – was higher, was now confirmed. His father Lord Brahmā had not only confirmed this, but was about to describe how everything in this material world was created by this higher being who was actually the Lord Himself! He braced himself to hear about the universal form of the Lord. Seeing his son's eagerness, Lord Brahmā smiled. Feeling encouraged, he closed his eyes, and meditating on the face of the Lord's universal form, began to describe the unimaginable.

"All the voices you hear in this world – from the chattering of the humans, the mooing of the cows, to the croaking of frogs – all come from the mouth of the Lord's universal body. The beautiful hymns . . ."

"Such as the Gāyatrī?"

Brahmā smiled at the attentiveness of his son.

"Yes. These beautiful hymns and mantras come from the seven layers of skin of the Lord, and His tongue produces all the tasty foodstuffs in this world."

Nārada tried extremely hard to see how the frothy milk from the cows, the sweet honey from the bees and the rice grains used for offering to the demigods, forefathers, and as eatables for people – all came from the Supreme Lord's own tongue!

"As we breathe in and out," continued Lord Brahmā, "these airs come from the nostrils of the Lord, and as our Lord smells, the herbs that people use to heal themselves are produced. All the various beautiful fragrances we can smell in this world . . ."

"Like the musk from the musk deer?"

"Yes."

"And lavender from the lavender plant?"

"Yes."

"And jasmine from the jasmine flower?"

"Yes, yes, yes!" laughed Lord Brahmā heartily as he watched his son's mind reel with enthusiasm at connecting his experiences to the Lord. "All these beautiful fragrances come from our Lord's breathing."

Nārada closed his eyes in gratitude and inhaled deeply, feeling the cool air enter his own nostrils and slowly fill his lungs. "This air. . ." he thought. "This air comes from a Lord higher than my own father; from His very own nostrils. The sweet scent I smell in the air comes from the breath of this Lord . . . of my Lord."

Exhaling, he smiled and opened his eyes again. Knowing this, how could anyone forget the Lord when He is present everywhere for us in His universal body?

Acknowledging his son's appreciation for the Supreme, Nārada's father continued to describe various features of this Supreme Lord:

From His eyes come all the forms
that one may see,

His hearing brings the skies
and the various melodies

Our sense of touch comes from His skin,

His bodily hairs are trees on Him,

The hairs on His head are the clouds in the sky.

His nails give us iron, stones, electricity

The warriors from His arms
fight all the duplicity

Take shelter in His steps forward

At His lotus feet we are no cowards

His genitals give us water, semen,

rains and children.

His evacuating outlet is death – it's deadly

His rectum is a place of misfortune,
hell and envy,

His back is where frustration lies,

Immorality within it's ties

. . . and downright dark, dark, dark ignorance.

His veins are the rivers

and His bones the mountains

His impersonal feature is the vast oceans

His belly is where the dead do rest

His heart is where the ghosts like to nest

. . . and His consciousness is where
dharma likes to dwell.

Lord Brahmā stopped. He looked at his son smiling. He could see something was troubling Nārada.

"Father, thank you." Nārada began hesitatingly. "So . . . there isn't an actual person higher than you. Our Lord is a large energy as big as the universe that produces everything in this world."

Nārada's voice wavered in disappointment. The hope of meeting his Lord and master face-to-face was dwindling. There was no such person. His Lord and master was an impersonal energy that produced everything in this world.

Lord Brahmā laughed. He was very pleased to see his son's expectation of the

Supreme Lord to be more than the universal form.

"O Nārada," he began, "as His gigantic universal body, our Lord covers everyone and everything in the material world – from me Lord Brahmā, to you and Lord Śiva down to the smallest ant. Yet . . ."

Lord Brahmā paused. Nārada hung onto his every word. Was there more to this Lord than His huge universal body?

"Yet?" prodded Nārada.

"Yet He remains only nine inches tall and always remains spiritual."

Nārada looked confused. So was the Lord as big as the universe or as small as nine inches? How can He be both?

"Imagine the sun," started Lord Brahmā, noticing his son's bewilderment. "The sun globe is a big ball of illuminating energy. It shines inwards and outwards. Our Lord's universal form is just like the heat and sun rays of the sun . . ."

"So is the sun globe like the small form of the Lord? The form that's only nine inches tall?"

"Yes, my son. His small form is known as the Supersoul."

Brahmā paused for a moment.

"You know Nārada, It's actually impossible to measure the full extent of our Lord's glories. All the material world, including the living entities who are attached to family life and the opulences all come from just a quarter of the Lord's energy. The rest of His energy is the spiritual world. This is a place far beyond the material world. A place where no one gets old or sick or dies. In the spiritual world, no one has anything to be worried or frightened about. The truth is, Our Lord is in charge of everything – everything material and everything spiritual."

"But father . . . ," Nārada interjected, "I see you create everything with your own powers and your own materials. Have I missed something?"

Brahmā chuckled. "O Nārada, I was born from a lotus flower that grew from the navel of Lord Mahā-Viṣṇu. At that time, there was nothing around me but darkness. There was no one except me and the body of Mahā-Viṣṇu. At that time, I just wanted to worship Him and perform sacrifices to please Him. But what could I do? I had nothing."

"So what did you do?"

"Well, everything I needed to perform the sacrifice I got from the Lord Himself – from different parts of His body to be exact. I created flowers, leaves, straw, a suitable time, utensils, grains, clarified butter, four priests, and so many other necessary things. In this way, I performed a sacrifice to the Lord by using the Lord.

"Thereafter, your nine brothers and other great personalities also performed sacrifices for the pleasure of the Lord."

Nārada shook his head in disbelief. All this time he'd truly believed his father, creator Lord Brahmā to be the Supreme Lord. Now Brahmā himself had revealed the supremacy of Lord Viṣṇu. His heart brimmed with exhilaration.

"So you see everything in this world

actually comes from Lord Viṣṇu. Yes I am the creator, Lord Śiva is the destroyer and Lord Viṣṇu maintains the material creation . . . but actually He is the main controller of all three."

Lord Brahmā wanted to ensure his son understood as much as he understood himself.

"So here's your answer," He continued with clarity. "The Supreme Lord is actually the cause of everything that happens. It is only because I very enthusiastically hold onto His lotus feet that what I do and say is perfect. Yes I am powerful, but even I cannot fully understand our Lord. Therefore, the only choice is to surrender to Him. Nārada, even He Himself can't estimate His own limits!

"Because you, me, Lord Śiva, and all living entities, are under the Supreme Lord's material energy, we are all bewildered and can only see this world according to our own limited abilities. So let us offer obeisances to Him whose glories we chant even if He can't be fully understood."

"Who is He?" asked Nārada. "Who is the original Supreme Personality of Godhead?"

"The original Supreme Personality of Godhead," answered his father, "is Lord Kṛṣṇa. He expands into Mahā-Viṣṇu who creates the material world in Himself and then absorbs it all again – yet He remains free from all contaminations. Any power, opulence or greatness you see in this world is only a tiny fragment of the wonders of Lord Kṛṣṇa!"

How was Nārada ever going to meet this person? It seemed as impossible as knowing His universal form.

"There is a way one can know Him," said Brahmā guessing his son's anxious thoughts.

"By travelling down your lotus stem to His navel?" ventured the sage.

"No."

"By flying to the spiritual world?"

"No."

Nārada was truly perplexed. When not even great demigods like his father Lord Brahmā or Lord Śiva could know Him fully, was there really a way for Nārada to know Him?

Nārada heaved a sigh. Although he still faced his father, his slouching back and morose expression hinted at the fading of any hope of actually finding his Lord Kṛṣṇa.

"Listen Nārada," said Brahmā sternly. "It can be done."

"But how?" asked Nārada hopelessly.

"You must be imbued with two important qualities. First, one must be free from the desire for anything material and secondly, one must not be disturbed by his senses."

"Impossible," retorted Nārada.

"Very much possible!" challenged Brahmā brightly. "O Nārada, now I will narrate to you the pastimes of the incarnations of Kṛṣṇa. These pastimes are always in my heart because they are very pleasing. Drink the nectar of this narration my son, because it will dry up the desire to hear other topics."

Thus, not only had Lord Brahmā given his son the formula of hearing about Kṛṣṇa's pastimes as the secret to attaining such qualities, he was also ready to start chanting the Lord's pastimes to begin the cleansing process! The son of Brahmā, Śrī Nārada was most fortunate indeed.

Key Messages

- Look them up in your *Śrīmad-Bhāgavatam.*
- Put them in your own words to help you memorize them.
- Discuss each one further.
- Apply them in your life.

Theme	References	Key Messages
Kṛṣṇa is never formless	2.6.1–12	Different parts of the Lord's universal form are the generating centers for various potencies, demigods, and qualities. The form of the Lord is different from ordinary mundane forms but even in His transcendental form, the Lord has voice, eyes, tongue, skin, etc. He is never a formless void.
Devotional service purifies our senses	2.6.1	All of our senses originate from the Lord's reservoir of senses. Therefore, we can achieve perfection of life by dedicating our senses to the loving devotional service of the Lord who is their creator and master. Devotional service alone purifies the sensual activities of the material world.
Taking exclusive shelter of Kṛṣṇa's lotus feet	2.6.7	Absolute dependence on the lotus feet of the Lord is called pure devotional service. His lotus feet grant fearlessness and all the needs of our life. Everything in creation, including demigods, is completely dependent on Lord Kṛṣṇa. Hence, it is not necessary to seek the shelter of anyone except the Supreme Lord Kṛṣṇa.
The importance of sacrifice	2.6.28	Sacrifice means dedicating our interests to satisfy someone else. We are all engaged in sacrifice for our family, friends, society, or nation. However, sacrifice becomes perfect when it is for the Supreme Lord who owns everything, is the friend of everyone, and is also the supplier of the ingredients for sacrifice!
The secret of Lord Brahmā's perfection	2.6.34	Lord Brahmā is perfect because he is a great devotee of Kṛṣṇa. Similarly, devotees engage their senses in devotional service of the Lord, and therefore their senses are not tempted by material enjoyment. If you are serious about being in touch with Kṛṣṇa in devotional service, your words and action will be perfect. A grain of devotion is more valuable than tons of faithlessness.
The only way to know Kṛṣṇa	2.6.35	Qualifications such as vast learning in the Vedic wisdom, mystic powers, self-realization, etc., are not enough for one who wants to know the Supreme Lord. The Lord can be known only by the sincere mood of eagerness for service, and not by any amount of material qualification.

Understanding the Story

Now it's time for you to check how well you understood the story by answering these multiple-choice questions. (Answers at the end of the chapter.)

1. Why was Nārada Muni bewildered?
   a) He saw darkness all around him even though Lord Brahmā had created the sun and moon.
   b) He thought Lord Brahmā was the Supreme but when he saw Lord Brahmā worshipped someone else, he wondered who was superior to him.
   c) Nārada Muni knew in his heart that Kṛṣṇa was the Supreme but he was puzzled when Lord Brahmā told him that he was the Supreme as he had created everything.
2. What did Nārada Muni inquire from his father, Lord Brahmā?
   a) He inquired about how the material world is created and maintained.
   b) He wanted to know why Lord Brahmā made a false claim that he was the Supreme.
   c) He asked how he can enjoy in the material world.
3. How did Lord Brahmā react to Nārada Muni's question?
   a) He feared that Nārada Muni will discover that he is not the Supreme.
   b) He ignored Nārada Muni's question as he was in deep meditation.
   c) He was overjoyed at the opportunity to glorify Kṛṣṇa as the Supreme Personality of Godhead.
4. Which form of Kṛṣṇa did Lord Brahmā start to describe to answer Nārada Muni's question?
   a) The Supreme Lord's universal form (*virāṭ-puruṣa*).
   b) Kṛṣṇa's original form as a two-handed blue-complexioned boy holding a flute.
   c) His form as Lord Rāma.
5. What is the purpose of Kṛṣṇa's universal form?
   a) It destroys the demons using magical powers.
   b) The body of this form provides everything needed for creation such as wind, clouds, plants, electricity, and our senses.
   c) It gives protection to the demigods so they can create and maintain the material world.
6. How big is the Lord's personal Paramātmā form that supports the entire creation?
   a) It is unlimited in size.
   b) Nine inches tall.
   c) 5,000 inches tall.
7. How big is the material creation compared to the spiritual world?

a) They are both similar in size.
b) The material world is much bigger than the spiritual world, being three fourths and one fourth respectively.
c) The material world is much smaller than the spiritual world, being one fourth and three fourths respectively.

8. Who is Mahā-Viṣṇu?
   a) He is Lord Brahmā's son who helps him with the creation of the material world.
   b) He is an expansion of Kṛṣṇa and runs the material world just like a principal runs a school for the government.
   c) He is Nārada Muni's son and travels all the universes singing glories of the Lord.
9. How was Lord Brahmā born?
   a) Lord Brahmā was born from the lotus flower that grew from the navel of Mahā-Viṣṇu.
   b) Lord Brahmā is eternal like Kṛṣṇa, so he was never born.
   c) Lord Brahmā was born from the darkness of night.
10. What was wonderful about Lord Brahmā's worship of Mahā-Viṣṇu after he was born?
   a) He was able to invoke all the demigods so they could glorify the Lord.
   b) He killed all the demons and offered their bodies to the Lord.
   c) He created all the articles of worship from the Lord's body and used it in His service.

Higher-Thinking Questions

Now it's time to deepen your understanding of Chapter 6 by delving into Śrīla Prabhupāda's purports for this chapter and reflecting upon the following questions.

1. Why is the Supreme Lord pleased by sacrifices when all the ingredients for such sacrifice are ultimately part of His universal form? If someone comes into your house, takes one of your possessions and offers it back to you, will you be pleased? Is this a fair comparison? If not, why not?
2. If you woke up to find yourself in complete darkness with absolutely no one else nearby, what would your reaction be and why? Compare your reaction to that of Lord Brahmā's as described in this chapter.
3. Why does Lord Brahmā provide such a detailed description of the anatomy and physiology of the universal form of the Lord? (Hint: Read the purport for *Śrīmad-Bhāgavatam* 2.6.10)

4. Is the *virāṭ-rūpa* just a product of imagination to help those who cannot understand Kṛṣṇa, or is it real? Does the Supreme Lord actually have a material universal form with a head, arms, legs, etc.?
5. If the Supreme Lord cannot be known or understood even by Lord Brahmā, Lord Śiva, and the demigods, what is the use of us performing devotional service in this human form of life which is much more insignificant compared to that of the demigods?
6. In the *Bhagavad-gītā* (Bg 15.15), Kṛṣṇa says *vedaiś ca sarvair aham eva vedyaḥ* – "By all the *Vedas*, I am to be known." Lord Brahmā is perfect in Vedic wisdom, but he still says that he is unable to understand the Supreme Lord. Why?

ACTIVITIES

In this section you will find many exciting things to do! They will get you thinking, moving, drawing, acting, and most importantly, having loads of fun!

Artistic Activities
. . . to reveal your creativity!

SENSE OF TOUCH

Description: Create a touch-and-feel collage to demonstrate how the Lord's skin is the generating center for all kinds of sensations of touch, and is the place for performing all kinds of sacrifice. (See **Resource 1** for an example.)

You will need: Card, pen, glue, bits and bobs.

Steps:

1. Draw around your hand five times.
2. Find five objects with different textures that could be glued to your different hands.
3. Stick the bits and bobs on the hands using glue. Make each hand a different texture, such as rough, spiky, smooth, etc.
4. Discuss the variety of textures on each hand.

A FRAGRANT PICTURE

Description: The Lord's breathing energies produce different fragrances. Create a scratch and sniff picture using beautiful scents to demonstrate this practically.

You will need: Scents – essential oils/food essences/perfume, PVA glue, acrylic or poster paint, card.

Steps:

1. Draw a picture of your choice and paint it, but leave the part of the picture you want to scent until Step 2.

2. For the scratch and sniff part, mix your desired color with some glue and carefully add some scent to it. For example, you could mix some red paint with strawberry essence, or purple paint with lavender oil, or blue with some perfume to paint Lord Kṛṣṇa's lotus feet. Remember, you only need a drop of scent as it can be very strong.
3. Once you have finished your painting, let it dry before you gently scratch and sniff your picture.

Critical Thinking Activities

. . . to bring out the spiritual investigator in you!

NARRATIONS IN ŚRĪMAD-BHĀGAVATAM

Description: In the purport to verse 2.6.46, Śrīla Prabhupāda says, "People who take interest in hearing *Śrīmad-Bhāgavatam* clear their heart of accumulated mundane filth."

Consider the following statement and share your thoughts on this with an adult: *Śrīmad-Bhāgavatam* gives detailed descriptions of Kṛṣṇa's names, form, qualities, activities, spiritual planets, incarnations, His devotees etc. The more we hear and understand about the nature of Kṛṣṇa and His devotees, the more we get attracted towards them. Based on your own study of *Śrīmad-Bhāgavatam*, answer the following:

- Do you relish hearing about Kṛṣṇa?
- Do narrations from the *Bhāgavatam* increase your material desires or spiritual desires?
- What are some of the names of Kṛṣṇa you have come across so far?
- What are the different incarnations mentioned in the third chapter of Canto 1?
- What qualities of Kṛṣṇa attract you the most?
- How would you describe the love of Kṛṣṇa's devotees like Queen Kuntī and the residents of Dvārakā?
- Narrate your favorite pastime which revealed Kṛṣṇa's opulence? (For example, Kṛṣṇa saving Mahārāja Parīkṣit)
- Can you name some qualities of the devotees of Kṛṣṇa?

LORD'S FORM DEBATE

Description: Some people claim that God is impersonal. How can you prove that He is not impersonal and that He in fact has a beautiful form?

Set up a debate. This activity can be done in pairs or in a group. One side will support the impersonal form and the other will argue against. Both sides will have to do some research to prove their argument. You may also take help from translations and purports of this chapter to collect some strong points.

Example: For the side debating for the personal form: "In any case, He – The Supreme Personality of Godhead – is never a formless void." (SB 2.6.10 purport)
The debate can be structured like this:

1. The first team should speak for 5–7 minutes, introducing their arguments.
2. The second team then presents their arguments, speaking for 5–7 minutes.
3. Both teams take three minutes to confer.
4. The first team begins the rebuttals with three minutes to speak.
5. The second team takes their opportunity for rebuttals, also for three minutes.

YAJÑA

Description: It is your job to research and find out what a *yajña* is. Also find out:

- Different kinds of *yajñas* that were performed in Vedic culture, and why they were performed.
- What ingredients are needed to perform these *yajñas*?
- What kind of mantras are usually chanted during these *yajñas*?
- Who is the beneficiary of these *yajñas*?

THE NATURE OF MATERIAL HAPPINESS

Description: Śrīla Prabhupāda describes the nature of material happiness as transient, meaning temporary. Can you think of a time when you were really happy because you received a material thing that you really wanted? Maybe you were given a new toy or game, a vacation, or something else. Now think about how you felt in the days following that. Make a graph of the level of your happiness, tracking the levels of intensity of your feelings for the event, starting from the day you felt most happy to now. Has the intensity of happiness increased, decreased or remained the same? From your analysis, what conclusion do you come to? Is it the same as the scriptures? Is material happiness permanent?

Theatrical Activities
. . . to bring out the actor in you!

VERSE MIME

Description: Choreograph a mime based on *Śrīmad-Bhāgavatam* verses 2.6.1–11. Miming involves using your facial expressions, arms, hands and whole body to communicate.

Play some background music or have someone read the verses. You can even set up a simple stage and wear a costume or mask if you like.

Research more about miming and use a mirror to practice getting your technique perfect. Then perform your mime to an audience.

Writing Activities . . . to bring out the writer in you!

PUNCTUATION PRACTICE

Description: The following passage is from the Story Summary, but someone forgot to punctuate it! Edit it, using punctuation marks: periods, commas, apostrophes, and quotation marks. Add capital letters. Check your answer against the edited version in the answer section.

o Nārada i was born from a lotus flower that grew from the navel of lord maha-Viṣṇu at that time there was nothing around me but darkness there was no one except me and the body of maha-Viṣṇu i just wanted to worship him and perform sacrifices to please him but what could i do i had nothing

so what did you do

well everything i needed to perform the sacrifice i got from the lord himself from different parts of his body to be exact i created flowers leaves straw a suitable time utensils grains clarified butter four priests and so many other necessary things in this way i performed a sacrifice to the lord by using the lord

thereafter your nine brothers and other great personalities also performed sacrifices for the pleasure of the lord

MISSING WORDS

Directions: After reading the Story Summary, choose the correct word(s) from the selection below to complete each sentence.

flowers	bewilderment	tongue	arms
fragrance	dwindling	explorer	clarified butter
original	illuminating	deer	wavered

1. Nārada's voice ______________ in disappointment. The hope of meeting his Lord and master face to face was ______________________.
2. "Imagine the sun," started Lord Brahmā, noticing his son's ______________________. "The sun globe is a big ball of ______________________ energy."
3. I created ______________, leaves, straw, a suitable time, utensils, grains, ____________________________, four priests, and so many other necessary things.
4. "Who is He?" asked Nārada. "Who is the __________________ Supreme Personality of Godhead?"
5. He felt like a curious ____________________ unexpectedly finding hidden treasure.
6. "These beautiful hymns and mantras come from the seven layers of skin of the Lord, and His ______________ produces all the tasty foodstuffs in this world."
7. "Like the _________ from the musk __________?"
8. The warriors from His ______ fight all the duplicity.

SEQUENCING

Description: Given below are a few of the events that have happened in Chapter 6. They are all mixed up. Arrange them in the order mentioned in the summary of the chapter.

1. It is only because I very enthusiastically hold onto His lotus feet that what I do and say is perfect.
2. All the material world, including the living entities who are attached to family life and the opulences all come from just a quarter of the Lord's energy.
3. Seeing his son's eagerness, Lord Brahmā smiled.
4. The sun globe is a big ball of illuminating energy. It shines inwards and outwards.

5. When not even great demigods like his father Lord Brahmā or Lord Śiva could know Him fully, was there really a way for Nārada to know Him?
6. Nārada closed his eyes in gratitude and inhaled deeply, feeling the cool air enter his own nostrils and slowly fill his lungs.
7. I created flowers, leaves, straw, a suitable time, utensils, grains, clarified butter, four priests, and so many other necessary things.
8. These airs come from the nostrils of the Lord, and as our Lord smells, the herbs that people use to heal themselves are produced.
9. His Lord and master was an impersonal energy that produced everything in this world.
10. Drink the nectar of this narration my son, because it will dry up the desire to hear other topics.

NEWS REPORT

Description: Write a news report about when Nārada Muni discovered that it is Lord Kṛṣṇa who is the original Supreme Creator and cause of all causes, and not his father Lord Brahmā. How did Nārada Muni feel about this news and how did it influence his perspective? First, read a few short news articles from *ISKCON News, Back to Godhead*, or a daily newspaper to become familiar with some of the language techniques that news reporters use in their writing (see below). Then use the "News Story – Writing Draft" section below to help you plan your report before you start writing. Let your creativity flow!

News Report – Features of News Articles

While you are reading a news article, see if you can identify the following features:

- An opening paragraph that provides information of the "Five W's": what, where, when, why, and who – and how.
- A catchy headline.
- A quote by someone involved in the story, or a witness.
- The article is written in the past tense.
- Powerful words are used to portray action.
- A photo is included with a caption.

News Story – Writing Draft

Use this writing draft to help you plan your news story. Then write a news story based on this draft.

1. List the main events in the story:____

   ____
2. Create a headline for your story:____
3. Write a quotation from someone in the story, or from a witness to an event in the story: ____
4. List the "5 W's"

   Who:____

   What:____

   Where:____

   When:____

   How:____
5. Draw a picture (this will be your photo) to capture the main event. Include a caption Sketch an idea below to recopy in final form with the news story:

SPELLING ERRORS

Description: There are one or more spelling mistakes in each of the following sentences. Write the correct spelling of each word in the space provided.

But his nagging sentement that something or someone was higher, was now confirmed. ____________________

All these beautiful fragrences come from our Lord's breathing. _________________

Nārada's father, acknowleding his son's appreciation for the Supreme, continued to discribe various features of this Supreme Lord. ____________________________

I see you create everything with your own powers and your own materiels.

____

I created flowers, leafs, straw, a suitable time, utensils, grains, claryfied butter, four priests, and so many other necessary things.____________________________

So let us offer obesances to Him whose glories we chant even if He can't be fully understood.______________________

WHAT DO YOU THINK?

Set 1: Tick those statements that you think are correct.

1. Nārada Muni had accepted his father, Lord Brahmā, as the Supreme because of his wonderful acts in creation.
2. Lord Brahmā glorified himself as the Supreme Personality of Godhead and described the process of material creation.
3. Our sense of touch comes from His eyes, His bodily hairs are trees on Him.
4. Lord Brahmā began, "O Nārada, as His gigantic universal body, our Lord covers everyone and everything in the material world from me Lord Brahmā, to you and Lord Śiva down to the smallest Ant."
5. All the material world, including the living entities who are attached to family life and the opulences all come from three-fourths of the Lord's energy.
6. This whole universe is situated in the Supreme Lord Brahmā.
7. Lord Brahmā simply surrenders to the Supreme Lord's lotus feet and begs to be delivered from the miseries of repeated birth and death.
8. Lord Viṣṇu is the master of everything in this material creation – the modes of nature, eternal time, mind, elements, the material ego, and all living entities.

Set 2: Inferring questions. Using what the author says and what you know, which of the following statements do you agree with or disagree with? Back up your

argument with reasons.

1. Whatever Lord Brahmā says has never been proved false because he is expert in all Vedic knowledge and has performed opulent sacrifices for Lord Viṣṇu.
2. In the material world, in His eternal form of Viṣṇu, the Supreme Lord maintains and controls all the affairs of the demigods, including Brahmā and Śiva.
3. The Supreme Lord expands Himself in the form of the *virāṭ-rūpa* because He has great attachment for the material universe, which is one fourth of His energies.

WORD JUMBLE

Description: The following words and phrases are from the Story Summary, but they are all jumbled up. Unjumble them. (The answers can be found in this chapter's Answers section).

JUMBLED	UNJUMBLED
EERAVNDL	
IHLYTARE	
GUEDTAITR	
MENAIGI EHT NSU	
FDEIRMNOC	
THRRESAEOFF	
MSNHY	
HAAM UISVN	
REONCTLLRO	
AANONTIRR	
TI NCA EB NDOE!	
FTURSEEA	

KEYWORDS

- Define the following keywords from the story.
- Use each word in a sentence (either in oral or written form).
- Complete a New Word Map at the back of the book for any new words.

KEYWORD	DEFINITION
Sentiment	
Unimaginable	
Revealed	
Expectation	
Appreciation	
Heave	

SUMMARY STORY

Description: In this chapter, Lord Brahmā has glorified the Supreme Lord on many occasions. Go through the summary and the chapter verses and identify 5–10 specific qualities of the Lord that have been glorified. Write a summary in your own words (no more than 200 words).

YOUNGER KIDS' WORD SEARCH

T	Q	C	T	X	S	O	J	L	I	I	J	S	Y	K	P	X	B	F	V
V	W	L	H	H	I	V	M	C	Y	D	H	U	U	V	R	R	A	L	Q
D	G	H	O	O	X	W	M	P	M	N	P	N	F	R	E	C	B	D	Y
Z	X	J	V	V	X	Z	O	C	U	I	S	L	U	P	C	M	G	D	A
I	C	V	N	F	R	N	O	D	Z	L	I	J	V	E	I	R	S	C	C
S	J	G	Q	H	A	K	F	R	A	F	N	W	P	L	O	I	T	V	L
K	K	P	H	Q	U	M	T	X	B	N	E	T	K	O	U	M	J	S	G
U	P	C	C	F	Q	F	C	G	I	U	E	Y	Q	A	S	R	P	T	O
K	N	Y	M	O	U	L	H	B	O	S	Y	D	D	M	A	N	J	U	T
K	P	R	P	U	Y	G	B	W	E	L	U	O	I	I	P	D	P	J	G
W	L	A	Z	S	X	Q	J	G	M	L	O	A	U	S	K	R	P	I	H
Z	H	T	Z	L	W	O	E	C	E	P	L	E	A	S	E	C	M	U	U
K	I	F	S	J	O	I	B	J	R	C	C	Y	A	G	B	R	E	H	Y
M	A	I	Y	F	X	L	O	S	Q	R	U	T	B	T	E	Q	M	V	H
R	P	C	T	N	H	P	V	R	U	X	S	T	M	F	V	P	O	G	H
S	F	S	Q	R	N	K	B	O	I	E	Z	A	K	X	B	K	W	B	I
M	B	L	I	L	Q	J	S	W	G	G	Y	I	J	Q	U	U	B	H	S
Q	Y	U	X	D	N	Y	D	T	F	S	L	B	P	U	Z	P	U	B	Z
K	E	R	E	D	J	A	H	H	M	H	A	T	K	Y	Z	M	S	S	S
L	R	W	Z	K	T	Z	V	P	G	O	L	Z	R	W	U	G	D	X	U

ACCEPT	
BELLY	
CLAIMS	
HERB	
LIMB	

PLEASE	
PRECIOUS	
RESIDE	
SOURCE	
TASK	

OLDER KIDS' WORD SEARCH

C	Y	E	J	N	J	Z	A	Q	H	Y	J	G	O	S	J	L	U	W	M
N	N	D	P	R	Q	C	B	V	E	A	X	K	D	E	Q	X	U	Z	X
F	D	E	W	Q	F	P	Z	H	J	V	M	Q	J	D	U	H	Z	V	I
R	A	T	W	L	A	Y	Z	K	L	W	S	D	Y	H	M	V	T	E	J
U	A	I	M	T	Z	Z	Y	K	P	X	F	E	T	D	S	Q	C	A	U
S	L	M	M	R	M	L	E	Z	Z	L	P	R	T	R	E	N	V	S	F
T	S	T	N	E	I	D	E	R	G	N	I	U	C	B	A	K	I	E	O
R	D	E	S	T	R	U	C	T	I	O	N	S	Y	R	S	G	R	E	G
A	E	I	N	G	A	N	I	Z	Y	N	Q	S	G	J	I	T	K	S	B
T	R	A	N	S	C	E	N	D	E	N	T	A	L	U	D	K	V	H	J
I	E	K	W	M	U	I	P	L	G	M	R	E	R	S	B	I	Q	U	K
O	D	W	Q	B	L	O	Y	R	J	F	T	R	R	S	B	D	U	U	O
N	L	T	W	W	O	O	I	I	U	K	H	J	A	J	U	C	G	N	Y
V	I	V	W	A	U	M	H	C	M	N	H	I	I	K	E	U	P	P	T
J	W	E	Z	L	S	Z	Q	W	S	E	A	D	W	U	N	C	U	U	T
S	E	G	P	X	L	P	S	W	L	N	C	Z	F	J	Z	W	T	E	R
N	B	X	J	M	Y	D	C	T	U	K	O	F	C	V	C	A	C	E	O
V	D	E	O	Q	R	X	U	A	N	P	C	C	B	T	E	Q	W	G	D
E	P	K	M	B	I	I	V	Y	K	G	U	E	K	C	U	S	N	Z	Y
E	N	Y	G	Q	E	K	B	G	Q	I	N	M	I	E	P	M	T	T	H

BEWILDERED	
CONSCIOUSNESS	
DESTRUCTION	
FRAGRANCE	
TRANSCENDENTAL	

INGREDIENTS	
INTERJECTED	
MIRACULOUSLY	
REASSURED	

Resource 1

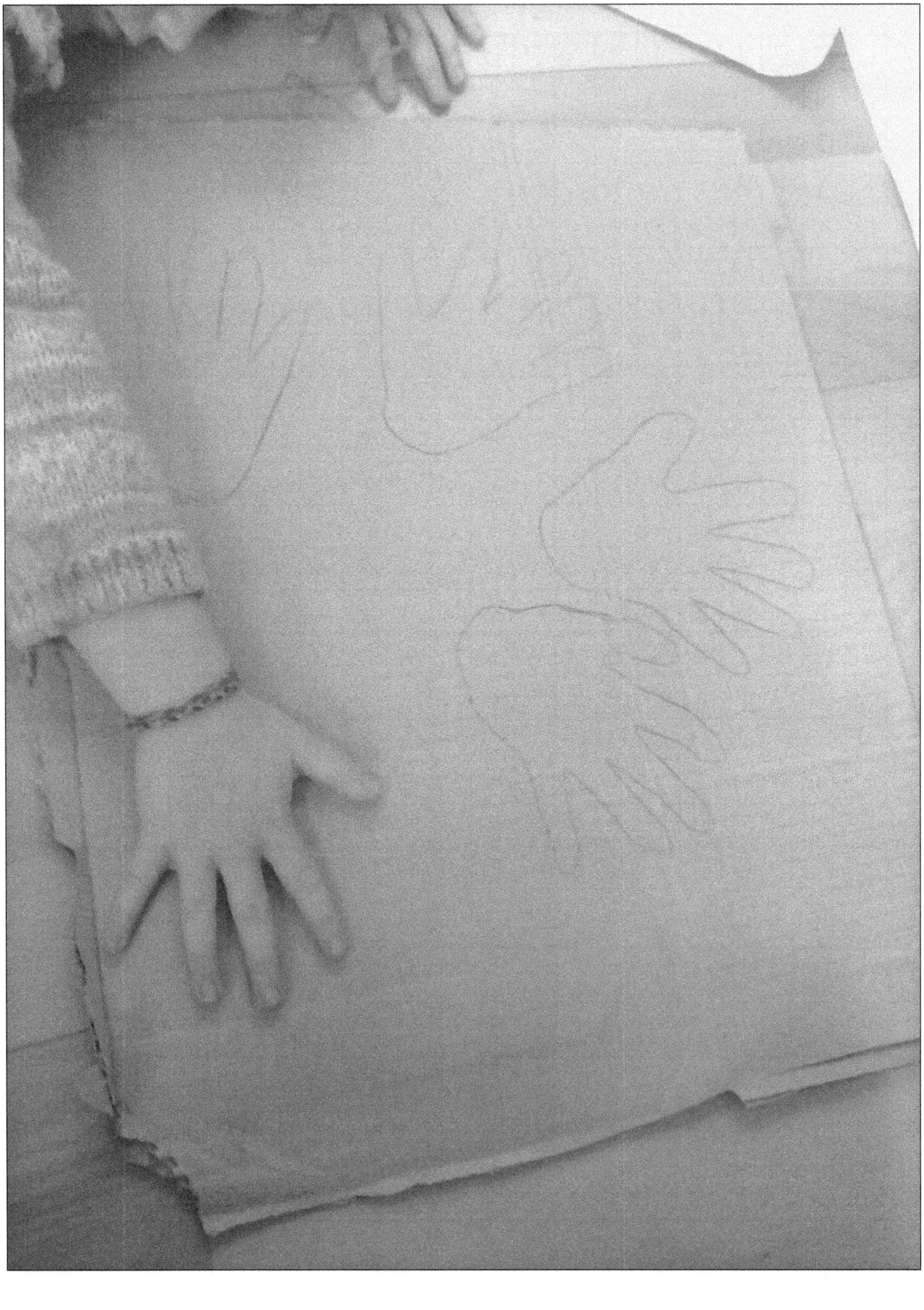

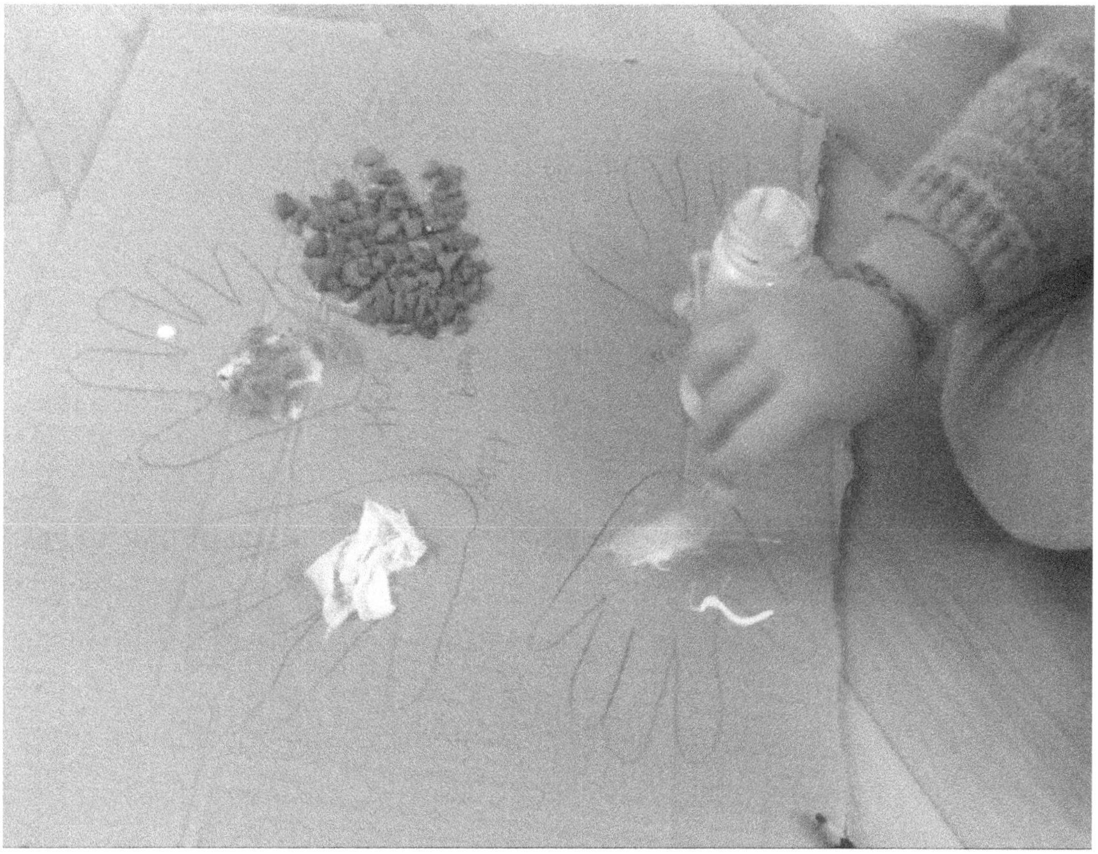

sticky
bumpy
soft
sharp
smooth

ANSWERS

Understanding the Story (pages 163-164)

1) b, 2) a, 3) c, 4) a, 5) b, 6)b, 7) c, 8) b, 9) a, 10) c

Punctuation Practice (page 169)

"O Nārada, I was born from a lotus flower that grew from the navel of Lord Maha-Viṣṇu. At that time, there was nothing around me but darkness. There was no one except me and the body of Maha-Viṣṇu. At that time, I just wanted to worship Him and perform sacrifices to please Him. But what could I do? I had nothing."

"So what did you do?"

"Well, everything I needed to perform the sacrifice I got from the Lord Himself – from different parts of His body to be exact. I created flowers, leaves, straw, a suitable time, utensils, grains, clarified butter, four priests, and so many other necessary things. In this way, I performed a sacrifice to the Lord by using the Lord.

"Thereafter, your nine brothers and other great personalities also performed sacrifices for the pleasure of the Lord."

Missing Words (pages 170)

1. wavered, dwindling
2. bewilderment, illuminating
3. flowers, clarified butter
4. original
5. explorer
6. tongue
7. musk, deer
8. arms

Sequencing (pages 170-171)

1. Seeing his son's eagerness, Lord Brahmā smiled.
2. These airs come from the nostrils of the Lord, and as our Lord smells, the herbs that people use to heal themselves are produced.
3. Nārada closed his eyes in gratitude and inhaled deeply, feeling the cool air enter his own nostrils and slowly fill his lungs.
4. His Lord and master was an impersonal energy that produced everything in this world.
5. The sun globe is a big ball of illuminating energy. It shines inwards and outwards.
6. All the material world, including the living entities who are attached to family life and the opulences all come from just a quarter of the Lord's energy.
7. I created flowers, leaves, straw, a suitable time, utensils, grains, clarified butter, four priests, and so many other necessary things.

8. It is only because I very enthusiastically hold onto His lotus feet that what I do and say is perfect.
9. When not even great demigods like his father Lord Brahmā or Lord Śiva could know Him fully, was there really a way for Nārada to know Him?
10. Drink the nectar of this narration my son, because it will dry up the desire to hear other topics.

Spelling Errors (page 173)

sentiment
fragrances
acknowledging, describe
materials
leaves, clarified
obeisances

What Do You Think? (pages 173-174)

Set 1:

1. Correct
2. Incorrect
3. Incorrect
4. Correct
5. Incorrect
6. Incorrect
7. Correct
8. Correct

Set 2:

1. False
2. True
3. False

Word Jumble (page 174)

JUMBLED	UNJUMBLED
EERAVNDL	LAVENDAR
IHLYTARE	HEARTILY
GUEDTAITR	GRATITUDE
MENAIGI EHT NSU	IMAGINE THE SUN
FDEIRMNOC	CONFIRMED
THRRESAEOFF	FOREFATHERS
MSNHY	HYMNS
HAAM UISVN	MAHA VIṢṆU
REONCTLLRO	CONTROLLER
AANONTIRR	NARRATION
TI NCA EB NDOE!	IT CAN BE DONE!
FTURSEEA	FEATURES

Keywords (page 175)

KEYWORD	DEFINITION
Sentiment	A view of, or attitude towards, a situation or event; an opinion. A feeling or emotion.
Unimaginable	Difficult or impossible to imagine or comprehend.
Revealed	Make (a secret) known to others. (Maybe something of divine which was unknown before). Cause or allow something to be seen.
Expectation	A strong belief that something will happen or be the case. A belief someone should achieve something.
Appreciation	Recognition and enjoyment of good qualities of someone. Full understanding of a situation.
Heave	Lift or haul with great effort; throw; pull, raise or move.

Younger Kids' Word Search (page 176)

T	Q	C	T	X	S	O	J	L	I	I	J	S	Y	K	P	X	B	F	V
V	W	L	H	H	I	V	M	C	Y	D	H	U	U	V	R	R	A	L	Q
D	G	H	O	O	X	W	M	P	M	N	P	N	F	R	E	C	B	D	Y
Z	X	J	V	V	X	Z	O	C	U	I	S	L	U	P	C	M	G	D	A
I	C	V	N	F	R	N	O	D	Z	L	I	J	V	E	I	R	S	C	C
S	J	G	Q	H	A	K	F	R	A	F	N	W	P	L	O	I	T	V	L
K	K	P	H	Q	U	M	T	X	B	N	E	T	K	O	U	M	J	S	G
U	P	C	C	F	Q	F	C	G	I	U	E	Y	Q	A	S	R	P	T	O
K	N	Y	M	O	U	L	H	B	O	S	Y	D	D	M	A	N	J	U	T
K	P	R	P	U	Y	G	B	W	E	L	U	O	I	I	P	D	P	J	G
W	L	A	Z	S	X	Q	J	G	M	L	O	A	U	S	K	R	P	I	H
Z	H	T	Z	L	W	O	E	C	E	P	L	E	A	S	E	C	M	U	U
K	I	F	S	J	O	I	B	J	R	C	C	Y	A	G	B	R	E	H	Y
M	A	I	Y	F	X	L	O	S	Q	R	U	T	B	T	E	Q	M	V	H
R	P	C	T	N	H	P	V	R	U	X	S	T	M	F	V	P	O	G	H
S	F	S	Q	R	N	K	B	O	I	E	Z	A	K	X	B	K	W	B	I
M	B	L	I	L	Q	J	S	W	G	G	Y	I	J	Q	U	U	B	H	S
Q	Y	U	X	D	N	Y	D	T	F	S	L	B	P	U	Z	P	U	B	Z
K	E	R	E	D	J	A	H	H	M	H	A	T	K	Y	Z	M	S	S	S
L	R	W	Z	K	T	Z	V	P	G	O	L	Z	R	W	U	G	D	X	U

Older Kids' Word Search (page 177)

C	Y	E	J	N	J	Z	A	Q	H	Y	J	G	O	S	J	L	U	W	M
N	N	D	P	R	Q	C	B	V	E	A	X	K	D	E	Q	X	U	Z	X
F	D	E	W	Q	F	P	Z	H	J	V	M	Q	J	D	U	H	Z	V	I
R	A	T	W	L	A	Y	Z	K	L	W	S	D	Y	H	M	V	T	E	J
U	A	I	M	T	Z	Z	Y	K	P	X	F	E	T	D	S	Q	C	A	U
S	L	M	M	R	M	L	E	Z	Z	L	P	R	T	R	E	N	V	S	F
T	S	T	N	E	I	D	E	R	G	N	I	U	C	B	A	K	I	E	O
R	D	E	S	T	R	U	C	T	I	O	N	S	Y	R	S	G	R	E	G
A	E	I	N	G	A	N	I	Z	Y	N	Q	S	G	J	I	T	K	S	B
T	R	A	N	S	C	E	N	D	E	N	T	A	L	U	D	K	V	H	J
I	E	K	W	M	U	I	P	L	G	M	R	E	R	S	B	I	Q	U	K
O	D	W	Q	B	L	O	Y	R	J	F	T	R	R	S	B	D	U	U	O
N	L	T	W	W	O	O	I	I	U	K	H	J	A	J	U	C	G	N	Y
V	I	V	W	A	U	M	H	C	M	N	H	I	I	K	E	U	P	P	T
J	W	E	Z	L	S	Z	Q	W	S	E	A	D	W	U	N	C	U	U	T
S	E	G	P	X	L	P	S	W	L	N	C	Z	F	J	Z	W	T	E	R
N	B	X	J	M	Y	D	C	T	U	K	O	F	C	V	C	A	C	E	O
V	D	E	O	Q	R	X	U	A	N	P	C	C	B	T	E	Q	W	G	D
E	P	K	M	B	I	I	V	Y	K	G	U	E	K	C	U	S	N	Z	Y
E	N	Y	G	Q	E	K	B	G	Q	I	N	M	I	E	P	M	T	T	H

7

Scheduled Incarnations with Specific Functions

STORY SUMMARY

Nārada was a meek and humble sage. Obedient and true to his dear father, he was Lord Brahmā's favorite son. Why? The Lord had many a child, yet here sat gentle sweet Nārada on a platform lower than his father. Legs crossed, head, neck, and back aligned as if the nectar he was about to hear required a clear pathway from the ears down to the innermost chambers of the heart. A wide expectant smile lit up his face and his eyes were wide with anticipation, transfixed on his father. This son wanted nothing more than to hear the glories of Lord Kṛṣṇa. Lord Brahmā was extremely happy and proud to see this, and his inclination to speak of Lord Kṛṣṇa to his son deepened.

"One day," began Lord Brahmā, edging forward on his lotus flower with a deep voice filled with mysteries, "when planet Earth was drowning in the nether regions of the Garbhodaka Ocean, our Lord who maintains this material world transformed into a boar with huge tusks."

"A boar?" interrupted the curious Nārada. Had he heard his father right?

"Yes, my son," confirmed his father. "The nether regions of the Garbhodaka Ocean are very dirty and our Lord incarnated as a boar -"

"…because boars like to go to dirty places!" piped up Nārada, enthused by the creativity of his Supreme Lord.

Brahmā laughed heartily. "Indeed! However, upon the Lord's saving the Earth, the first ever demon appeared. His name was

Hiraṇyākṣa. They fought for a while and eventually the Lord pierced him with His tusk."

At this, Brahmā jolted his four heads down and ahead, pretending to pierce his own imaginary demon. Nārada chuckled in glee. What a wonderful process of purification! Just hearing stories such as these would free one from material attachment? Face flushed with enthusiasm, he waited to hear more.

"Now Svāyambhuva Manu was the great father of mankind. He had a daughter called Ākūti and she married a nice young man called Ruci. Together they had a son called Suyajña. Suyajña was so great that he filled the post of Indra at a time when no one else was qualified to fill it. Consequently, all the miseries in the upper, middle, and lower planetary systems were completely diminished."

"How?" enquired a confused Nārada, "How can any living entity possibly do something like that?"

"He wasn't any normal living entity. His grandfather Manu called him Hari."

"Hari? As in the Supreme Lord, Hari?"

"Yes! Suyajña was Lord Kṛṣṇa."

"Father, is there a reason you told me who his parents were?" asked Nārada.

"Son, your attentiveness to details brings such joy to my heart! Yes there is a very good reason. In time, people will claim to be Hari. They will claim to be Suyajña. They will claim to be the Supreme Personality of Godhead. Intelligent people will look back and see what I have said and will know."

"They will know that it wasn't just anyone called Suyajña or Hari, but the son of Ruci the progenitor and his wife Ākūti, the daughter of Svāyambhuva Manu!" said Nārada. Ingenious idea! Bewildered people of Kali yuga were sure to acknowledge many powerful men as

the Supreme Personality of Godhead. Naming the parents of the actual incarnations is bound to help verify who the true incarnations are.

Brahmā continued: "The Lord then came as Kapila – the son of Kardama Muni and his wife Devahūti, along with nine other sisters. In this incarnation, He spoke to His mother about self-realization. In that very lifetime her heart was cleansed and she was liberated. As Lord Dattātreya, the son of Atri, He granted both material and spiritual blessings to those who took shelter of the dust of His lotus feet."

Lord Brahmā paused. His drifting eyes and the appearance of a gentle smile of reminiscence indicated to Nārada that the next incarnation would have had some connection to Brahmā himself.

"The Lord is so kind," began Brahmā. "As I performed my austerities whilst creating this world, the merciful Lord was really quite happy with my service. As a result, He incarnated as the four Kumāras. You see, when Lord Śiva destroyed the previous creation, all the spiritual truths were destroyed along with it. However, these four Kumāras appeared and explained the truths so nicely that the sages understood them immediately and with great clarity."

"You must be the most austere person!" exclaimed Nārada, still transfixed on his father's ability to create this world.

"Oh well, actually the Lord exhibited His own austerity to a wondrous degree," replied Brahmā rather proudly. "He appeared in twin forms as Nara-Nārāyaṇa in the womb of Mūrti, the wife of Dharma and the daughter of Dakṣa. One day, Cupid sent his companions to try and break his austerities."

"Oh no!" exclaimed Nārada.

"They were unsuccessful of course. But not only that! They were mesmerized as they watched many more beauties like themselves

emanating from Him!"

"Ha! They must have not realized that everything beautiful emanates from our Lord! Was He angry at their foolishness?" asked Nārada.

"No my son, not at all. Great people like Lord Śiva himself can also vanquish Cupid and his followers, but not without getting angry. When anger comes, Lord Śiva is not able to overcome the effects of his own wrath, but Lord Kṛṣṇa is so great that He is never affected by any kind of wrath!"

"Like when Bhṛgu kicked the Lord in the chest…"

"Yes! The Lord was only concerned that Bhṛgu would have hurt his foot because His chest was too hard!" Imagining this, they both threw back their heads in laughter and love for Their sweet Lord Kṛṣṇa.

Lord Brahmā continued to briefly describe the pastimes of various incarnations of the Lord. He described how the Lord appeared to Dhruva after the young boy performed austerities in the forest due to his step mother piercing his gentle heart with sharp words. And the merciful King Pṛthu, who fixed all misgivings of the earth, before descending again as Lord Ṛṣabhadeva, the son of King Nābhi and Sudevī, to emulate the power of controlling the senses to calm the mind.

He continued by mentioning the Lord's incarnations as Hayagrīva the horse, Matsya the fish, and Kūrma the tortoise who served as a pivot for the Mandara Mountain when the demigods and demons churned the ocean of milk to extract nectar. O how the two laughed at the sleepy Lord who felt an itch and required the mountain to scratch His back!

Brahmā then described how the Lord came as Nṛsiṁhadeva, and how Hiraṇyakaśipu was ferocious enough to challenge the Lord but ultimately lost. The Lord placed him on His

thighs, pierced him with His nails, rolled His eyebrows in anger and roared loudly showing His fearful teeth and mouth.

Nārada, thrilled to the core, listened to the story of the elephant Gajendra who picked up a lotus flower with his trunk to offer to the Lord amidst the pain of having his leg trapped by the sharp teeth of a crocodile. Immediately the Lord came to his rescue aboard His bird carrier Garuḍa, and with His *cakra* cut the mouth of the crocodile to free His devotee before lifting him by his trunk!

Shaking his head in awe, Nārada heard the story of Vāmana the dwarf incarnation of Kṛṣṇa. After asking for a mere three steps of land from the powerful King Bali, He was able to acquire all the lands of the universe. In fact, this was done in just two steps, and although his spiritual master had warned Bali not to fulfil his promise, he was insistent and offered his own head as the third step for the Lord.

Brahmā spoke of Lord Dhanavantari who came to cure the diseases of the living entities and establish a medical science in the universe, and of powerful Paraśurāma who slayed 21 generations of kings with his sharp chopper as they strayed from the path of the dharma.

The creator then spoke of the glorious Lord Rāma. He described how Rāma entered the forest with His dear brother Lakṣman and beautiful wife Sītā, residing there for many years before vanquishing the ten-headed demon Rāvaṇa for his offence of kidnapping the pure Sītā. Lord Rāma had looked over at the Kingdom of Rāvaṇa – Laṅkā – across the ocean with red hot eyes. This glare was hot enough to burn the residents of the ocean! Trembling in fear, the ocean made way for Him. O how proud Rāvaṇa was when his own chest broke to pieces the trunk of the great Airāvata – the elephant of Indra! Proudly, he loitered about the battlefield laughing in joy at his prowess but did not last long before the tingling sound of Lord Rāma's bow.

"These demons do lumber upon the earth frequently," remarked an exasperated Brahmā as he contemplated the effects of the continuous burdensome demons. "That gives reason time and time again for our beautiful Lord to incarnate and perform such miraculous feats! Sometimes He also comes in His original form…"

"As opposed to an incarnation?" asked Nārada.

"Yes. As Lord Kṛṣṇa Himself in His original form," replied Brahmā. His voice took on a softer tone as he envisioned the beauty of His Lord's curling thick locks, "with His beautiful black hair."

There was no doubt that Lord Kṛṣṇa is the Supreme Lord. For who could kill a giant witch at the tender age of three months? Or uproot two enormous Arjuna trees as tall as the sky when He was just a crawling baby? Or as a young cowherd boy, revive His friends who lost their lives by drinking poisonous water, and then jump into that poisoned river to fight a venomous snake with numerous hoods before saving everyone from an encumbering forest fire all in one day?

This young boy Kṛṣṇa, naughty as He was, being chastised by His mother Yaśodā who tried to tie Him up, opened His little mouth in which was revealed the whole universe. How could He be anything other than the Supreme Personality of Godhead? This young boy saved His father Nanda Mahārāja from the Sea God Varuṇa and even His friends from being trapped in a cave. At the age of only seven, He was able to protect all the inhabitants of Vṛndāvana from the onslaught of a terrible storm by holding up the great Govardhana Hill for seven days and seven nights with the little finger of His left hand! He even protected the cowherd girls during the rāsa dance when He heroically chopped off the head of Śaṅkhacūḍa as the demon attempted to kidnap the young maidens.

"The Supreme Personality is so kind, Nārada," said Brahmā, his face still glowing at the memory of the feats of the Lord as a young cowherd boy. "Every demon He killed was never to be born again. They either merged with His light or went straight back to Godhead. Such is the kindness of our Lord."

"Will this be His final appearance in this world?" asked Nārada.

"Not quite," replied his father. "He will come as Vyāsa to write the Vedas, and then as Buddha when atheism is rampant among the populace, before finally incarnating as Kalki at the end of Kali yuga when there is no sign of God consciousness remaining in the world."

Brahmā stopped. Hesitating, he addressed his son softly.

"Nārada..."

"Yes father?" Nārada was receptive. He knew his father was about to ask something of him. Whatever it was, it was bound to be connected to the service of the Lord. He excitedly awaited the order which could only be for his own well-being and that of the

world.

"The only way to understand Kṛṣṇa is to serve Him with love and devotion, and surrender to His pure devotees. There is no other way. Please don't concern yourself with trying to control your mind or meditate, it is devotion that gets one to Kṛṣṇa easily."

"How father? How can I best serve Lord Kṛṣṇa with love and devotion?"

Brahmā motioned for his son to come forward. The sincerity of the eager sage endeared him to his father who warmly took hold of his hand. Looking into his son's eyes, Brahmā made a heartfelt appeal.

"The Lord briefly described His activities to me," began Brahmā in a low voice, "and now I have described them to you. Lord Kṛṣṇa's activities must be described, appreciated, and heard. This is how we can best serve Him with love and devotion. Expand on these pastimes. Tell everyone about them, for this is the only way they can be freed from the illusions of this world."

Nārada nodded without moving his gaze. This instruction was to become his life and soul.

Key Messages

- Look them up in your *Śrīmad-Bhāgavatam.*
- Put them in your own words to help you memorize them.
- Discuss each one further.
- Apply them in your life.

Theme	References	Key Messages
How to recognize an authentic incarnation	2.7.2	Authorized scriptures include details of the Lord's incarnations such as the name, place of birth, name of parents, etc. This helps us guard against the invention of unauthorized incarnations of God by less intelligent persons. We should never accept any cheap edition of an incarnation without reference to the authorized scriptures.
Guidance by a pure devotee	2.7.8	Prince Dhruva was initiated by the pure devotee Nārada Muni and achieved perfection by chanting the Lord's name. In fact, the Lord incarnated Himself just to satisfy Prince Dhruva. This shows the importance of being guided by pure devotees, who can help us achieve the highest perfection of meeting the Lord.
Chanting the holy name is the same as going on a pilgrimage	2.7.15	We go to places of pilgrimage to be freed of sinful reactions. You can receive the same benefit by simply chanting the Lord's holy names! For pure devotees, such chanting and earnest remembrance of the Lord is sufficient. There is no need to go on pilgrimage.
Why does the Lord incarnate?	2.7.15	Any of Kṛṣṇa's numerous potencies can vanquish demons without the Lord having to come Himself. However, the Lord still descends to this earth so we can hear about His pastimes. The authorized scriptures have many descriptions of His wonderful activities so that people in general can get purified and make progress in spiritual life.
Giving up temporary material possessions to gain eternal spiritual wealth	2.7.17-18	Bali Mahārāja recognized that the Brahmāna begging him for land was Viṣṇu Himself but he still gave up everything he possessed. In return, the Lord became his constant companion and doorman. From this, we learn that we do not lose anything by giving everything to the cause of Kṛṣṇa. In fact, we gain the invaluable gift of Kṛṣṇa's personal service for eternal life, bliss and knowledge.
Kṛṣṇa is always God. No one else can ever become God.	2.7.27	Lord Kṛṣṇa is the Supreme Personality of Godhead under all circumstances – as a baby in His mother's arms, as a young boy, as Lord Nṛsiṁhadeva, etc. He does not have to undergo any austerities or penances to become God. By performing severe austerities, some people can attain godly qualities but no one can ever become God.
Surrender is the key to spiritual life	2.7.46	If we are sincere about wanting to go back to Godhead, Kṛṣṇa sends a bona fide person to guide us. In the material world, we usually need some qualification to perform a material service. However, the only qualification for devotional service is surrender to the guru and Kṛṣṇa. As soon as one surrenders, spiritual life begins.

Understanding the Story

Now it's time for you to check how well you understood the story by answering these multiple-choice questions. (Answers at the end of the chapter.)

1. What is the best way to lose interest in ordinary topics?
   a) To live in a secluded place with no access to even the internet.
   b) Chanting the Lord's glories and hearing about His pastimes when he appeared as various avatars.
   c) Simply wait until we get older as we will naturally lose interest in ordinary topics then.
2. Why is it important to know about the birth, activities, parents, and be able to name of some of the Lord's innumerable incarnations?
   a) It makes us appear more intelligent than others who do not have this information.
   b) We can score good marks when we are examined on the scriptures.
   c) The authorized scriptures contain this information so that less intelligent people cannot just invent bogus incarnations of the Supreme Lord. No one – past, present, or future – can be accepted as the Lord's incarnation if his father's name and his place of birth is not stated in the scriptures.
3. What are the various forms in which the Lord incarnates?
   a) Human, animal, and aquatic
   b) He only appears in the human form.
   c) The Lord only appears in His original form as Kṛṣṇa.
4. Does Kṛṣṇa take on the ordinary qualities of these forms?
   a) Yes, Kṛṣṇa lives like an ordinary human or animal, etc., when He appears in these forms.
   b) No, He is eternally the Supreme Lord in all circumstances. He vanquishes demons, pleases His devotees, and performs pastimes that are inconceivable to our tiny minds.
   c) Sometimes He forgets that He is the Lord and acts in an ordinary way and at other times He acts like the Supreme Lord.
5. In which form did the Lord rescue Bhūmidevī and kill Hiraṇyākṣa, the first demon?
   a) As a fish (Matsya).
   b) As a boar (Varāha).
   c) As a tortoise (Kūrma).
6. What was the Lord's role when he appeared as Lord Kapila?
   a) He appeared as half-man half-lion and killed the demon Hiraṇyakaśipu to protect His devotee Prahlāda.

b) He assisted in churning of the Milk Ocean by carrying Mount Mandara on His back.
c) He appeared as the son of Kardama Muni and Devahūti and instructed His mother about self-realization.

7. The Lord incarnated as Nārada Muni's brothers. What were their names?
   a) The four Kumāras – Sanaka, Sanandana, Sanātana and Sanat kumāra.
   b) Jaya and Vijaya
   c) Nara and Nārāyaṇa ṛṣis
8. What did the Lord do when he incarnated as Vyāsadeva?
   a) He killed all the kṣatriya rulers who were troubling the population.
   b) He divided the Vedas into branches so that men whose intelligence has been reduced by time can understand and benefit from them.
   c) He killed all the demons present on earth at that time.
9. What did the Lord do when He appeared in His original form as Kṛṣṇa, the Supreme Personality of Godhead?
   a) He decided to forget that He was the Lord and lived like an ordinary person.
   b) He made everyone realize that He was the Supreme Lord so everyone could worship Him.
   c) He vanquished many demons and performed activities for the pleasure of His devotees such as lifting Govardhan Hill, Dāmodara-līlā and the rāsa-līlā dance with the gopīs.
10. What is the duty of a devotee?
    a) To spread this science of God, the *Śrīmad-Bhāgavatam*, all over the world.
    b) To keep the knowledge of *Śrīmad-Bhāgavatam* a secret from all except from the pure devotees of the Lord.
    c) To speak *Śrīmad-Bhāgavatam* only on Ekādaśī.
11. Why is it important to spread the Lord's glories?
    a) It is a good way of making money as people like to pay a lot of money for this type of knowledge.
    b) It will benefit all living entities and help them develop transcendental devotional service towards Him.
    c) It will make us famous.

Higher-Thinking Questions

Now it's time to deepen your understanding of Chapter 7 by delving into Śrīla Prabhupāda's purports for this chapter and reflecting upon the following questions.

1. Lord Kṛṣṇa is so powerful that even the mightiest demon is insignificant compared to Him. Why does He then incarnate personally in order to fight with and kill demons? Does the Lord like to fight?
2. The demons are also jīvas who are the Lord's part and parcel. Why does He then favor devotees and fight with demons? Why does He not treat demons the same as devotees?
3. In Vṛndāvana, Yoga-māyā covers the residents so that they are no longer aware that Kṛṣṇa is the Supreme Lord. They see Him just as the most special, sweet member of their village. Why does Kṛṣṇa do this? If your dearest friend happened to be Kṛṣṇa Himself, would you want to know?
4. In verse 7, Lord Brahmā says, "Such wrath can never enter into the heart of Him [the Lord], who is above all this. So how can lust take shelter in His mind?" What is the relationship between anger and lust? Which arises first and what is the root cause of both? How can we conquer them? Consult Bhagavad-gītā (2.62-64).
5. In verse 7, Lord Brahmā says that wrath never enters the heart of the Supreme Lord. However, verses 14 and 24 describe the wrath of Lord Nṛsiṁhadeva and Lord Rāma respectively. How do we understand this apparent contradiction?
6. In this chapter, Lord Brahmā reveals the secret of how even sinful people can become liberated from the clutches of the illusory energy. Which verse contains this secret and what is the recommendation?

ACTIVITIES

In this section you will find many exciting things to do! They will get you thinking, moving, drawing, acting, and most importantly, having loads of fun!

Action Activities . . . to get you moving!

LĪLĀ - AVATĀRA CHALLENGE

Description: The goal of this game is to read about and understand the various transcendental incarnations of Lord Kṛṣṇa mentioned in this chapter.

- The game can be played between two children or between a child and a parent.
- Each player should read about at least 8-10 incarnations mentioned in this chapter.
- To begin the game, one player gives up to three clues related to a particular incarnation. For example, if you were giving some clues about Lord Vāmana, you could say:
    1. Kṛṣṇa came to protect the demigods from a powerful demon.
    2. The Lord did not use any weapon in this incarnation.
    3. Though Kṛṣṇa subdued the demon, the demon was not angry with the Lord, rather he wanted to please the Lord.
- If the opponent correctly names the avatāra after the first clue, she gets three points, after two clues, she gets two points, and gets one point if it takes her three clues.
- If the opponent fails to answer after three clues, the first player gets two points.
- The game is continued until the players run out of ideas.

Variation: Instead of giving verbal clues, children can act them out.

AVATĀRA MEMORY GAME

Test your memory with this fun game

You can play this game with a partner or in a group. One person will start the game by saying, "When Lord Kṛṣṇa incarnated, He came as Varāha." The next person will continue by repeating the incarnation already mentioned and adding one more. For example: "When Lord Kṛṣṇa incarnated, He came as Varāha, then Kapila." Each person repeats what the previous person said and adds one more incarnation to the list! Whoever accurately repeats the longest list of incarnations wins! You can give bonus points to the team which tells the purpose of each incarnation.

Artistic Activities
. . . to reveal your creativity!

STAINED GLASS WINDOW HANGING

Description: Create a "stained glass effect" hanging to remind you of the incarnations of Kṛṣṇa

You will need: Colored card, scissors, pencil, colored cellophane (look through recycled packaging or whatever you can find around that is colorful and translucent) decorative bits and bobs, glue, something to stick your hanging on the window, such as adhesive putty.

Steps:
1. Draw a silhouette of an incarnation of Kṛṣṇa on your colored card. For example, if you want to draw Matsya, draw a silhouette of a fish.
2. Cut out the silhouette carefully from the center, leaving the rest in place. Younger children may need help with this.
3. Stick the translucent colored paper behind the silhouette and using glue around the sides.
4. Turn your stained glass window hanging over so you can add detail to the front. Paint on a tilak, add some sequins for a garland.
5. Once you are finished, stick your hanging to the window and see the light shine through.

SUPER HERO

Description: Everybody loves a super hero – Superman, Spider-Man, Wonder Woman. Lots of comics, movies and products advertise these pretend characters. Kṛṣṇa's incarnations have much more amazing powers than any cartoon character, and His pastimes are much more exciting than any movie! For this activity, choose one incarnation and write a list of His special abilities and characteristics, His pastimes and His bodily features. Now make some promotional material for your Kṛṣṇa super hero! Perhaps make a poster? Some badges? A comic book? You can even make a TV advert and record it using a digital camera or tablet. Think about how movies are promoted and come up with something cool!

Critical Thinking Activities
. . . to bring out the spiritual investigator in you!

DAŚĀVATĀRA INVESTIGATION

In this chapter, Lord Brahmā has described more than 20 different incarnations of the Supreme Lord, each with a specific purpose. There are also ten incarnations known as the Daśāvatāra that are known as the main incarnations. Your task is to use the Śrī Daśāvatāra-stotra by Śrīla Jayadeva Gosvāmī and understand the glories of each of the ten incarnations described in the stotra.

Ask your parents or other devotees to help you locate a copy of the Śrī Daśāvatāra Stotra. Find out how to sing it!

Are all the ten incarnations described in this chapter? Are there any differences between the activities described in the stotra and what Lord Brahmā narrates to Nārada Muni?

THE SUPREME LORD'S QUALITIES

We learn from this chapter that in each incarnation, the Supreme Lord accomplishes one or more objectives and prominently exhibits certain qualities and pastimes. Go through the incarnations and list 2-3 incarnations in which, in your opinion, the Lord especially displays the following qualities:

- Compassion towards His devotees and protecting His devotees
- Wrath for evil-doers and irreligious persons
- Sharing of transcendental knowledge to help elevate the common people

Explain your answer. Are there incarnations where more than one of the above qualities are equally prominent?

GLORIES OF BHAKTI YOGA

Verse 48 of this chapter states: "In such a transcendental state there is no need of artificial control of the mind, mental speculation or meditation, as performed by the jñānīs and yogīs. One gives up such processes, as the heavenly King, Indra, forgoes the trouble to dig a well."

Śrīla Prabhupāda explains that many people try to find God by difficult methods such as mental speculation or meditation. A devotee never really performs any of these austerities, but he still knows the Supreme Lord better than others simply because he continuously hears and chants the glories of the Lord. By this process, he also gets all the benefits that a mental speculator or meditator gets.

From the *Śrīmad-Bhāgavatam*, identify personalities who were looking for God in different ways. Find out what method they used to understand God, and to what extent they succeeded. Then find out whether a devotee practicing bhakti yoga can get these benefits through his or her easy method. Use a table like the following to summarize your findings.

Which personality from the Bhāgavatam?	What method did they adopt?	What benefit did they get?

Now describe what you found out about how a bhakta gets all these benefits by bhakti-yoga:

Benefit	How it is obtained through bhakti yoga.

INCARNATION JUMBLE

Description: Three incarnations have been jumbled up in Resource 1. Find out who They are and identify all the boxes that are related to the pastimes of Their appearances, by choosing three different colors and coloring in the boxes. This chapter should help you identify the three incarnations but remember that all details of each incarnation are not necessarily found in this chapter. For some boxes, you will need to investigate elsewhere in the *Śrīmad-Bhāgavatam* to understand the related incarnation.

GUESS THE INCARNATION

Description: Below is a list of illustrations of objects or scenes. Each is associated with a particular incarnation of the Supreme Lord. Your task is to identify the object in the illustration and on the right of it, write the incarnation and pastime of Kṛṣṇa where that object or scene features. Note that for some objects or scenes, there may be multiple associations. In such cases, do not worry if your answer does not exactly match the one provided in the answers section.

1.		______________________
2.		______________________

3.		
4.	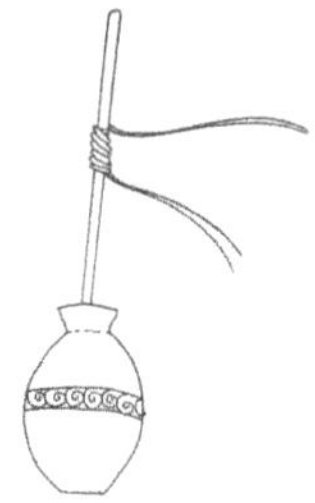	
5.		
6.		
7.	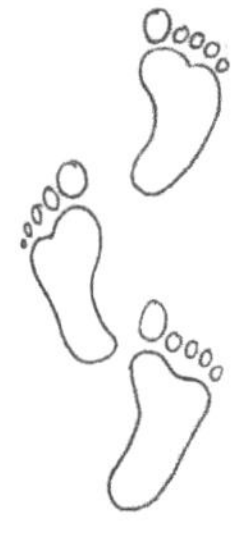	

8.	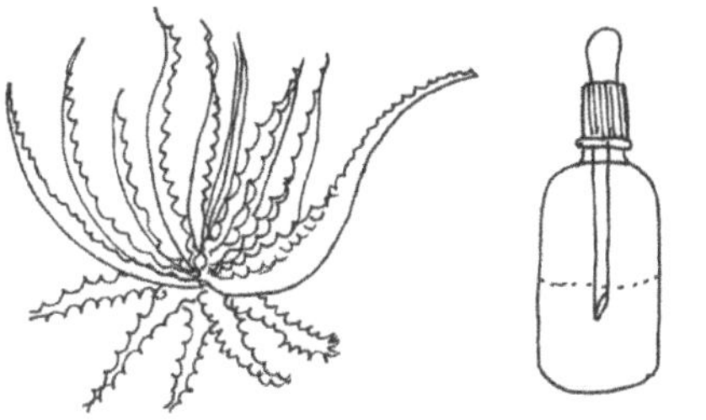	
9.	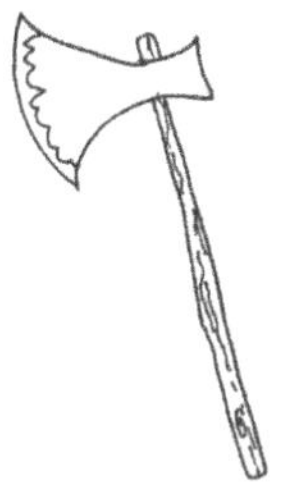	
10.		
11.		
12.	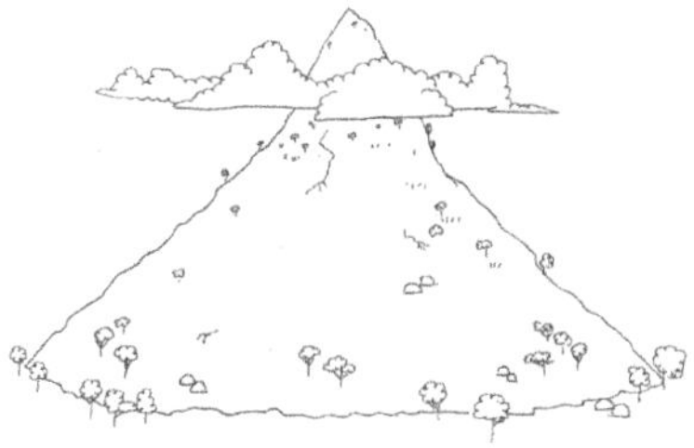	

Introspective Activities

. . . to bring out the reflective devotee in you!

- Read Verse 50 and its purport that describes how we (conditioned souls who have material bodies) are trying to lord it over the material world.
- Think about what makes up your body –bones, blood, skin, hair and other things! No matter how many parts of the body you can name, none of them is you – because you are the one who lives in the body!
- Now consider what makes up your world – all the things you can see, hear, feel, taste and smell make up your world. How many different things can you think of?
- Now ponder what Śrīla Prabhupāda says in this purport. The reason we have a material body is because we are trying to be the boss of our world! He also says that the way to be happy and go back to our real spiritual home is explained in the scriptures like *Śrīmad-Bhāgavatam*. Instead of trying to be the master of our world, we should become the servant of Lord Kṛṣṇa, who is the Original Creator of everything in our world. Remember our world is made up of our body and all the things we can see, hear, feel, taste and smell.
- Think about whether you usually act like a master or like a servant. Most of us normally act like we are the master! Just for fun, try to be someone's servant for a day to see how it feels. Does acting as a servant make you feel better or worse than acting as a master? Now spend a day (or half a day) at your local temple and be Kṛṣṇa's servant - ask the devotees to give you some service to do for Kṛṣṇa. See how it feels to be Kṛṣṇa's servant for a day!

Writing Activities... to bring out the writer in you!

READING AND COMPREHENSION 3-2-1

Description: After reading this chapter, use this reading strategy to summarize key events, to focus on important points of interest, and to clarify areas that you may be unsure about.

3 things you found out

2 things you found interesting and why

1 question you still have

ADVERTISING KṚṢṆA!

Description: Create a three-page leaflet, informing people in your local area about Kṛṣṇa, how to get to know Him, and the benefits derived from building a relationship with Him. Use the points below to help you:

Before you start

- Plan the layout on paper.
- Research the subject by reading the summary and śāstra .
- Conduct a survey to include some data. (For example, how many people know about Kṛṣṇa? Do they know His pastimes? Which pastimes? How do they get to know Kṛṣṇa?)
- Collect quotes and take relevant photos.

Include

- A logo designed by yourself
- A brief contents section
- Facts and figures
- Photos with appropriate captions
- Quotes
- Survey results
- Information about how applying spiritual knowledge of Kṛṣṇa and serving Him can help us with our personal relationships... (family, friends).

CONNECTIVE WORDS

Connectives are words that link sentences together or make a sentence longer.

Learning Objective: To extend sentences and use connective words.

Task: For each sentence, select a joining word from the box below, and then finish the sentence in your own words. You will usually add a comma before the connective word, unless it is at the beginning of the sentence. The first one is done for you as an example (the added part is underlined).

and	so	but	when	because

Bali Mahārāja lost all his material possessions in charity to Lord Vāmanadeva, <u>but he gained the invaluable treasure of transcendental service to the Supreme Lord.</u>

1. The Lord appears as the supreme chastiser at the end of Kali-yuga

   ____

2. ______________________________ served as a resting place for the Mandara Mountain.
3. ______________________________ subdued Kāliya by dancing on him.
4. Indra sent constant heavy rains for seven days on the land of Vraja ______________

   ____

SEQUENCING

Given below are few of the events that have happened in Chapter 7 – Scheduled Incarnations with Specific Functions. They are all mixed up. Arrange them in the order mentioned in the summary of the Chapter.

1. At this, Brahmā jolted his four heads down and ahead, pretending to pierce his own imaginary demon.
2. "Oh well actually, the Lord exhibited His own austerity to a wondrous degree," replied Brahmā rather proudly.
3. A wide expectant smile lit up his face and his eyes were wide with anticipation, transfixed on his father.

4. As Lord Dattātreya, the son of Atri, He granted both material and spiritual blessings to those who took shelter of the dust of His lotus feet.
5. He described how the Lord appeared to Dhruva after the young boy performed austerities in the forest due to his step mother piercing his gentle heart with sharp words.
6. The only way to understand Kṛṣṇa is to serve Him with love and devotion, and surrender to His pure devotees.
7. This young boy Kṛṣṇa, naughty as He was, being chastised by His mother Yaśodā who tried to tie Him up, opened His little mouth in which was revealed the whole universe.
8. O how the two laughed at the sleepy Lord who felt an itch and required the mountain to scratch His back!
9. Our Lord who maintains this material world immediately transformed into a boar with huge tusks.
10. He described how Rāma entered the forest with His dear brother Lakṣman and beautiful wife Sītā, residing there for many years before vanquishing the ten-headed demon Rāvaṇa for his offence of kidnapping the pure Sītā.

SPELLING ERRORS

There are one or more spelling mistakes in each sentence. Write the correct spelling of each word in the space provided.

1. A wide expectent smile lit up his face and his eyes were wide with antecipation; transfixed on his father. ________, ________
2. The neither regions of the Garbhodaka Ocean are very dirty and our Lord incarnated as a boar ________________
3. Suyajña was so great that he filled the post of Indra at a time when there was no one to fill it, and concequently, all the miseries in the upper, middle and lower planetary systems were completely deminished _________, ___________
4. "Oh well actually, the Lord exhibited His own austeirity to a wondurous degree," replied Brahmā rather proudly. __________, __________
5. And the merciful King Pṛthu, who fixed all misgivings of the earth, before discending again as Lord Ṛṣabhadeva, the son of King Nābhi and Sudevī, to emulate the power of controlling the senses to calm the mind. ______________
6. Brahmā then described how the Lord came as Nṛsiṁhadeva, and how Hiraṇyakaśipu

was ferocius enough to chalenge the Lord. _________,___________

7. Or as a young cowherd boy revieve His friends who lost their lives by drinking poisonous water, and then jump into that poisoned river to fight a venumous snake with numerous hoods. _________,___________

KEYWORDS ACTIVITY

- Explain the meanings of the following keywords from the summary.
- Use each word in a sentence (either in oral or written form).
- Find at least one synonym and one antonym.
- Identify the word's part of speech (noun, verb, adjective, pronoun, or adverb).

Key Word *(part of speech)*	**Definition**	**Synonym & Antonym**
chastised (________________)		**Syn.** **Ant.**
uproot (________________)		**Syn.** **Ant.**
atheism (________________)		**Syn.** **Ant.**
briefly (________________)		**Syn.** **Ant.**
wondrous (________________)		**Syn.** **Ant.**
heartily (________________)		**Syn.** **Ant.**

FACT FILE

Read about Suyajña in this excerpt from the Chapter Summary.

"Now Svāyambhuva Manu was the great father of mankind. He had a daughter called Ākūti and she married a nice young man called Ruci. Together they had a son called Suyajña. Suyajña was so great that he filled the post of Indra at a time when no one else was qualified to fill it. Consequently, all the miseries in the upper, middle and

lower planetary systems were completely diminished." "How?" enquired a confused Nārada, "How can any living entity possibly do something like that?" "He wasn't any normal living entity. His grandfather Manu called him Hari." "Hari? As in the Supreme Lord, Hari?" "Yes! Suyajña was Lord Kṛṣṇa." "Father, is there a reason you told me who his parents were?" asked Nārada. "Son, your attentiveness to details brings such joy to my heart! Yes there is a very good reason. In time, people will claim to be Hari. They will claim to be Suyajña. They will claim to be the Supreme Personality of Godhead. Intelligent people will look back and see what I have said and will know." "They will know that it wasn't just anyone called Suyajña or Hari, but the son of Ruci the progenitor and his wife Ākūti, the daughter of Svāyambhuva Manu!" said Nārada. Ingenious idea! Bewildered people of Kaliyuga were sure to acknowledge many powerful men as the Supreme Personality of Godhead. Naming the parents of the actual incarnations is bound to help verify who the true incarnations are.

Fill in the fact file below. Use the word/phrase bank for help.

Name:

His parents' names:

What he did which was so amazing:

Describe how this was possible:

Describe why is it was so important to identify who his parents were:

Word Bank

Filled the post of Indra
Suyajña
Ruci
Hari
people of Kali
Completely diminished
will claim
upper, middle and lower planetary systems
Ākūti
the progenitor

JUMBLED WORDS

Description: The following words are from the story summary, but they are all jumbled up. Unscramble them. (The answers can be found in this chapter's Answers Section).

JUMBLED	UNJUMBLED
RSATFNIDEX	
MELBHU	
IEIRSMES	
ARGDABAKHO CNAEO	
AYETDTTRAA	
NMAAEEST	
QVNAIHSU	
RDNJAGAE	
PAHRS	
HLEOW	

WHAT DO YOU THINK?

Set 1 – Tick those statements that you think are correct.

1. Lord Brahmā described various incarnations and pastimes of the Supreme Lord that were revealed to him by Śrīla Vyāsadeva himself.
2. Devotional service to the Lord is the best way of surrendering to Him.
3. When He was just a few months old, Lord Kṛṣṇa saved the residents of Vṛndāvana from Indra's wrath by lifting Govardhana Hill!
4. Lord Vyāsadeva divides the Vedas into branches so that men whose intelligence has been reduced by time can understand and benefit from them.
5. The incarnation that inaugurated the knowledge of medicine in this universe was Dhanvantari.
6. As the dwarf Vāmana, the Lord appeared as the son of Devahūti and took away all the lands of Bali Mahārāja.
7. The Lord's incarnation as Kapila is superior to His descent as Matsya (fish) because the human form of life is superior to the aquatic form.
8. The Lord is so full of compassion for the fallen souls that even the demons killed by Him attain His lotus feet.
9. Hearing *Śrīmad-Bhāgavatam* helps living entities develop transcendental devotional service towards Lord Kṛṣṇa.

Set 2 – Inferring questions. Using what the author says and what you know, which of the following statements do you agree with or disagree with? Back up your argument with reasons.

1. The authorized scriptures mention details such as the place of birth of various incarnations so that men of less intelligence can go to those holy places of pilgrimage and get purified.
2. Bali Mahārāja lost his kingdom because he disobeyed his spiritual master Śukrācārya who warned him not to give land in charity to Vāmanadeva. The lesson of this story is to never disobey our spiritual master.
3. Because Kṛṣṇa is always God, He can perform superhuman acts at any age that are inconceivable to any of us.

Younger Kid's Word Search

C	W	S	W	I	X	M	V	E	T	T	L	B	E	F	G	D	L	T	S
F	L	V	U	F	D	I	A	V	R	Y	N	T	P	N	A	Y	I	O	P
E	Y	U	C	O	C	S	S	L	V	N	O	W	Y	B	E	B	U	O	R
A	J	A	T	R	I	E	Y	T	U	D	K	D	G	E	I	R	X	T	E
T	B	R	U	C	T	R	P	O	L	E	V	E	D	H	C	M	G	F	A
S	O	E	N	E	H	I	U	H	W	X	I	I	X	E	S	X	T	Y	D
X	L	M	X	J	Q	E	Y	C	S	W	O	E	C	C	Y	G	K	T	J
C	Z	D	I	Z	Y	S	S	H	U	C	Q	T	I	F	S	L	K	Z	M
C	R	Y	Q	O	U	J	K	R	P	T	V	P	T	K	L	W	R	Z	A
T	M	Y	C	F	I	E	E	Z	M	W	O	B	T	I	A	H	F	B	Y
S	A	F	M	R	V	F	N	R	O	T	T	Y	B	Q	G	U	V	W	T
W	V	E	J	M	J	S	U	I	U	X	C	Y	U	W	G	I	L	K	E
U	R	M	F	A	U	R	Z	E	M	I	E	A	F	D	E	W	G	F	G
Z	A	A	H	E	B	W	G	D	E	Y	T	K	E	Z	E	Y	B	J	I
C	Q	E	T	S	D	H	Y	X	M	I	O	Z	U	S	I	U	C	W	L
0	Z	W	T	H	Q	S	B	L	C	D	R	T	L	W	I	D	H	O	B
M	I	S	C	H	I	E	F	S	U	X	P	R	E	S	C	U	E	D	0
R	P	A	M	F	N	V	N	D	T	J	K	E	R	U	T	K	Q	K	X
I	N	V	E	N	T	M	E	U	W	E	L	V	E	C	N	A	L	G	I
G	A	G	C	F	Q	Z	M	W	Q	K	G	Q	F	C	T	K	I	T	D

AQUATICS	
CLUTCHES	
CRUEL	
CURIOUS	
DEFEAT	
DEVELOP	
DUTY	
ENERGY	

EXHIBIT	
FEATS	
GLANCE	
HUED	
INVENT	
MISCHIEF	
MISERIES	

OBLIGE	
PROTECT	
RESCUED	
SOURCE	
SPREAD	
TOPICS	
WRATH	

Resource 1

Devahūti	DUSK	KĀLIYA
POISON	PLAYING BALL	PRAHLĀDA
AERIAL MANSION	YAŚODĀ	KARDAMA MUNI
NALAKUVERA	SĀṄKHYA PHILOSPHY	ṢAṆḌA
NINE SISTERS	VIŚVĀVASU	VIŚVĀVASU
PILLAR	RĀSA DANCE	HERMITAGE
BINDU SAROVAR	GOVARDHANA	HALF MAN HALF LION
BRAHMĀ'S BENEDICTION	KAYĀDHU	YAMUNĀ
VṚNDĀVANA	AMARKA	PŪTANĀ
SVAYAMBHUVA MANU	DEMONIAC KING	CAGE OF SERPENTS
LAMENTATION	KURUKṢETRA	LORD'S TEACHINGS
STEALING BUTTER	HIRAṆYAKAŚIPU	FLUTE

ANSWERS

Understanding the Story (pages 194-195)

1)b, 2)c, 3)a, 4)b, 5)b, 6)c, 7)a, 8)b, 9)c, 10)a, 11)b

Guess the incarnation (pages 203-205)

1. A hermitage with a lake represents Kardama Muni's hermitage where **Lord Kapiladeva** appeared to instruct his mother Devahūti about Sāṅkhya philosophy.
2. A temple/hut in the Himālaya mountains represents Badarikāśrama where the Deity **Nara-Nārāyaṇa** is worshipped.
3. An airplane going to the spiritual world reminds us of Dhruva Mahārāja to whom the Lord appeared as **Pṛśnigarbha**.
4. A churning rod represents the Mandara Mountain that was used to churn the Ocean of Milk, while being supported by the Lord in the form of a transcendental tortoise (**Kūrma**).
5. A palatial pillar reminds us of **Lord Nṛsiṁhadeva** who emerged from a pillar and killed the king of the demons Hiraṇyakaśipu.
6. An elephant offering a lotus reminds us of Gajendra who surrendered to **Lord Nārāyaṇa** who appeared before him seated on Garuḍa. The Lord then rescued Gajendra by killing the crocodile who had captured his leg.
7. Three steps remind us of **Lord Vāmanadeva** who asked Bali Mahārāja for only three steps of land but then encompassed the entire universe with only two!
8. Medicinal preparations represent knowledge in medicine that was inaugurated by the Personality of Godhead in His incarnation **Dhanvantari**.
9. The axe is representative of the Lord incarnating as sage **Paraśurāma** who killed all the miscreant kings twenty-one times with His powerful axe.
10. The arrow reminds us of **Lord Rāma**, son of Daśaratha, who appeared along with His plenary expansions and killed the demon Rāvaṇa.
11. The pen and scroll represent the Lord in His incarnation as **Vyāsadeva**, who compiled the vast Vedic literature.
12. The beautiful Govardhana mountain represents the Lord when He comes in His original, most attractive form of **Kṛṣṇa**.

Sequencing (pages 208-209)

1. A wide expectant smile lit up his face and his eyes were wide with anticipation, transfixed on his father.
2. Our Lord who maintains this material world immediately transformed into a boar with huge tusks.

3. At this, Brahmā jolted his four heads down and ahead, pretending to pierce his own imaginary demon.
4. As Lord Dattātreya, the son of Atri, He granted both material and spiritual blessings to those who took shelter of the dust of His lotus feet.
5. "Oh well actually, the Lord exhibited His own austerity to a wondrous degree," replied Brahmā rather proudly.
6. He described how the Lord appeared to Dhruva after the young boy performed austerities in the forest due to his step mother piercing his gentle heart with sharp words.
7. O how the two laughed at the sleepy Lord who felt an itch and required the mountain to scratch His back!
8. He described how Rāma entered the forest with His dear brother Lakṣman and beautiful wife Sītā, residing there for many years before vanquishing the ten headed-demon Rāvaṇa for his offence of kidnapping the pure Sītā.
9. This young boy Kṛṣṇa, naughty as He was, being chastised by His mother Yaśodā who tried to tie Him up, opened His little mouth in which was revealed the whole universe.
10. The only way to understand Kṛṣṇa is to serve Him with love and devotion, and surrender to His pure devotees.

Spelling Errors (pages 209-210)
expectant; anticipation
nether
consequently; diminished
austerity; wondrous
descending
ferocious; challenge
revive; venomous

Keywords Activity (page 210)

Key Word *(part of speech)*	**Definition**	**Synonym & Antonym**
chastised (verb)	a) To have punished or reprimanded; b) To have censored severely.	**Syn.** scold, discipline **Ant.** praise
uproot (verb)	a) pull something out of the ground b) to remove or destroy	**Syn.** eradicate **Ant.** plant, establish
atheism (noun)	a) The disbelief or the lack of belief of the existence of God	**Syn.** skepticism, irreligion **Ant.** belief, faith
briefly (adverb)	a) for a short time; fleetingly b) using few words; concisely	**Syn.** in brief, to sum up **Ant.** at length, permanently
wondrous (adjective)	a) inspiring a feeling of wonder or delight; marvelous.	**Syn.** amazing, extraordinary **Ant.** boring, ordinary
heartily (adverb)	a) to a great degree; very (especially with reference to personal feelings). b) with all sincerity. c. with gusto	**Syn.** genuinely **Ant.** heavily, unhappily.

Fact File (pages 210-211)
Name: Suyajña
His parents' names: Ruci, the progenitor, and his wife, Ākūti, the daughter of Svāyambhuva Manu.

What he did which was so amazing: He filled the post of Indra at a time when there was no one to fill it, and as a result, all the miseries of the upper, middle and lower planetary systems were completely diminished.

Describe how this was possible: This was possible because Suyajña was an incarnation of the Supreme Personality of Godhead Himself!

Describe why it was so important to identify who his parents were: It is important because unscrupulous people of Kali Yuga will claim to be the Lord Himself. Therefore, the only way to really identify the different incarnations of the Lord is to check His parentage. In this case, Suyajña's father is stated to be the progenitor of the universe, Ruci, and His mother as Ākūti, the daughter of the great Manu, Svāyambhuva. With this parentage clearly described, it is easy to discredit unscrupulous imitators.

Jumbled Words (page 212)

1. transfixed
2. humble
3. miseries
4. Garbhodaka Ocean
5. Dattātreya
6. emanates
7. vanquish
8. Gajendra
9. sharp
10. whole

What do you think (page 213)

Set 1:

1. Incorrect
2. Correct
3. Incorrect
4. Correct
5. Correct
6. Incorrect
7. Incorrect
8. Correct
9. Correct

Set 2:

1. False
2. False
3. True

Younger Kid's Word Search (page 214)

C		S				M							E					T	S
F	L		U			I								N			I	O	P
E		U		O	C	S									E	B	U		R
A			T	R	I	E	Y	T	U	D					I	R			E
T			U	C		R	P	O	L	E	V	E	D	H	C		G		A
S		E			H	I	U						X	E	S			Y	D
	L					E		C				E		C					
						S	S						I						
												p							
T											O				A				
	A									T	T			Q					
W		E									C		U						E
	R		F								E	A		D					G
		A		E							T				E				I
			T		D					I	O					U			L
				H					C		R						H		B
M	I	S	C	H	I	E	F	S			P	R	E	S	C	U	E	D	O
I	N	V	E	N	T								E	C	N	A	L	G	

8

Questions by King Parīkṣit

Story Summary

Mahārāja Parīkṣit, after hearing about the Lord's different incarnations, became very curious and began asking his spiritual master, Śukadeva Gosvāmī about matters contained in the Bhāgavatam. He wanted to ask the sage many questions because he just could not miss this precious opportunity.

The King asked, "O Sage! Who did Nārada Muni speak to about the transcendental qualities of the Lord?"

The King was humbly asking with all sincerity. He wanted to completely absorb himself in the *Śrīmad-Bhāgavatam* and the Supersoul within. He knew that anyone who hears the *Śrīmad-Bhāgavatam* and takes its matters seriously will have the Lord manifested in his or her heart, and like autumnal rains the Lord will cleanse the heart. After such cleansing, a pure heart can never turn away from the lotus feet of Lord Kṛṣṇa.

Mahārāja Parīkṣit continued, "Śukadeva Gosvāmī, kindly explain to me how the spirit, which is transcendental, acquires a material body. Is it by some accident or is there a cause? What is the difference between the body of the Lord and that of the common living entity? And is Brahmā – who came from a transcendental lotus originating from the Lord's navel – the same quality as the Lord? Please tell me who is the Supersoul lying in the heart of every living entity? How is He untouched by material energy, but at the same time within and outside of each atom?"

The King seemed perplexed by just thinking of the Lord's great creation but he needed to know everything. He continued his inquiry: "What is the actual position of the planets and those who rule them within the gigantic body of the Lord? Can you tell me about the duration of time between creation and annihilation, sub-creation, and the nature of time indicated by past, present and future? What about the duration of life of the different living beings like the demigods and human beings in different planets of the universe? What is the cause of duration of such lifetimes, both short and long?

"Kindly explain to me, O Sage, how one receives a high or low birth. How does the creation of the different universes, the four directions, the sky, planets, stars, mountains, rivers, seas and islands as well as their inhabitants take place?

"Please describe the inner and outer space of the universe by specific divisions, the activities of the great souls and the different caste systems and other classifications."

The King pondered for a minute and continued, "Can you tell me about the different ages of creation and their durations? What are the religions, occupations and principles for people? What about creation and its causes and development?

"What is the process of devotional service

and the method of attaining mystic powers? What are the realizations and the opulences of those who develop mystic powers? How do they become detached from their subtle body?"

Śukadeva Gosvāmī smiled from ear to ear, absorbing the questions the King was asking. He listened carefully.

"What about the basis of Vedic literatures, including history and common scriptures? There is so much to understand!

"Please Sage, explain to me how the living beings are generated, maintained and destroyed. Please tell me the advantages

and disadvantages of serving the Lord in devotion. What about the Vedic rituals, rites and injunctions? What about the procedures of religion, economic development, and sense gratification?"

Mahārāja Parīkṣit was ever so curious and continued to inquire, "How are the living beings created, and how do the unfaithful appear in the world? How do the unconditioned living entities exist?

"How does the Supreme Lord enjoy His pastimes within the world only to then completely destroy the world during annihilation and remain the only witness to it all?"

"Please, O Sage, satisfy me by answering these questions. I have been drinking the nectar of the Lord's message and I do not feel exhausted whatsoever from my fasting. I eagerly await your answers!"

Śukadeva Gosvāmī, satisfied with the king's questions, spoke, "Dear King, the science of God was first spoken to Brahmā when he was first born… and I shall tell you the story."

Key Messages

- Look them up in your *Śrīmad-Bhāgavatam.*
- Put them in your own words to help you memorize them.
- Discuss each one further.
- Apply them in your life.

Theme	References	Key Messages
Hearing through bona fide disciplic succession	2.8.1, 2.8.25	Hearing from a bona fide spiritual master in a bona fide chain of disciplic succession is the same as hearing from the Supreme Lord Himself! This is because the instructions are passed down from spiritual master to disciple without any modification. Transcendental knowledge such as the *Śrīmad-Bhāgavatam* is distributed only by this descending process. Mental speculators cannot distribute Vedic knowledge.
The power of devotional service	2.8.5	Devotional service to Kṛṣṇa is the best method for cleaning our heart of unwanted things. While there are other methods like empiric knowledge, which may help for some time, the effects are not permanent. Only devotional service is so powerful that a pure devotee can cleanse his/her heart for good, as well as those of others in his/her association.
The right topics for inquiry	2.8.16	Devotees of Lord Kṛṣṇa are curious about all aspects of Kṛṣṇa's creation – material and spiritual. They are searchers of real knowledge and not just sentimental. In addition to the material creation, devotees should also inquire about the character and activities of other pure devotees of the Lord.
Kṛṣṇa's devotees are greater than the greatest yogī	2.8.20	Great yogīs possess many mystic powers such as the ability to become very small or become lighter than air. However, Kṛṣṇa's devotees are even more powerful than the yogīs even without such mystic powers. Just as a child is powerful because of the strength of his parents, Kṛṣṇa's devotees are fully surrendered to Him and the Lord lovingly protects them by His unlimited power!
A disciple must be inquisitive	2.8.24	To progress quickly in spiritual life, the disciple must be very inquisitive about self-realization. In fact, the disciple should approach the spiritual master to put forward various inquiries about topics related to Kṛṣṇa and His creation. A bona fide spiritual master can enlighten the disciple in every way for the disciple's benefit.

Understanding the Story

Now it's time for you to check how well you understood the story by answering these multiple-choice questions. (Answers at the end of the chapter.)

1. Knowing that he was going to die soon, how did Parīkṣit Mahārāja want to spend his last days?
   a) Hearing about his family from his beloved wife.
   b) Looking for mystic yogīs who could help him live a little longer.
   c) Fully absorbed in narrations of the glories of Kṛṣṇa and His devotees.
2. Why was Parīkṣit Mahārāja listening to Śukadeva Gosvāmī narrate the glories of Kṛṣṇa and His devotees?
   a) Parīkṣit Mahārāja knew that if Kṛṣṇa saw that he was interested to hear His pastimes then Kṛṣṇa would not send the snake bird to kill him. This way he could live longer.
   b) By doing this, he and all other listeners were being purified of all material contamination. Also, he knew that if one regularly and seriously hears the *Śrīmad-Bhāgavatam*, Kṛṣṇa spontaneously enters into the devotee's heart and attaches the jīva to Himself.
   c) Śukadeva Gosvāmī had threatened Parīkṣit Mahārāja with a curse if he did not let him narrate the glories of Kṛṣṇa and His devotees.
3. What did Parīkṣit Mahārāja do when Śukadeva Gosvāmī finished narrating a conversation between Nārada Muni and his father Lord Brahmā describing how Kṛṣṇa creates, maintains, and annihilates the material universes through various expansions?
   a) Parīkṣit Mahārāja accepted the transcendental potency of the *Śrīmad-Bhāgavatam* and wanted Śukadeva Gosvāmī to answer all possible questions that may arise in the mind of a serious student of the Bhāgavatam – about the Supreme Lord, the living beings, material nature, time, prescribed duties (karma), and religious principles (dharma).
   b) Parīkṣit Mahārāja accepted the transcendental potency of the *Śrīmad-Bhāgavatam* and decided what he had heard so far was sufficient to help him die peacefully.
   c) Parīkṣit Mahārāja decided to continue his search for a true spiritual master who could impart better knowledge to him than Śukadeva Gosvāmī.
4. What kind of questions did Parīkṣit Mahārāja ask Śukadeva Gosvāmī about the Lord?
   a) He wanted to know for certain whether the Lord would let him be killed by a snake bird after seven days, or if the Lord would make some arrangement to keep him alive.

   b) He enquired about the difference between our body and the Lord's body and how the Supreme Lord remained untouched by His creation even though it rests in Him and He resides in the heart of every living entity?
   c) He wanted to know if God really existed or if He was an imaginary person created by the sages in order to fool people.
5. What kind of questions did Parīkṣit Mahārāja ask Śukadeva Gosvāmī about the living entities?
   a) He asked about the nature of living entities. How does the spirit soul acquire a material body? How are living entities generated, maintained, and annihilated? How do unconditioned souls exist?
   b) He asked Śukadeva Gosvāmī how he can prove to all the people that the body was only a combination of chemicals and did not have a soul.
   c) He wanted to know how living entities could live in their current bodies forever looking young and beautiful.
6. How can we understand how the Supreme Lord created this magnificent and perfect world?
   a) With the help of our senses and mind.
   b) By using powerful machines like telescopes and microscopes.
   c) While our imperfect senses are useless when it comes to understanding the science of creation, pure devotees of the Lord can impart such knowledge to others in the form of *Śrīmad-Bhāgavatam*.
7. What did Parīkṣit Mahārāja enquire about yoga?
   a) Parīkṣit Mahārāja was interested to know that out of many kinds of spiritual practices such as karma-yoga, dhyāna-yoga, aṣṭāṅga-yoga, and bhakti-yoga, which was the most beneficial path to be followed by a sincere devotee.
   b) Parīkṣit Mahārāja wanted to know if meditation by holding his breath would prolong his life.
   c) Parīkṣit Mahārāja wanted to know if he should promote various yoga exercises in his kingdom.
8. What did Parīkṣit Mahārāja enquire about karma?
   a) He wanted to know due to which past karma he had been cursed to be killed by a snake bird.
   b) He asked Śukadeva Gosvāmī how living entities experienced their karma during their life-span. What was the relationship between one's karma, the influence of the three modes of material nature (sattva, rajas and tamas) and the different life-forms that one could acquire?
   c) He enquired what kind of karma he was creating for himself by hearing Bhāgavatam and

if that would save him from being killed by a snake bird.

9. How did Parīkṣit Mahārāja feel whilst listening to narrations from Śukadeva Gosvāmī and enquiring about various topics?
   a) Whatever Śukadeva Gosvāmī had spoken so far was such nectar that although Mahārāja Parīkṣit was fasting until the time of his death, he did not feel tired at all.
   b) Mahārāja Parīkṣit was almost fainting as he had not eaten or slept in many hours.
   c) Mahārāja Parīkṣit felt refreshed as he took rest and ate prasāda every few hours so he could continue to hear Śukadeva Gosvāmī's narrations and enquire about various topics.
10. How did Śukadeva Gosvāmī feel about Parīkṣit Mahārāja's numerous questions?
    a) Śukadeva Gosvāmī felt that Parīkṣit Mahārāja had asked too many questions and seven days would not be enough time to answer them all.
    b) As these questions were sincere inquiries about the Supreme Lord, Śukadeva Gosvāmī was immensely pleased with Parīkṣit Mahārāja and proceeded to answer all his questions.
    c) Śukadeva Gosvāmī was upset that in order to answer Parīkṣit Mahārāja's numerous questions he would have to postpone his visit to the Himalayas.

Higher-Thinking Questions

Now it's time to deepen your understanding of Chapter 8 by delving into Śrīla Prabhupāda's purports for this chapter and reflecting upon the following questions.

1. Why do so many purports in the *Śrīmad-Bhāgavatam* warn you against hearing from "professional" reciters who narrate the Bhāgavatam for money? When Parīkṣit Mahārāja heard the Bhāgavatam from Śukadeva Gosvāmī, how was that different from hearing from a professional reciter?
2. In Verse 1, Parīkṣit Mahārāja says that those who hear from Nārada Muni are "as fortunate as those instructed by Lord Brahmā". Explain.
3. Verse 4 says: "Persons who hear *Śrīmad-Bhāgavatam* regularly and are always taking the matter very seriously will have the Personality of Godhead Śrī Kṛṣṇa manifested in their hearts within a short time." What does 'taking the matter very seriously' mean to you? In addition to regularly reading or hearing the *Śrīmad-Bhāgavatam*, name a few things you can do in practice that will show that you are taking the matter very seriously.
4. The effect of devotional service in general, and specifically the *Śrīmad-Bhāgavatam*, is compared to the action of "autumnal rains upon pools of muddy water". Understand and then explain this analogy in your own words.

5. Parīkṣit Mahārāja was a pure devotee, and was interested in spending the last days of his life exclusively hearing about the pastimes of Kṛṣṇa. Why then did he ask Śukadeva Gosvāmī so many questions that were not directly about Kṛṣṇa-kathā – e.g., about creation, time, planetary systems, religious principles, etc.?

ACTIVITIES

In this section you will find many exciting things to do! They will get you thinking, moving, drawing, acting, and most importantly, having loads of fun!

Analogy Activities . . . to bring out the scholar in you!

SUNSHINE AND DARKNESS

kṛṣṇa—sūrya-sama; māyā haya andhakāra
yāhāṅ kṛṣṇa, tāhāṅ nāhi māyāra adhikāra

Translation: Kṛṣṇa is compared to sunshine, and *māyā* is compared to darkness. Wherever there is sunshine, there cannot be darkness.

In the purport to *Śrīmad-Bhāgavatam* 2.8.3, Śrīla Prabhupāda states that Lord Kṛṣṇa is like the sun, and material contamination is like darkness. Consequently, wherever the Supreme Personality of Godhead is present, there cannot be darkness or ignorance.

Reflections and Questions:

1. Think about how when it is dark we cannot see things as they are. It is even difficult to see ourselves or someone sitting next to us. Similarly, when we are not aware that we are part and parcel of Kṛṣṇa, we are not able to truly see ourselves.
2. Kṛṣṇa is the sun and devotees of Kṛṣṇa are like the moon reflecting the light of the sun. Discuss with a friend how devotees help us get out of darkness.
3. Are Kṛṣṇa conscious activities such as chanting the holy names, reading and discussing *Śrīmad-Bhāgavatam*, and observing festivals as powerful as Kṛṣṇa to bring light into our hearts?

DEVOTEES AND THE LOTUS FEET OF KṚṢṆA

Description: Śrīla Prabhupāda explains how after taking shelter of Lord Kṛṣṇa, a devotee becomes satisfied just like a traveler reaching home after a long journey. After that, the devotee does not leave Lord Kṛṣṇa's service even if he is faced with difficulties in the execution of the service.

Interview a few devotees in your temple or yātrā to find out how they came to Kṛṣṇa consciousness. Ask them how they felt before and after coming to Kṛṣṇa consciousness, and note down the words they use to describe their experiences.

VISA TO DIFFERENT WORLDS

"Then again, kindly describe how the proportionate accumulation of the reactions resulting from the different modes of material nature act upon the desiring living being, promoting or degrading him among the different species of life, beginning from the demigods down to the most insignificant creatures." (Example taken from purport of Verse 14)

Have you ever been to another country? Do you remember what you or your parents had to do to travel to another country? Usually, we need a set of documents (such as a passport, a visa, etc.) to travel abroad. To obtain these documents, we need to first qualify ourselves by meeting the requirements set by the government of the foreign country.

In purport 14, Śrīla Prabhupāda explains how going to a higher planet is very similar—we cannot go there by space craft. We need to first qualify ourselves by following the rules described in the Vedic literatures to deserve entry to the higher planets. There are different requirements to enter the different planets.

Compare the two examples and make a collage or a chart. You can make it very creative and informative. For example, you could find information about the unique visa requirements for a country you know about, and of the requirements to go to any of the higher planets (refer to websites of different consulates and to Śrīla Prabhupāda's books). From the exercise, appreciate that it is a reasonable expectation that we need to qualify ourselves to go to the higher planets.

Artistic Activities
. . . to reveal your creativity!

QUESTION MARK THREAD ART

Description: Create a vibrant question mark thread art.

You will need: Cardboard, a pencil, a nail, hammer, a needle, embroidery thread

Steps:
1. Draw an outline of a question mark.
2. Using a hammer and nail gently make holes around the outline of the question mark and around the border.
3. Sew backwards and forwards between the holes around the border to the outline of your question mark until most of your background is colored in with lines of thread.

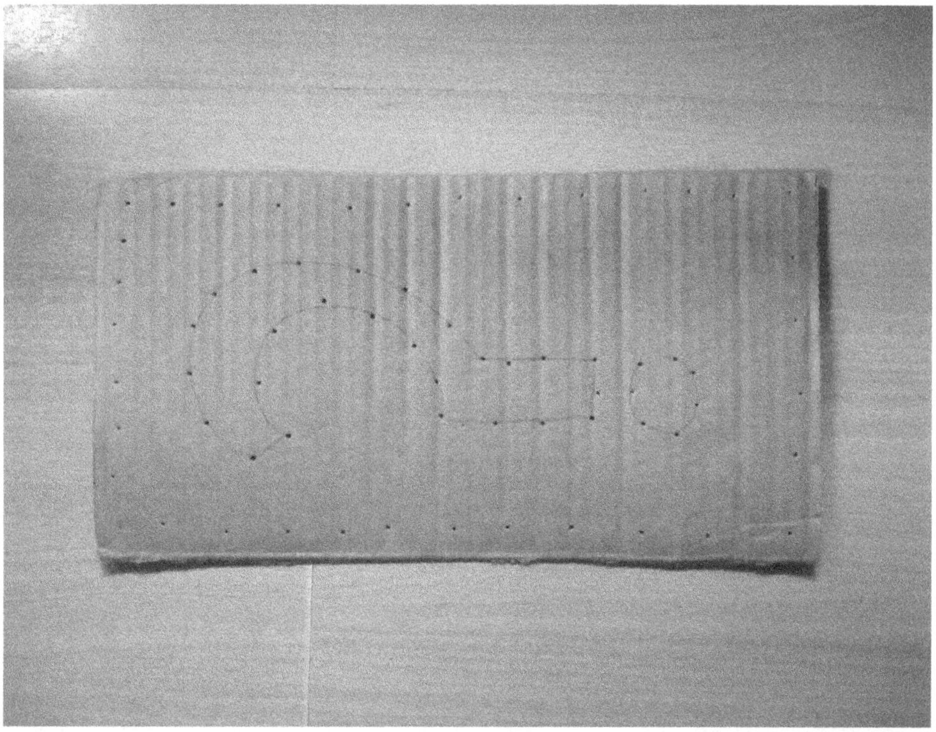

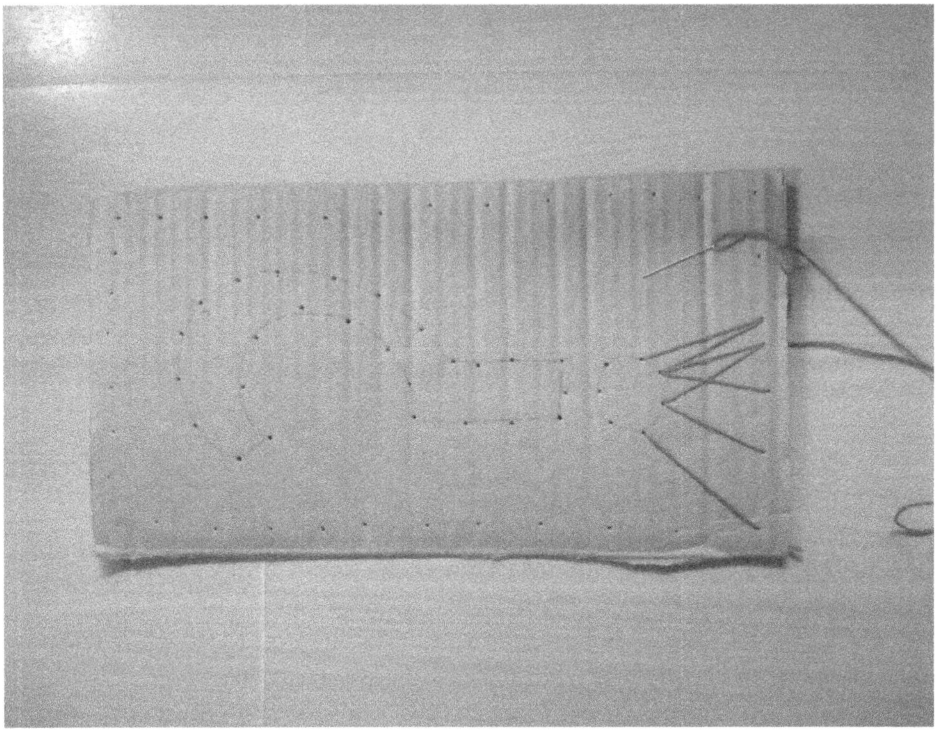

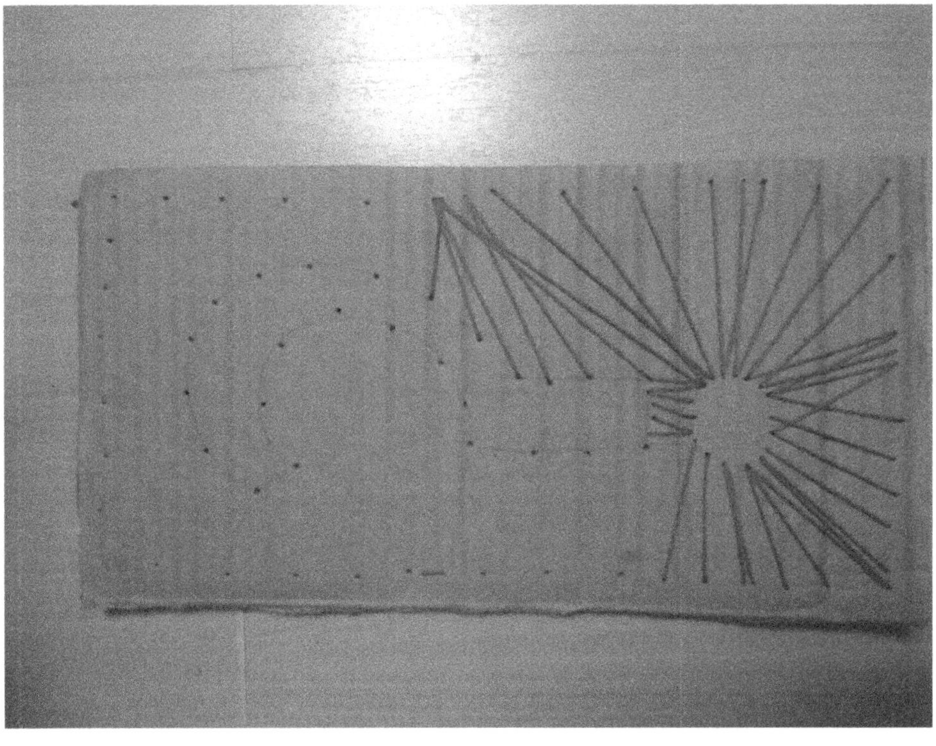

DOT QUESTION MARK COLLAGE

Description: Make a question mark collage to help you think about Parīkṣit Mahārāja's inquisitiveness.

You will need: Paper, stick glue, scissors, old magazines.

Steps:

1. Choose two colors.
2. Cut lots of circles out of pictures from an old magazine which contain your chosen colors.
3. Draw an outline of a question mark.
4. Glue circles of one color onto the inside of your question mark, and the other on the outside.

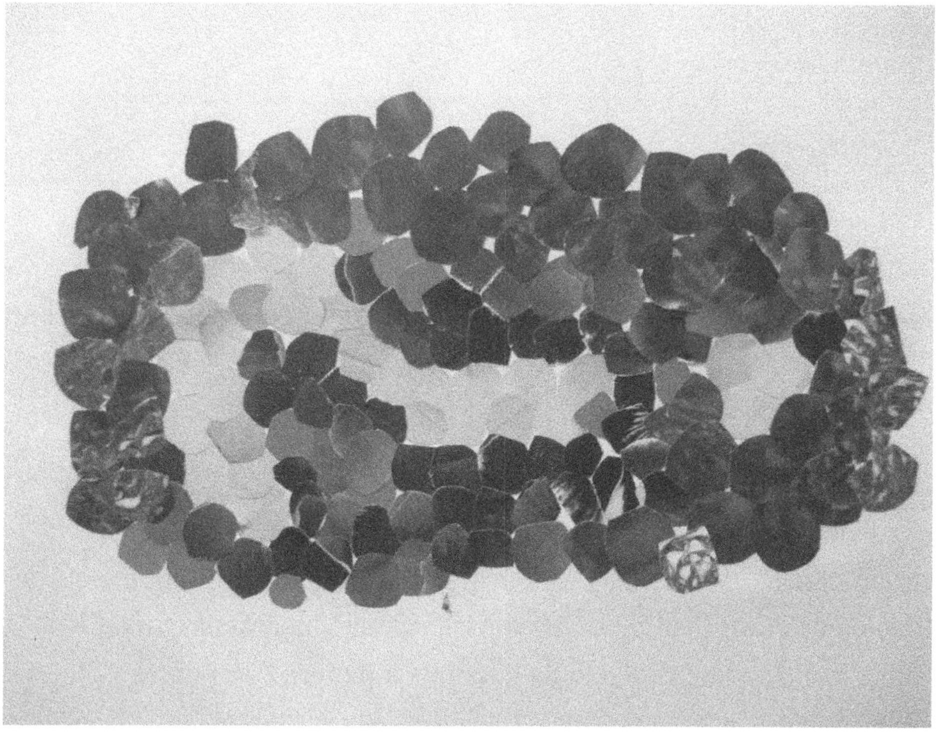

Q WRITING ART

Description: Turn your questions and observations into a dramatic piece of art.

You will need: Paper, pencils, pens

Steps:

1. Using a pencil, very gently draw the outline of the letter Q.
2. Go through the story summary and using your pen, write along the outline and also inside, the questions that were asked by Parīkṣit Mahārāja to Śukadeva Gosvāmī.
3. You can use different colored pens to create a pattern or rainbow…be as creative as you like.

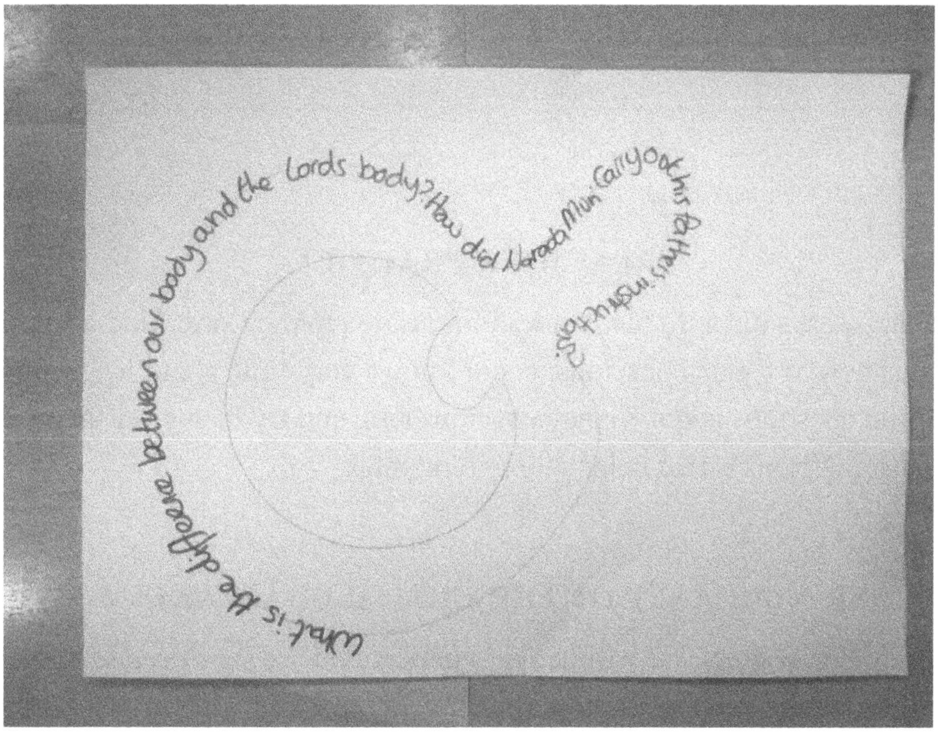
What is the difference between our body and the Lords body? How did Narada Muni carry out his fathers instructions?

What is the difference between our body and the Lords body? How did Narada Muni carry out his fathers instructions? How does the soul aquire a body?

Critical Thinking Activities

. . . to bring out the spiritual investigator in you!

PREACHING PRACTICE

Parīkṣit Mahārāja asks his guru many questions related to the Lord. Find a friend or a relative who is new to Kṛṣṇa consciousness or knows very little about it. Encourage them to ask you questions about Kṛṣṇa consciousness, and try to answer them. You can write down the questions if that helps you to remember.

SIGNIFICANCE OF THE ŚRĪMAD-BHĀGAVATAM

Description: In this activity, we will begin to understand the significance of the Śrīmad-Bhāgavatam! Study the summary and purports, using the following prompts to guide you:

- What is the Śrīmad-Bhāgavatam "full of"?
- What does it mean to fully engage in hearing the Śrīmad-Bhāgavatam?
- Who benefits by hearing the Śrīmad-Bhāgavatam?
- What will happen if you constantly read the Śrīmad-Bhāgavatam?

Present your research in one or more of the following ways:

- Design and write a leaflet about the significance of the Śrīmad-Bhāgavatam. Create an attractive layout with a mix of illustrations and text.
- Draw a mind map based on what you found out and visually show the glories of the Śrīmad-Bhāgavatam.
- Compile an index of verses in glorification of the Śrīmad-Bhāgavatam. Try your hand at writing an original poetic verse or two!
- Cut out a flower shape and write "Śrīmad Bhāgavatam" in the middle in fancy writing. Then select some quotes and verses you are most inspired by and write them on each petal of the flower.

THOUGHT BUBBLES

Directions: In this chapter, Mahārāja Parīkṣit is asking the great sage Śukadeva Gosvāmī a number of very good questions whose answers will benefit everyone. Your mission is to go through this chapter and identify seven questions that are asked by Parīkṣit Mahārāja. Express each question in as brief and simple a manner as possible. Then write each question in the thought bubbles below!

Introspective Activities
. . . to bring out the reflective devotee in you!

TRICKING THE MIND

In the purport to verse 25, Śrīla Prabhupāda says: "No one can be independent except Nārāyaṇa; therefore no one's knowledge can be perfect, for everyone's knowledge is dependent on the flickering mind." It is important to know that what we think and feel, and also how we perceive things through our senses, are influenced by Kṛṣṇa's illusory energy and cannot give us the real truth. Therefore, it is important to receive knowledge from realised souls through the paramparā. If we trust our mind and senses too much we may end up in a lot of trouble!

Exercise: Do a Google Images search under your parents' supervision for "optical illusions for kids" and see how many ways our eyes deceive us! Then try to think about your own life and some mistakes your mind has made. Perhaps you were angry at somebody for doing something bad to you but after some time you found out that it wasn't them who had done it at all, so you were angry at them for no reason!

COMPARE AND CONTRAST

Description: When was the last time you heard someone ask more than fifteen questions in a row in a classroom? In this age, most students can hardly sit in a classroom for more than an hour and may ask perhaps two questions throughout its duration. However, Mahārāja Parīkṣit spent seven days asking hundreds of questions!

Compare and contrast the modern student and the student represented by Mahārāja Parīkṣit in the *Śrīmad-Bhāgavatam*. What are their differences? Are there any similarities between the two? Think of the unique time and circumstance Mahārāja Parīkṣit was asking his questions. Give some examples and describe how we can learn from Mahārāja Parīkṣit.

A sample entry is provided to get you started (next page).

Mahārāja Parīkṣit	**Similarities**	**Modern Student**
Eager to acquire transcendental knowledge about the Supreme Lord and His creation.	Both are interested in acquiring knowledge.	Focuses mainly on acquiring material knowledge with the objective of getting a well-paying job.

Writing Activities . . . to bring out the writer in you!

ACTION WORDS ACTIVITY SHEET

a) Action words (verbs) are doing words. They describe the "action." For example: "I will quickly run to the temple" and "We will jump into the Ganges". Can you think of your own examples? How do you determine if a word can be a verb? (You can precede it with either 'to', a noun, or one of the personal pronouns: 'he', 'she', 'it', 'I', 'you', 'we', or 'they'.)

b) Circle the action words in the box below. Now fill in the blank spaces with action words from the box.

spend	transcendental	relish
sincere	asked	perform
acquire	impart	entities

1. He was determined to ______________ his last days fully absorbed in narrations of the glories of Kṛṣṇa and His devotees.
2. In conclusion, Lord Brahmā had ______________ Nārada to widely preach the science of God.
3. What wonderful activities did different incarnations of the Lord ______________ when they appeared in different ages.
4. Only pure devotees of the Lord can __________________ such knowledge to others.
5. Whenever devotees assemble, they always ______________ transcendental topics related to Kṛṣṇa.
6. What are the powers that a yogī can ______________ ?

PUNCTUATION PRACT ICE

Description: The following passage is from the Story Summary, but someone forgot to punctuate it! Edit it by using punctuation marks: periods, commas, apostrophes, and quotation marks. Add capital letters. Check it against the edited version in the answer section.

the king was humbly asking in all sincerity he wanted to completely absorb himself in the *Śrīmad-Bhāgavatam* and the supersoul within he knew that anyone who hears the *Śrīmad-Bhāgavatam* and takes its matters seriously will have the lord manifested in their hearts and like autumnal rains the lord will cleanse the heart after such cleansing a pure heart can never turn away from the lotus feet of lord Kṛṣṇa

maharaj Parīkṣit continued Śukadeva Gosvāmī kindly explain to me how the spirit which is transcendental acquires a material body is it by some accident or is there a cause what is the difference between the body of the lord and that of the common living entity and is Brahmā who came from a lotus originating from the lord's navel the same quality as the lord please tell me who is the supersoul lying in the heart of every living entity how is he untouched by material energy but at the same time within and outside of each atom

A BOOK OF QUESTIONS AND ANSWERS

Description: Create a book based on questions by Parīkṣit Mahārāja and answers by Śukadeva Gosvāmī. You are the author, so get busy writing and researching. Do some illustrating as well!

Steps:

1. Read the summary of Chapter 2.8 and select at least six questions that you would like to investigate and write about.
2. Browse Śrīla Prabhupāda's book: "Perfect Questions, Perfect Answers". You can also find it online on: http://www.vedabase.com/en/pqpa
3. Your book should have an Introduction and a Conclusion just like in Perfect Questions, Perfect Answers.
4. Make each of your questions a chapter in the book. So, if you have six questions, you will need at least eight sheets of paper to form the book.
5. For each chapter, select a suitable title, and write the question on top of the page, below the title.
6. With the help of an adult, look for the answer given by Śukadeva Gosvāmī or other devotees following in the footsteps of Śukadeva Gosvāmī.
7. For each question, write your answers on a separate sheet of paper and review them a few times. After you have made required corrections, write the final answer below the question in each chapter of your book.

8. Continue until you have answers for all questions.
9. If you want, you could add drawings to enhance your book.
10. Now design front and back covers for your book.
11. Assemble all your covers and chapters in proper order and staple them together neatly. Your book is now ready!

SENTENCE WRITING EXERCISE
CONNECTIVES ("Connecting words")

Connectives are words that link sentences together or make a sentence longer.

Learning Objective: To extend sentences and use connective words.

Task: For each sentence, select a joining word from the box below, and then finish the sentence in your own words. You will usually add a comma before the connective word, unless it is at the beginning of the sentence. The first one is done for you as an example (the added part is underlined).

and | so | but | when | because

The Lord is always within the heart of the living being, <u>but He becomes manifested by one's devotional service.</u>

1. ______________________________ pure devotees can deliver the whole world by the strength of their devotional service.
2. Although he was fasting, Mahārāja Parīkṣit did not feel tired at all ______________

   ______________________________.
3. ______________________________ the incarnation of the Lord may be confirmed by the description of His activities in the authorized scriptures.
4. Śukadeva Gosvāmī was very pleased at hearing all of Parīkṣit Mahārāja's questions

   ______________________________.

5. ____ Parīkṣit Mahārāja was also anxious to know of things he had not been able to ask.

KEYWORDS ACTIVITY

- Explain the meanings of the following keywords from the summary.
- Use each word in a sentence (either in oral or written form).
- Find at least (1) synonym and (1) antonym.
- Identify the word's part of speech (noun, verb, adjective, pronoun, or adverb).

Key Word *(part of speech)*	**Definition**	**Synonym & Antonym**
incarnation (________________)		**Syn.** **Ant.**
acquires (________________)		**Syn.** **Ant.**
perplexed (________________)		**Syn.** **Ant.**
sage (________________)		**Syn.** **Ant.**
patiently (________________)		**Syn.** **Ant.**
development (________________)		**Syn.** **Ant.**

'MAHĀRĀJA PARĪKṢIT'S QUESTIONS' WORD JUMBLE

Description: Unjumble the words to reveal the different questions by the King! For bonus points, answer all the unscrambled questions.

SCRAMBLED QUESTION	UNSCRAMBLED
oWh idd ardaNa kepsa ot?	
Si het odyb ttaaiend yb oems ccdeniat or si rehte a useac?	
htaW si het upeSrsolu?	
Si mhBara het ames uiltqay sa the oLdr?	
hWta rea het imet uraiotdns fo eacrtoin nda nnhailaiont?	
hatW rea eht iferfetnd estac ysstmes adn terho ssclafiiacitons?	
oHw odes het ysmtic tchade rofm ish ltbues odyb?	
htaW rea het adtavangse and disvangestada fo reingvs het rodL?	
hWat rea het Videc itaurls, itesr, nda juctoinsin?	
hatW rea het sicba edciV ittlauersre?	

DEAR DIARY

Description: Imagine yourself to be Parīkṣit Mahārāja. You have less than seven days to live and you have been hearing topics related to Kṛṣṇa from the mouth of Śukadeva Gosvāmī. Write a diary entry about what effect that is having on you and all the questions that are still in your mind about Lord Kṛṣṇa, His devotees, and His creation.

OLDER KIDS' WORD SEARCH

X	Y	C	N	E	T	O	P	A	P	M	O	B	M	P
C	S	U	O	E	N	A	T	N	O	P	S	D	A	S
U	N	C	O	N	D	I	T	I	O	N	A	L	G	L
R	E	M	A	E	V	I	T	I	S	I	U	Q	N	I
I	V	B	T	U	S	E	I	R	I	U	Q	N	I	N
O	A	U	S	N	S	H	R	O	V	O	A	J	F	O
U	T	B	T	N	I	P	C	S	S	I	Y	U	I	I
S	O	B	E	T	A	N	I	M	A	T	N	O	C	S
B	U	M	A	T	C	F	F	C	T	T	D	N	E	N
N	M	D	D	C	E	T	A	L	I	H	I	N	N	A
I	S	I	F	H	I	Z	R	V	U	O	Y	O	T	P
S	X	C	A	P	M	Q	D	C	K	E	U	R	N	X
Q	D	C	S	T	I	G	G	V	P	G	N	S	F	E
I	E	O	T	G	U	L	A	F	W	N	B	C	P	K
Z	T	T	V	Q	K	E	S	R	J	K	W	W	E	A

ANNIHILATE	
AUSPICIOUS	
CONTAMINATE	
CONVERSATION	
CURIOUS	

EXPANSION	
IMMENSE	
INFLUENCE	
INQUIRIES	
INQUISITIVE	

MAGNIFICENT	
POTENCY	
SPONTANEOUS	
STEADFAST	
UNCONTIONAL	

ANSWERS

Understanding the Story (pages 226-228)
1)c, 2)b, 3)a, 4)b, 5)a, 6)c, 7)a, 8)b, 9)a, 10)b

Thought Bubbles (page 239)
The following are simplified versions of seven of the many questions Mahārāja Parīkṣit asks Śukadeva Gosvāmī. Your list may differ from the one below.

1. What is the difference between the Lord's body and ours?
2. How are we born and maintained, and how do we die?
3. What is the nature of time?
4. How does a soul get a body?
5. How long does each species live?
6. What are the pastimes of the Lord in different ages?
7. How does the mystic yogi become detached from his body?

Action Words Activity Sheet (page 242)

spend	transcendental	**relish**
sincere	**asked**	**perform**
acquire	**impart**	entities

1. He was determined to <u>spend</u> his last days fully absorbed in narrations of the glories of Kṛṣṇa and His devotees.
2. In conclusion, Lord Brahmā had <u>asked</u> Nārada to widely preach the science of God.
3. What wonderful activities did different incarnations of the Lord perform when they appeared in different ages.
4. Only pure devotees of the Lord can <u>impart</u> such knowledge to others.
5. Whenever devotees assemble, they always <u>relish</u> transcendental topics related to Kṛṣṇa.
6. What are the powers that a yogī can <u>acquire</u>?

Punctuation Practice (pages 242-243)

The King was humbly asking with all sincerity. He wanted to completely absorb himself in the *Śrīmad-Bhāgavatam* and the Supersoul within. He knew that anyone who hears the *Śrīmad-Bhāgavatam* and takes its matters seriously will have the Lord manifested in his or her heart, and like autumnal rains the Lord will cleanse the heart. After such cleansing, a pure heart can never turn away from the lotus feet of Lord Kṛṣṇa.

Mahārāja Parīkṣit continued, "Śukadeva Gosvāmī, kindly explain to me how the spirit, which is transcendental, acquires a material body. Is it by some accident or is there a cause? What is the difference between the body of the Lord and that of the common living entity? And is Brahmā – who came from a transcendental lotus originating from the Lord's navel – the same quality as the Lord? Please tell me who is the Supersoul lying in the heart of every living entity? How is He untouched by material energy, but at the same time within and outside of each atom?"

Keywords Activity (page 245)

Key Word *(part of speech)*	**Definition**	**Synonym & Antonym**
incarnation (noun)	a) A person who embodies in the flesh a deity, spirit, or quality. b) (with reference to reincarnation) each of a series of earthly lifetimes.	**Syn.** personification, epitome **Ant.** antithesis
acquire (verb)	a) Buy or obtain (an asset or object) for oneself. b) Learn or develop (a skill, habit, or quality).	**Syn.** grasp, receive **Ant.** lose, forfeit
perplexed (adjective)	a) Completely baffled; very puzzled.	**Syn.** baffled, confounded **Ant.** composed, untroubled

sage (adjective)	a) wise, prudent	**Syn.** knowledgeable, discerning **Ant.** unperceptive, unwise
patiently (adverb)	a) In a way that shows tolerance of delays, problems, or suffering without becoming annoyed or anxious.	**Syn.** tolerantly **Ant.** impatiently, hastily
development (noun)	a) An event constituting a new stage in a changing situation. b) A new and advanced product or idea.	**Syn.** evolution, expansion **Ant.** regression, demise

'Mahārāja Parīkṣit's Questions' Word Jumble (page 246)

Scrambled Question	Unscrambled
oWh idd ardaNa kepsa ot?	Who did Nārada speak to?
Si het odyb ttaaiend yb oems ccdeniat or si rehte a useac?	Is the body attained by some accident or is there a cause?
htaW si het upeSrsolu?	What is the Supersoul?
Si mhBara het ames uiltqay sa the oLdr?	Is Brahmā the same quality as the Lord?
hWta rea het imet uraiotdns fo eacrtoin nda nnhailaiont?	What are the time durations of creation and annihilation?

hatW rea eht iferfetnd estac ysstmes adn terho ssclafiiacitons?	What are the different caste systems and other classifications?
oHw odes het ysmtic tchade rofm ish ltbues odyb?	How does the mystic detach from his subtle body?
htaW rea het adtavangse and disvangestada fo reingvs het rodL?	What are the advantages and disadvantages of serving the Lord?
hWat rea het Videc itaurls, itesr, nda juctoinsin?	What are the Vedic rituals, rites, and injunctions?
hatW rea het sicba edciV ittlauersre?	What are the basic Vedic literatures?

Older Kids' Word Search (page 248)

	Y	C	N	E	T	O	P						M	
C	S	U	O	E	N	A	T	N	O	P	S		A	
U	N	C	O	N	D	I	T	I	O	N	A	L	G	
R			A	E	V	I	T	I	S	I	U	Q	N	I
I				U	S	E	I	R	I	U	Q	N	I	N
O			S		S		R						F	O
U			T	N	I	P		S					I	I
S			E	T	A	N	I	M	A	T	N	O	C	S
		M	A				F	C		T			E	N
	M		D		E	T	A	L	I	H	I	N	N	A
I			F						U	O		O	T	P
			A							E	U		N	X
			S								N	S		E
			T									C		
													E	

9

Answers by Citing the Lord's Version

Story Summary

Śri Śukadeva Gosvāmī was relishing his recitation of transcendental knowledge to King Parīkṣit. He continued to speak in a deep voice, "O King, although the living entity is in pure consciousness in his original state, he is still influenced by the external energy of the Lord and controlled by Him."

Mahārāja Parīkṣit listened attentively. "Is there no real meaning to pure consciousness unless one remembers that he is a servant of the Lord and serves Him with transcendental love? Is it all connected to the Lord?" he asked.

Śukadeva Gosvāmī answered, "There is indeed no meaning, O King, for Kṛṣṇa is the source of everything. How can there be meaning without the source? Dear King, the illusioned living entity in this material world can appear in many different bodies to learn the process of remembering and serving the Lord. Specifically, the conditioned soul can take one of 8,400,000 species of life within this universe!"

Mahārāja Parīkṣit questioned, "8,400,000 species of life?! How does a conditioned soul attain a particular species of life or body?"

"Great question!" Śukadeva Gosvāmī exclaimed. "The body one receives is determined by the conditioned soul's material desires. For example, souls that desire to eat flesh and blood are born with a tiger's body, where it is easy and natural to eat flesh. If they desire and deserve to enjoy heavenly pleasure, they are born with a demigod's body and get the ability to enjoy such pleasures. However, the true spiritual journey begins when the living entity starts to enjoy the transcendence beyond time and material energy and becomes free from the material concepts of "I" or "mine", realizing that everything belongs to Lord Sri Kṛṣṇa, who is the source of all creation!"

"Is it illusory for me to think of this body as mine?" Mahārāja Parīkṣit inquired.

"That is exactly right." Śukadeva Gosvāmī replied. "Everything is Kṛṣṇa's property! Thinking in terms of "I" or "mine" only causes more bondage in this world. The way to be free from these concepts is to accept Lord Vāsudeva (Kṛṣṇa) as the Supreme Lord and proprietor of everything."

Mahārāja Parīkṣit gave the subject matter a little more thought and bowed respectfully. "O great sage, can you tell me now about the Supreme Lord's conversation with Lord Brahmā at the beginning of creation?"

"Yes of course. I will be happy to share the story with you in detail."

Śukadeva Gosvāmī began to narrate Lord Brahmā's conversation with his son, the great sage, Nārada Muni, about the material creation and the Supreme Lord's instructions to him. The story began when Lord Brahmā appeared on the lotus flower originating

from the navel of Garbhodakaśāyī Viṣṇu. He was alone and all he could see was darkness everywhere. Looking around from side to side, he was unable to trace the source of his lotus seat. "Who is my creator?" Brahmā wondered. He could not see anyone. Lord Brahmā felt within him an immense desire to create the universe, but he realized he did not know how or even where to start! At that moment, he heard two sounds - "ta" and "pa" – repeated twice from somewhere nearby. He looked around trying to find the speaker, but could see no one.

Nārada pondered and asked his father, "ta-pa… you mean 'penance', father?"

"Yes son, penance," Lord Brahmā replied. "And because I did not know how or where to start the process of creating this material universe, I took this voice as a divine and transcendental instruction to perform penance. So, I sat on my lotus flower and meditated for over 1,000 celestial years! (1 celestial year = 6x30x12x1,000 of our earth years) Talk about tapa!" Brahmā laughed and continued to speak.

His eyes widening, he said "After 1000

celestial years of meditation, my dear son, to my great fortune, do you know what happened? The Lord was so merciful to me that He allowed me to see His effulgent Nārāyaṇa form!"

"What a sight that must have been!" replied Nārada, imagining what the Lord's transcendental form and features looked like.

"Nārada, you wouldn't believe it until you see it with your own eyes!" Lord Brahmā said recalling the Lord's brilliance. By the Lord's mercy, Lord Brahmā saw not just His brilliant four-handed Nārāyaṇa form but the entire spiritual sky glowing around Him. Lord Brahmā could see the Supreme Lord's personal abodes of Goloka and Vaikuṇṭha and all the devotees serving Him in their own transcendental ways. The people of Vaikuṇṭha were all glowing and brilliantly situated. Some had the most marvellous flower airplanes! Lord Kṛṣṇa in His Nārāyaṇa form was seated on a golden throne. He was wearing yellow robes, earrings, and had a helmet on His head. The goddess of fortune Lakṣmī Devī served His lotus feet and sang His glories. On the Lord's chest were the lines of the goddess of fortune and He was surrounded by His different energies.

Seeing the Supreme Lord of Vaikuṇṭha in His full glory, Lord Brahmā's heart was filled with joy. His eyes brimming with tears of love, he bowed before the Lord.

Śukadeva Gosvāmī continued, "O King, Lord Brahmā is showing his humility and intelligence by bowing down before the Lord. He serves as an example for all of us so that we too can attain the perfection of life and see the Lord's transcendental form!"

Mahārāja Parīkṣit smiled and bowed his head. Gratitude filled his heart, for he knew how fortunate he was to hear about this pastime of the Lord.

Śukadeva Gosvāmī continued, "The Lord looked upon Brahmā knowing how intensely he had meditated to serve Him. He knew Brahmā was ready to begin the act of material creation and shook his hand in approval, just like friends shake hands with each other.

"Giving Lord Brahmā a loving smile, the Supreme Lord spoke, 'O Brahmā, My son, impregnated with the Vedas, I am so very pleased with your penance and your desire to create! I wish you good luck in your endeavour and you may ask me anything you desire. But please remember that the ultimate benediction is to see Me by realization as opposed to anything material. You have seen My abodes perfectly due to your submissive attitude, discipline, and faith in My instructions. May all the living entities you create become as submissive as you and gain the ultimate benediction as you already have!'

The Supreme Lord continued: "Dear Brahmā, it was I who gave you your first order by speaking the two syllables "ta" and "pa". Know, dear son, that it is this very penance (*ta-pa*) by which I create, maintain and destroy the whole universe. It is My heart and soul and My internal potency. Through this penance only will all the conditioned souls be free from material bondage. And it is only performed by engaging in devotional service unto Me. Therefore, one who follows the principles rigidly is sure to achieve success."

The Lord also explained to Lord Brahmā that if anything appears to be without relation to Him, it has no reality at all but is only His illusory material energy mahā-māyā. In contrast, anything that is dovetailed in relationship with the Lord is known as His superior spiritual energy yoga-māyā.

Lord Brahmā, astounded at how fortunate he was to associate with the Lord Himself, said, "O Lord, although I know that You are the supreme director situated in everyone's heart and You are aware of all the living entities' endeavours by Your superior intelligence, I still pray to You, O Lord, to kindly fulfil my desire to know the secrets of creation."

The Lord waited to hear Brahmā's questions. Lord Brahmā cleared his throat, and asked, "O Lord, can you tell me about Your different forms in the material world and the transcendental world? How is it that You manifest different energies? How do You play with these energies? You play like a spider covering itself by its own energy and Your determination is infallible. How is this? And how can I generate living entities without being conditioned by such activity?"

Lord Brahmā was feeling more and more eager to hear the answers to his own questions. "Lord, You have shaken hands with me like a friend, so I assure You I will create different types of living entities while always being in Your service. Please allow me to never find myself prideful and think that I am You, the Supreme Personality of Godhead. "

The Lord replied, "Please know, dearest Brahmā, that knowledge about Me as mentioned in the scriptures is confidential and revealed only to My dear devotees who can realize such knowledge by My causeless mercy. May all My qualities, eternal form, transcendental existence, color and activities be awakened within you by factual realization out of My causeless mercy!"

The Lord's eyes widened as if transmitting knowledge and realization into the heart of Brahmā. After a moment, He continued to speak the famous four verses of the *Śrīmad Bhāgavatam* describing the essence of its message (2.9.33-36).

"It was I, O dear son, who existed before the creation, when there was nothing but Me", the Lord said. "Material nature, which is the cause of this material creation, did not exist then, but material nature is Me, and what remains after its annihilation is also Me. I exist within everything that is created and simultaneously exist outside of everything."

Nārada Muni who was hanging on to his father's every word, inquired from Lord Brahmā, "So the Lord is inside everything and outside everything at the same time, father?"

"Yes," Lord Brahmā replied, "Because everything is the creation of the Lord - from the soul to the material bodies we are in to the very air we breathe."

Śukadeva Gosvāmī continued, "The Lord then said to Brahmā, 'The special person who earnestly searches for the Absolute Truth in all circumstances, in all space and time, both directly and indirectly, ultimately concludes that the Absolute Truth is Me, the Supreme Personality of Godhead, who is the cause and creator of all that exists.'"

Brahmā nodded his head with agreement; still worrying about whether he may become prideful in his own creative process.

The Supreme Lord, as if reading Lord Brahmā's mind, said, "O Brahmā, do not worry about pride! Just follow this conclusion with a steady mind and you will not be overcome with pride, neither in the partial or final devastation."

The Supreme Personality of Godhead, Hari, being seen in His transcendental form, instructing Lord Brahmā, then disappeared.

Śukadeva Gosvāmī continued, "Lord Brahmā, knowing he had just seen the perfect conclusion to the bhakti-yoga process by seeing the Lord's transcendental form began creating the universe and its multiple living entities. Brahmā now understood the purpose of his creation, which was to give souls a chance to return home, back to Godhead by taking up the process of self-realization or bhakti-yoga! Thus, Lord Brahmā, the forefather of all living entities, situated himself in acts of regulative principles, desiring self-interest for the welfare of all living entities."

"What a noble man you are, father!" Nārada said. "You are an example of how one must lead a regulated life before being situated in any exalted position." Nārada bowed before his father and with good manners, meekness and sense control, inquired from him in detail about the transcendental knowledge his father was given by the Lord.

Thus, the father told the whole *Bhāgavatam* with satisfaction to his son Nārada. Later, Nārada would instruct the powerful Vyāsadeva who meditated upon the Lord on the bank of the Sarasvatī River.

Key Messages

- Look them up in your *Śrīmad-Bhāgavatam.*
- Put them in your own words to help you memorize them.
- Discuss each one further.
- Apply them in your life.

Theme	References	Key Messages
Why are we in the material world?	2.9.1	Kṛṣṇa is our original Father. He wishes for us to be situated in our pure consciousness as part and parcel of Him. Unfortunately, some living entities (us!) misused our partial independence and desired to become as powerful as Him. To fulfil our desire, Kṛṣṇa put us in this material world in a dreaming state where we think we are the controller and try to enjoy. Someday we will hopefully realize the futility of this effort and desire to go back to Godhead.
Penance in bhakti yoga is the key to self-realization	2.9.4-9, 2.9.24	As the (secondary) creator of the universe, Lord Brahmā sets an example for us to follow. He undertook severe penance in bhakti-yoga and he was thus able to see the transcendental, fully spiritual form of Kṛṣṇa. For us, penance means following the orders of the Lord through a bona fide spiritual master and striving to always please Kṛṣṇa's senses through bhakti-yoga, however painstaking it may be. If we do this perfectly, we will get the same result as Lord Brahmā – seeing Kṛṣṇa in person.
Difference between Vaikuṇṭha and the material world	2.9.10	n the spiritual realm of Vaikuṇṭha, living entities are free from lust. They only want to serve the Lord. There is no influence of māyā. There is no creation or annihilation because the destructive effect of time does not exist. The duration of life is unlimited and everything is eternal, full of knowledge and full of bliss. The Lord is the chief leader and no one competes with Him for leadership. Everyone gets unlimited bliss just by being His follower.
How to know Kṛṣṇa?	2.9.31-32	We can obtain transcendental knowledge about Kṛṣṇa only if Kṛṣṇa Himself makes it known. One must be very dear to Kṛṣṇa to know Him, and one becomes dear to Kṛṣṇa only if one becomes a devotee and performs devotional service.
Śrīmad-Bhāgavatam in a nutshell	2.9.33-36	(1) The Supreme Lord Kṛṣṇa is the cause of all causes. He exists before material creation, He exists within and outside the creation, and He continues to exist when the material creation is annihilated. (2) The whole cosmic manifestation emanates from Him. When we forget that everything is related to Kṛṣṇa, we are said to be influenced by the illusory energy of Kṛṣṇa. (3) The material elements (earth, water, etc.) exist within this universe and at the same time outside of it. Similarly, Kṛṣṇa, by His different energies is within everything in material creation and at the same time situated outside of it – i.e., in the kingdom of God (Vaikuṇṭha-loka). (4) To unfold the mystery of bhakti-yoga is the highest objective for the inquisitive.

Understanding the Story

Now it's time for you to check how well you understood the story by answering these multiple-choice questions. (Answers at the end of the chapter.)

1. What did Parīkṣit Mahārāja expect from Śukadeva Gosvāmī?
   a) To be able to answer all the questions he was going to ask Śukadeva Gosvāmi as he was the most learned sage.
   b) To be able to answer some of the questions he was going to ask Śukadeva Gosvāmi as it was not possible for anyone to know all the answers.
   c) He wanted Śukadeva Gosvāmī to answer not just the questions he had asked, but also those he had not even asked so that any serious student of the Bhāgavatam would be satisfied.
2. On which topics did Parīkṣit Mahārāja ask questions of Śukadeva Gosvāmī?
   a) He asked how to save himself from the curse of being bitten by a snake bird so he could return to his kingdom to rule safely.
   b) He asked about the Supreme Lord, the living beings, material nature, time, prescribed duties, and religious principles.
   c) Out of fear of imminent death, Parīkṣit Mahārāja was confused about what to ask Śukadeva Gosvāmī.
3. How well did Śukadeva Gosvāmī answer Parīkṣit Mahārāja's questions?
   a) He systematically answered all the questions, starting with basic knowledge that we are not this body but the spirit soul.
   b) He did not have full knowledge of *Bhāgavatam* and therefore only gave the answers he knew.
   c) He could not give any answers as he was not paying attention to Parīkṣit Mahārāja's questions.
4. According to Śukadeva Gosvāmī what is the connection between the spirit soul and the material body?
   a) The spirit soul resides in the material body and therefore it is like a bodily organ such as the heart, brain, etc.
   b) There is no connection between the spirit soul and the material body.
   c) There is a connection when we are awake and the connection is lost when we are asleep.
5. What explanation did Śukadeva Gosvāmī give for the spirit soul acquiring a material body?
   a) Śukadeva Gosvāmī said he did not know how it all started.

b) He explained that the chemical reaction from which the soul is created also creates a material body for it as a by-product.

c) He explained that when the soul wants to become the supreme controller and supreme enjoyer like Kṛṣṇa, the Lord's energy gives the soul different material bodies to act out its desires and keeps the soul in the illusion that it is the body.

6. Why did Śukadeva Gosvāmī say that human form of life was very special?
   a) It is only in this form that the spirit soul can understand the Supreme Lord and render service unto Him. The Lord then helps the spirit soul to give up the illusion that it is the body.
   b) It can create things that other forms cannot create, such as buildings, cars, internet, etc.
   c) This was the first form of life that Lord Brahmā created.
7. Why was Lord Brahmā bewildered at the beginning of creation?
   a) He could not understand all the different forms present around him.
   b) He was the first created being and he could not understand who he was, how he came into existence, and what the purpose of his life was.
   c) He saw Lord Śiva and Lord Viṣṇu standing before him and wondered who the Supreme Lord was out of the two.
8. How did Lord Brahmā come out of his bewilderment?
   a) Lord Brahmā asked Lord Śiva various questions to clear his doubts.
   b) He wept in his state of bewilderment and waited for someone to appear to help him.
   c) Being initiated by the Supreme Lord on the path of penance, Lord Brahmā took up severe penance for one thousand celestial years to come out of his bewilderment.
9. How did the Supreme Lord reward Lord Brahmā for his penance?
   a) He gave Lord Brahmā many powers so he could do whatever he wanted to be happy.
   b) Pleased with Lord Brahmā's penance, the Supreme Lord revealed to him His personal transcendental abode called Vaikuṇṭha.
   c) He made Lord Brahmā very powerful so he could continue with his penance for several thousand years more.
10. What did the Supreme Lord say to Lord Brahmā before disappearing from his vision?
   a) He told Lord Brahmā the essence of the *Bhāgavatam* and said that this knowledge was confidential and could only be understood by His devotees.
   b) He instructed Lord Brahmā to always pray to Lord Śiva and serve him with devotion.
   c) He told Lord Brahmā that his goal of life was to perform penance and therefore he should delegate the work of creation to Lord Śiva.

Higher-Thinking Questions

Now it's time to deepen your understanding of Chapter 9 by delving into Śrīla Prabhupāda's purports for this chapter and reflecting upon the following questions.

1. What is the "first sinful will" of the living entity as described in this chapter? Can you think of a few day-to-day examples that illustrate this "sinful" tendency?
2. Can you identify which of the many questions asked by Mahārāja Parīkṣit in the previous chapter are answered by Śukadeva Gosvāmī in this chapter?
3. Read verse 14 which describes the typical occupation of the residents of Vaikuṇṭha. If we perform devotional service according to Śrīla Prabhupāda's instructions and do japa and kīrtan, can we claim to be doing exactly the same activity as residents of Vaikuṇṭha? If yes, why do need to strive to get out of this material world and go to Vaikuṇṭha planets?
4. Verse 17 in this chapter describes the Supreme Lord in relation to His energies. We have seen a similar mention in an earlier chapter. Look up the word for word translations and compare the descriptions – *"adhyarhaṇīyāsanam āsthitaṁ paraṁ vṛtaṁ catuḥ-ṣoḍaśa-pañca-śaktibhiḥ"* [SB 2.9.17] with *"apaśyat puruṣaṁ pūrṇaṁ māyāṁ ca tad-apāśrayām"* [SB 1.7.4]. Why is it important for devotees to know this relationship between the Lord and His energies?
5. One of the verses (and the associated purport) in this chapter states the highest perfectional stage of life and provides the secrets of attaining this stage. Find the verse! Think of at least two things you can start doing or continue doing in your life so you can achieve what Lord Brahmā achieved.
6. The purport of verse 34 states "The independence of the individual living entity is not real independence, but is just the reflection of the real independence existing in the Supreme Being, the Lord." However, we are also told that we are in the material world because we misused our independence and desired to enjoy separately from Kṛṣṇa – this means we do have real independence. Is this contradictory? If not, what is wrong or missing in the logic presented here?

ACTIVITIES

In this section you will find many exciting things to do! They will get you thinking, moving, drawing, acting, and most importantly, having loads of fun!

Analogy Activities . . . to bring out the scholar in you!

THE WEB OF CREATION

kṛṣṇa—sūrya-sama; māyā haya andhakāra
yāhāṅ kṛṣṇa, tāhāṅ nāhi māyāra adhikāra

Verse 28: "O master of all energies, please tell me philosophically all about them. You play like a spider that covers itself by its own energy, and Your determination is infallible."

In this verse, the Lord's work to create, maintain and destroy the material universe is compared to the expert way a spider weaves its web, stays in it, and ultimately destroys it. On the internet, find a video that shows how the spider spins its web and uses it. Read the part of the purport which compares the Lord's way of working to a spider's. In what ways do you think that they are similar, and in what ways are they dissimilar? Does this mean that the spider is as expert as the Supreme Lord?

	Similarities	Dissimilarities
Spider		

	Similarities	Dissimilarities
Supreme Lord		

SEEING KṚṢṆA

"All living beings require factual light from the Lord to see Him directly, just as the sun can be seen only by the direct light of the sun." (Purport SB 2.9.34).

Śrīla Prabhupāda uses this analogy to explain why we cannot see the Supreme Personality of Godhead by artificial means, just as we cannot see the sun by lamps or man-made flashlights.

Understanding the analogy:

1. When the sun rises, it reveals itself. Also when the sun rises, we don't see just the sun, but we also see ourselves and the world around us.
2. Similarly, the Supreme Lord reveals Himself to someone by the light of His causeless mercy. That mercy is manifested when someone pleases Kṛṣṇa with his/ her loving devotional service.

3. When one sees Kṛṣṇa, one can also perceive the different energies of Kṛṣṇa and one's true self as a spiritual entity and eternal servant of Kṛṣṇa.
4. An example of such realization can be found in the first canto of *Śrīmad-Bhāgavatam* when Vyāsadeva fixed his mind perfectly on Kṛṣṇa through bhakti-yoga and saw the Lord along with His external energy.

Learning Activity: Create your own acrostic poem with the word 'Kṛṣṇa'. An acrostic poem uses the letter given in a word/topic to begin each line of the poem. Each line in the poem should relate to the above analogy.
Here is an example for the word 'Sun':

Shows itself, myself and all that is around.
Unless it shines, it is all dark and not bright.
No way to see it unless it shows itself.

Critical Thinking Activities
... to bring out the spiritual investigator in you!

ACHIEVING SUCCESS BY THE POWER OF BHAKTI

Description: In this chapter, we understand how by the power of bhakti yoga, Lord Brahmā got the strength to create the universe. Śrīla Prabhupāda, by the strength of his devotion, also did great things that are impossible for an ordinary person to accomplish.

- Research Śrīla Prabhupāda's achievements and list them.
- Understand how Śrīla Prabhupāda undertook a lot of personal austerity for the sake of the Lord's mission, and how he fully dedicated himself to executing the instruction of his spiritual master, in much the same way as Lord Brahmā had done.

Present your data and understanding to the rest of the class as a poster or a presentation

FIRST LETTER QUESTION GAME

Description: In this game, the letter in the question on the left is the first letter of the answer. Ask your partner the questions in the left column. At first, you may need to rephrase the questions so your partner understands the game – e.g., "What word starting with the letter "N" is the name of the person who said Kṛṣṇa would soon be returning to the spiritual world?"

Question	Answer
What V was the name of the land where devotees can fly on flower airplanes?	
What N is the name of Kṛṣṇa who wears yellow robes, a helmet on His head, and has Goddess Lakṣmī at His feet?	
What V is Lord Brahmā impregnated with?	
What M is one name of the Lord's external energies?	
What S type of insect does the Lord act like while creating the material world, yet remaining aloof from its entanglement?	
What SPOG is another name for Kṛṣṇa, the cause and creator of all that exists.	

What B is another name for the process of self-realization?	
What P was Lord Brahmā worried about regarding his duty in creating the material universe?	

AUSTERITY: A REQUIREMENT FOR PROGRESS

Description: Lord Brahmā got the strength to create this universe only after much austerity. This is the way of the material world – to achieve anything in this world, we need to perform hard work. Even material achievements come only after hard work and austerity, so we can imagine the amount of hard work we must do to achieve spiritual success.

- Think of a couple of material achievements people covet, and write down the kinds of sacrifice, hard work and austerity they take up to achieve them.
- Think of some spiritual goals devotees try to attain and write down the austerities they need to go through to attain them.

You can complete the assignment by writing it out as a short story, illustrating it as a comic strip, or using case studies of real people. Which kind of austerity do you think yields more lasting results? Why?

CATUR-ŚLOKA MIND MAP

Description: Let's gain a deeper understanding of the four very important verses of this chapter – verses 2.9.32, 33, 34, 35. An effective technique is to make a mind map (or Spider diagram) to help you understand all the aspects of the verse thoroughly.

A mind map is a diagram used to visually outline information. It is often created around a single word or text, placed in the center, to which related ideas, words, and concepts are added. Search the internet for various examples.

You can start by writing the translations of these verses in four different bubbles on four separate sheets. Read the purports to understand the main points of each verse. Then, you can branch off the mind map by noting down the main points. For each main point, look for any examples or analogies that Śrīla Prabhupāda has mentioned.

WHAT'S THE QUESTION?

Description: Lord Kṛṣṇa has spoken the summary of *Śrīmad Bhāgavatam* in four verses to Lord Brahmā. Read the translations and purports of verses SB 2.9.31-35 with a partner.

Instead of asking questions from your study of these 5 verses, first provide an answer from the answer list below to your partner. Your partner must then come up with an appropriate question for your answer! Answers from verses 2.9.31-32 are given in the list. You can come up with your own answers from the rest of the verses.

For example, for the answer, "love of Godhead" your partner may respond with the question, "What is the qualification for knowing the mystery of the Personality of Godhead".

Answer list:

1. Love of Godhead

2. Association of devotees
3. Yogamāyā potency
4. Śri Brahmā Samhita
5. Protection of devotees
6. *Śrīmad Bhāgavatam*
7. Śri Govardhan Hill

Variation: Depending upon the length of the purport you can set a time limit for your partner to look up the questions to make it more challenging. Next, he/she will give you answers from the next verse and you have to formulate questions for them.

Theatrical Activities
. . . to bring out the actor in you!

Description: Make a complete puppet show about the creation story to perform for your friends and community.

Steps:

- Make a set using a cardboard box.
- For the scenery, paint a big bubble with an ocean scene on the bottom half and sky on the top. This will represent our universe.
- Make a lotus flower. Then make puppets or cut out pictures. You will need to make Lord Nārāyaṇa (four-handed form), Lord Garbhodakaśāyī Viṣṇu (lying down on Ananta Śeṣa), and Lord Brahmā. Then glue them onto cardboard.
- Lord Viṣṇu should be lying down and Lord Brahmā should be behind Him sitting in the lotus on a stem. You can push a stick through a hole in the bottom of the box so when pushed up, the lotus will rise up as if growing from Lord Viṣṇu.
- Cut out or draw an extra background of the Vaikuṇṭha planets.
- Children can choose or make music.
- Lights go on as music gets quieter.
- Someone can blow bubbles to fall on the scene.

Narrator: Once upon a time, far, far away, Lord Viṣṇu way lying down in the Garbhodaka ocean.

Lord Brahmā sitting on the lotus flower rises up from behind Lord Viṣṇu until fully grown.

Lord Brahmā: Oh my! Where am I? Well I know I am on a lotus, but I am so high up I can't even see where it begins! Where have I come from? I am supposed to create the material world and I can't even figure out how I was created. Anyone desiring perfect knowledge must seek the mercy of the Supreme Lord. There is no other way.

Voice from off stage: ...ta... pa... ta... pa...

Brahmā: Tapa? Tapasyā! Austerity! My Lord has spoken. But where is He? I have four heads looking in every direction, but I can't see anyone. I must follow His instruction.

Narrator: Thus Lord Brahmā meditated for a really, really, really long time. He had a vision of the Vaikuṇṭha planets.

Vaikuṇṭha planets' background appears in one corner then Lord Nārāyaṇa appears.

Lord Brahmā offers obeisances. Lord Nārāyaṇa comes forward and shakes Brahmā's hand.

Nārāyaṇa: I am very pleased with your penance Brahmā. You can ask from Me anything you like.

Brahmā: The Lord just shook my hand as if we were friends. Okay, thinking heads on…what should I ask for? Umm, please tell me how You in Your transcendental form appear to have a material body. How do you manifest these energies for creation? How can I create without being conditioned by pride in my creative abilities?

Narrator: Lord Nārāyaṇa then recited the catur-śloka, the four most important verses of *Śrīmad-Bhāgavatam* to Lord Brahmā. Let's listen really carefully...

Lord Nārāyaṇa: O Brahmā, it is I, the Personality of Godhead, who was existing before the creation, when there was nothing but Myself. Nor was there the material nature, the cause of this creation. That which you see now is also I, the Personality of Godhead, and after annihilation what remains will also be I, the Personality of Godhead.

O Brahmā, whatever appears to be of any value, if it is without relation to Me, has no reality. Know it as My illusory energy, that reflection which appears to be in darkness. Please know that the universal elements enter into the cosmos and at the same time do not enter into the cosmos; similarly, I myself also exist within everything created, and at the same time I am outside of everything.
A person who is searching after the Supreme Truth, the Personality of Godhead, must certainly search for it up to this, in all circumstances, in all space and time, and both directly and indirectly.

Lord Nārāyaṇa then disappears.

Lord Brahmā: Thank you my Lord, I shall start my service now.

Children sing:
Hare Kṛṣṇa Hare Kṛṣṇa Kṛṣṇa Kṛṣṇa Hare Hare
Hare Rāma Hare Rāma Rāma Rāma Hare Hare

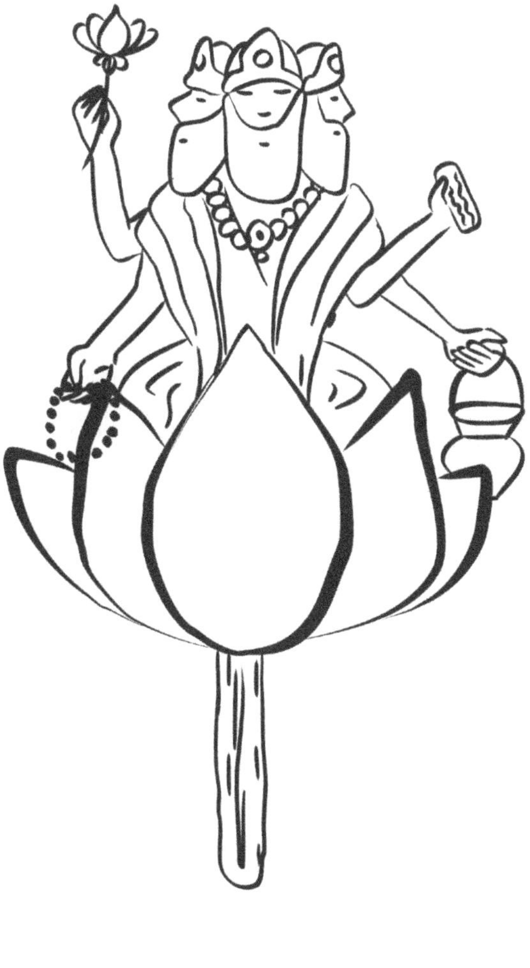

Deep in the ocean on a lotus petal bed
looking around Brahmā scratched His heads
Where have I come from what shall I do,
how can I create, oh I wish I knew!

Then from far away he heard a voice
Tapa it said, he knew he had no choice.
He sat in meditation for a really long time
until he saw the spiritual world divine.

The Lord appeared to his vision and kindly said
the catur śloka to him so he would not be misled
The Lord then disappeared and Brahmā then knew
how to serve his Lord of rain-cloud blue.

Hare Kṛṣṇa Hare Kṛṣṇa Kṛṣṇa Kṛṣṇa Hare Hare
Hare Rāma Hare Rāma Rāma Rāma Hare Hare

Music fades away and lights go down.

Introspective Activities
. . . to bring out the reflective devotee in you!

WHO AM I?

- Try to think of as many ways as you can to describe yourself. E.g., are you a boy or a girl? Are you happy or are you sad? Are you good at singing or good at running?
- Make a list as long as you can. Then go through your list and cross out anything that describes your body (e.g. tall/ short/ brown hair, etc.)
- Now go through your list again and cross out anything that describes your mind (e.g. happy/friendly/funny, etc.)

There should be **nothing** left on your list, because all the ways we can describe ourselves are ways of describing our body and our mind. In the first purport of this chapter, Śrīla Prabhupāda explains that the soul is different from the body and from the mind! So why do we feel like we are the body? It is because of Kṛṣṇa's magic power called māyā. Sometimes people say that I am not this body but it is "my" body. Śrīla Prabhupāda says in the first purport that this is also not correct – only because of māyā are we dreaming and thinking in terms of "I" and "mine".
Think about the differences and similarities of dreams and waking life. Why does Prabhupāda compare our waking life to a dream?

Artistic Activities
. . . to reveal your creativity!

COSMIC MAP

Description: With the help of an adult, draw a cosmic map of the material and spiritual planets. Before you start, you should know that the material world (where we all live) is just one fourth of the whole cosmic manifestation. The rest is the spiritual world.
To start with, you can use two sheets of paper.

On Sheet 1:

1. Draw an elliptical shape at the bottom of the page to represent the material world. The remaining sheet will be spiritual world.
2. The spiritual world is separated from the material creation by the Virajā River or the Kāraṇa Ocean.

3. Above the material world, you can draw lots of Vaikuṇṭha planets ruled by various incarnations of Lord Kṛṣṇa, such as Lord Nṛsiṁha, Varāha, etc., in the spiritual sky.
4. Above them draw Lord Rāma's abode, Ayodhyā.
5. The topmost planet is GolokaVṛndāvana where Kṛṣṇa lives with His pure devotees.

On sheet 2:

1. Start by drawing 14 elliptical shapes in a row. These shapes will depict 14 planetary systems in our universe. Draw large concentric circles representing coverings of earth, water, fire, air and ether around the universe.
2. Our planetary system is the middle system known as Bhūrloka.
3. There are six planetary systems above us – Bhuvarloka, Svargaloka, Maharloka, Janaloka, Tapoloka and Satyaloka (Lord Brahmā's abode).
4. There are seven planetary systems below us – Atala, Vitala, Sutala, Talātala, Mahātala, Rasātala and Pātāla.

Color your maps. You can also research additional information with the help of your parents and include that.

CATUR-ŚLOKA PAPER CHAIN

Description: Create a catur-śloka paper chain to remind you of the revelation of Lord Kṛṣṇa.

You will need: A2 or larger thick paper, scissors, pencil, pens

Steps:

1. Fold your paper lengthwise and cut it in half creating a long strip.
2. Fold your long strip in half and then fold it one more time. Fold them in such a way as to create four accordion-like pleats of equal size.
3. Draw a lotus on the top-most pleat making sure the petals on each side touch the edges of the paper.
4. Now cut around your lotus silhouette so that when you unfold the pleats, you will have a chain of four lotuses. If you don't get a chain of lotuses, search the internet for "paper doll chains" to get an idea of how to do this using lotuses instead of

drawing dolls.

5. Unfold your lotus flower chain and write one of the catur-śloka (Verses 33 thru 36 of this chapter) on each flower or one verse in Sanskrit or English across the flowers and decorate them.

DECORATIVE STONES

Description: Using your own realizations from Chapter 9, decorate simple stones to remind you of the pastime described in this chapter.

You will need: Pencil and paper, stones, paints, brushes

1. Read the story summary again and note down things that you found inspiring. What could you apply from the pastime? How could you practically do that? Make a plan.
2. Beautifully paint your stones to remind you of the pastime and your intention. For example, you may paint the word 'tapa' on your stone and leave it by your bed to remind you of the need of austerity.

Writing Activities . . . to bring out the writer in you!

COMPARATIVE ANALYSIS

Description: In the purport of verse 37 in this chapter, Śrīla Prabhupāda says, "As in the Bhagavad-gītā, Tenth Chapter, the Personality of Godhead, Lord Kṛṣṇa, has summarized the whole text in four verses, namely *ahaṁ sarvasya prabhavaḥ,* etc., so the complete *Śrīmad-Bhāgavatam* has also been summarized in four verses, as *aham evāsam evāgre*, etc."

Your task:

1. Read the translations and purports of the four summary verses in Bhagavad-gītā (Chapter 10, verses 8-11, and the four summary verses in the *Śrīmad-Bhāgavatam* (Chapter 9, verses 33-36).
2. In your own words, write a comparison between the two sets of summary verses – what are the common themes you can detect; are there some points that are in the Bhagavad-gītā summary that are not emphasized so much in the *Śrīmad-Bhāgavatam* summary, etc.

SPEECH WRITING

Description: Imagine you are a witness when Lord Nārāyaṇa comes and speaks to Lord Brahmā. Write a speech to read at this auspicious time. You can use some of the points below to help you:

- Introduce Lord Brahmā.
- What is your relationship to him?
- What events in his life would you mention to glorify him?
- Describe how we can continue to benefit from his association by following his instructions and his devotion to the Lord.

READING AND COMPREHENSION 3-2-1

After reading the story summary for this chapter, use this reading strategy below to summarize key events, to focus on important points of interest, and to clarify areas you may be unsure about.

3 New things you discovered

2 Interesting facts. Why are they interesting?

1 Question you still have

SENTENCE MATCH UP

Match the first part of the sentence on the left with the part of the sentence on the right to correct and finish the sentence.

1. The body one receives is determined by	a) and was overcome with joy in his heart.
2. The story began when Lord Brahmā appeared	b) the conditioned soul's material desires.
3. Lord Brahmā saw the Supreme Lord in His fullest glory	c) from somewhere nearby.
4. I exist within everything created and	d) who meditated upon the Lord on the bank of the Sarasvatī River.
5. Thinking in terms of "I" or "mine"	e) on his lotus flower from the abdomen of Garbhodakaśāyī Viṣṇu.
6. At that moment, he heard two sounds, "ta" and "pa",	f) desiring self-interest for the welfare of all living entities.
7. Later Nārada would instruct the powerful Vyāsadeva	g) simultaneously exist outside of everything.
8. Thus Lord Brahmā, the forefather of all living entities, situated himself in acts of regulative principles,	h) only causes more bondage to this world.

WHAT WORDS FIT THE CLUES?

Read the sentence clues in the table and identify the correct corresponding word or phrase from the box to make both sentences true.

Penance	Śukadeva Gosvāmī	
Material desires	8,400,000 species of life	Humility

Sentence Clues	Answer from the box above
There is this number of species in the material world. A person can transition from one species to this number of species.	
This determines what body a soul receives. Is the reason we are in this material world.	
He was describing *Śrīmad Bhāgavatam* to the King. His name means 'parrot'.	
Lord Brahmā heard this within his heart and began to perform it. After 1,000 years of it, the Lord showed Himself to Lord Brahmā.	
What Lord Brahmā showed by bowing down to the Lord. What is needed to chant the Holy Names of the Lord.	

MISSING WORDS ACTIVITY SHEET

Directions: After reading the story summary, choose the correct word from the box below to complete the sentences.

sight	father	transmitting
dreamer	Nārada	Brahmā
transcendental	unable	"ta" and "pa"
working	alone	

1. Thus, the _________ told the whole *Bhāgavatam* with satisfaction to his son, _____________.
2. The Lord's eyes widened as if ______________ knowledge and realization into the heart of ______________.
3. "What a ___________ that must have been!" replied Nārada, imagining what the Lord's _____________________ form and features looked like.
4. He was ____________ and all he could see was darkness everywhere. Looking around from side to side, he was ____________ to trace out the source of his lotus seat.
5. At that moment, he heard two sounds, _____________ repeated twice, from somewhere nearby.
6. It's like a ____________'s seeing his own body _______________!"

SPELLING ERRORS

There are one or more spelling mistakes in each sentence. Write the correct spelling of each word in the space provided.

Śri Śukadeva Gosvāmī was relishing his receitation of transcendental knowledge to King Parīkṣit. _________________

So then, how does a conditioned soul attein a particular speicis of life or body?

________, __________

Lord Brahmā felt within him an immence desier to create the universe, but realized he did not know how or even where to start! ________________

"Giving Lord Brahmā a loving smile, the Supreme Lord spoke, 'O Lord Brahmā, my son, impregneted with the Vedas, I am so very pleased with your penunce and your desire to create! ________, _________

Dear Brahmā, it was I who gave you your first order by speaking the two syllabels "ta" and "pa" deep into your heart. ________________

Thus Lord Brahmā, the fourfather of all living entities, situated himself in acts of regulative principles, desiring self-interest for the welfare of all living entities.

____

Nārada bowed before his father and with good maners, meekness and sense control, inquired from him in detail about transcendental knowledge his father was given by the Lord. ________________

SEQUENCING

Given below are few of the events that have happened in Chapter 9 Answers by Citing the Lord's Version. They are all mixed up. Arrange them in the order mentioned in the summary of the chapter.

1. Lord Kṛṣṇa in His Nārāyaṇa form was seated on a golden throne.
2. Mahārāja Parīkṣit questioned, "8,400,000 species of life?! How does a conditioned soul attain a particular species of life or body?"
3. Seeing the Supreme Lord of Vaikuṇṭha in His full glory, Lord Brahmā's heart was filled with joy.
4. However, the true spiritual journey begins when the living entity starts to enjoy the transcendence beyond time and material energy and becomes free from the material concepts of "I" or "mine", realizing that everything belongs to Lord Sri Kṛṣṇa, who is the source of all creation!"
5. The Lord also explained to Lord Brahmā that if anything appears to be without relation to Him, it has no reality at all but is only His illusory material energy mahā-māyā.
6. Thus, Lord Brahmā, the forefather of all living entities, situated himself in acts of regulative principles, desiring self-interest for the welfare of all living entities."
7. The story began when Lord Brahmā appeared on the lotus flower originating from

the navel of Maha-Viṣṇu.

8. Sri Śukadeva Gosvāmī was relishing his recitation of transcendental knowledge to King Parīkṣit.
9. The Supreme Personality of Godhead, Hari, being seen in His transcendental form, instructing Lord Brahmā, then disappeared.
10. "And because I did not know how or where to start the process of creating this material universe, I took this voice as a divine and transcendental instruction to perform penance.

LORD BRAHMA SEEKING HIS SOURCE

In this activity, you will be creating your very own children's book. The target audience for your book is children between 4 to 6 years of age. Look at some children's books for those ages to get an idea of the illustrations and the type of language that is used. Your book must also be concise. Go through the story of Lord Brahma as described in this chapter to pick out the key events to include in your book.

It is a good idea to plan your book first before you start assembling it. Depending on how many events you wish to include in your book, you can decide to use more or less pages than the number given in the instructions below.

What you need

- 4 sheets of white paper (Letter size or A4 size).
- 1 sheet of white or colored card (thicker paper for the book cover; same size as the other sheets).
- Scissors, glue, coloring pencils or pens, decorative bits and pieces.

Instructions

1. Fold the four sheets of paper and one sheet of card width-wise.
2. Put them together and staple the center fold to make a booklet with the card as the outside cover and the white paper as the inside pages.
3. Write the title on the front cover: "How I Found My Source!" by Lord Brahma and draw a picture to accompany this.
4. On each left-hand page inside the book, include a caption that briefly describes each part of Lord Brahma's journey.

5. On the right-hand page opposite the caption, draw a picture to illustrate the scene described.
6. Decorate your book cover and inside pages to make it attractive to young children!

KEYWORDS

Define the following keywords from the story.

- Use each word in a sentence (either in oral or written form).
- Complete a New Word Map at the back of the book for any new words.

Keyword	Definition
Cite	
Utopia	
Misconceive	
Multifarious	
Altruism	
Untinged	
Penance	
Syllable	

WHAT DO YOU THINK?

Set 1 - Tick the statements that you think are correct.

1. Śukadeva Gosvāmī wanted Parīkṣit Mahārāja to answer all possible questions that may arise in the mind of a serious student of the Bhāgavatam.
2. Non-devotee living entities are illusioned by the will of the Lord because they want to become like Him.
3. All material activities are permanent.
4. By giving up the illusion of "I" and "mine" through service to the Lord, the living entity can be situated once again in his original transcendental position.
5. Pleased with Lord Brahmā's penance, the Supreme Lord revealed to him His personal transcendental abode called Vaikuṇṭha.

6. The Supreme Lord said to Brahmā. "Dear Brahmā, it was I who ordered you to undergo penance ('tapa')."
7. The Supreme Lord was pleased to hear Lord Brahmā's questions and spoke the entire science of the *Śrīmad*-Bhāgavatam in great detail.
8. Everything in the material universe emanates from Brahmā, but at the same time he is untouched by material contamination.

WORD SEARCH

N	O	I	T	A	R	B	I	V	M
A	S	A	U	H	D	F	C	E	A
E	P	O	P	U	L	E	N	C	E
N	E	J	U	O	P	U	L	N	N
H	C	E	N	R	A	F	A	A	U
A	I	N	E	G	C	D	R	N	T
T	A	M	U	N	N	E	A	E	R
M	L	A	N	U	E	A	T	P	O
K	S	E	M	A	N	A	T	E	F
O	D	T	G	I	O	R	I	M	Y
S	O	R	I	G	I	T	I	M	L
P	R	S	U	R	S	G	R	Q	E
H	S	E	I	T	U	D	H	T	C
A	J	N	F	O	L	T	A	N	S
R	G	G	P	S	L	L	T	S	T
K	I	A	E	U	I	E	A	H	A
B	A	G	N	H	U	S	R	O	C
C	D	E	A	L	D	O	B	U	Y
B	E	N	V	I	N	A	S	R	K
D	N	K	C	E	N	G	A	M	E
A	N	N	L	A	T	E	M	U	N

Annihilate
Duties
Ecstasy
Emanate
Enchant
Engage
Fortune
Illusion
Mundane
Opulence
Source
Special
Throne
Vibration

ANSWERS

Understanding the Story (pages 260-261)

1)c, 2)b, 3)a, 4)b, 5)c, 6)a, 7)b, 8)c, 9)b, 10)a

First letter question game (pages 267-268)

Vaikuṇṭha
Nārāyaṇa
Vedas
Mahāmāyā
Spider
Supreme Personality of Godhead
Bhakti-yoga
Pride

Sentence match up (pages 279-280)

1)b, 2)e, 3)a, 4)g, 5)h, 6)c, 7)d, 8)f

What Words fit the Clues? (pages 280-281)

8,400,000 species of life
Material desires
Śukadeva Gosvāmī
Penance
Humility

Missing Words Activity Sheet (page 282)

father, Nārada
transmitting, Brahmā
sight, transcendental
alone, unable
"ta" and "pa"
dreamer, working

Spelling Errors (pages 282-283)

recitation
attain; species
immense; desire
impregnated; penance

syllables
forefather
manners

Sequencing (pages 283-284)

1. Sri Śukadeva Gosvāmī was relishing his recitation of transcendental knowledge to King Parīkṣit.
2. Mahārāja Parīkṣit questioned, "8,400,000 species of life?! How does a conditioned soul attain a particular species of life or body?"
3. However, the true spiritual journey begins when the living entity starts to enjoy the transcendence beyond time and material energy and becomes free from the material concepts of "I" or "mine", realizing that everything belongs to Lord Sri Kṛṣṇa, who is the source of all creation!"
4. The story began when Lord Brahmā appeared on the lotus flower originating from the navel of Mahā-Viṣṇu.
5. "And because I did not know how or where to start the process of creating this material universe, I took this voice as a divine and transcendental instruction to perform penance.
6. Lord Kṛṣṇa in His Nārāyaṇa form was seated on a golden throne.
7. Seeing the Supreme Lord of Vaikuṇṭha in His full glory, Lord Brahmā's heart was filled with joy.
8. The Lord also explained to Lord Brahmā that if anything appears to be without relation to Him, it has no reality at all but is only His illusory material energy mahā-māyā.
9. The Supreme Personality of Godhead, Hari, being seen in His transcendental form, instructing Lord Brahmā, then disappeared.
10. Thus, Lord Brahmā, the forefather of all living entities, situated himself in acts of regulative principles, desiring self-interest for the welfare of all living entities."

Keywords (page 285)

Keyword	Definition
Cite	to write or say the words (of a book, a person, etc.); refer to something as evidence or as justification
Utopia	an ideal place (usually imaginary) where everything is perfect; paradise
Misconceive	poorly planned; poorly thought out

Multifarious	of many different kinds; diverse
Altruism	desire to help others without any selfish motives
Untinged	not even the least affected (by something)
Penance	act of doing a good deed to make up for past wrongs; punishment inflicted on oneself to repent for something you have done wrong
Syllable	a unit of pronunciation having one vowel sound, with or without surrounding consonants, forming the whole or part of a word

What do you think? (pages 285-286)

1. Incorrect
2. Correct
3. Incorrect
4. Correct
5. Correct
6. Correct
7. Incorrect
8. Incorrect

Word Search (page 286)

N	O	I	T	A	R	B	I	V	
	S							E	
	P	O	P	U	L	E	N	C	E
	E		U					N	N
	C			R			A	A	U
	I				C	D		N	T
	A				N	E		E	R
	L			U				P	O
		E	M	A	N	A	T	E	F
					O				
					I				
					S				E
	S	E	I	T	U	D		T	C
		N			L		A	N	S
		G			L	L		A	T
		A			I			H	A
		G		H			R	C	S
		E	I			O		N	Y
		N	V		N			E	
	N			E					A

10

Bhāgavatam Is the Answer to All Questions

Story Summary

Śukadeva Gosvāmī was very pleased that the sages of Naimiṣāraṇya were so inquisitive about the transcendental pastimes of the Lord. They were wise and knew that the soul experiences pleasure only by hearing the transcendental pastimes of Lord Sri Kṛṣṇa.

Śukadeva Gosvāmī explained to Mahārāja Parīkṣit that the *Śrīmad-Bhāgavatam* is divided into 10 subject matters – creation, sub-creation, planetary systems, the Lord's protection, creative impetus, change of Manus, the science of God, returning home - back to Godhead, liberation and the summum bonum (absolute conclusion).

Taking a deep breath, Śukadeva Gosvāmī clasped his hands together, and closed his eyes remembering the story he had heard from his father, Vyāsadeva. "It was a grand display of creation. Mahā-Viṣṇu, the first expanded puruṣa incarnation of the Lord, was lying in the Causal Ocean, inhaling and exhaling. At each breath, innumerable universes were being created and destroyed from the pores of His transcendental body."

"Ah, from His pores?" asked Mahārāja Parīkṣit.

"Yes!" replied Śukadeva Gosvāmī. "The Lord simultaneously created the original creation and its elements - sixteen items of matter composed of the five elements (fire, water, earth, air and sky), along with sound, form, taste, smell, touch, and eyes, ears, nose, tongue, skin and mind throughout space and in this universe. All of these creations were produced by His external energy."

"Wow, the Lord created these elements all at once? How wonderful!" said the King.

"Actually, the Lord is very clever, and do you know why? Because He has so many incarnations! He has His original two-handed form in Goloka Vṛndāvana. The *Śrīmad-Bhāgavatam*, which is His sound incarnation is also non-different from Him. By His causeless mercy, Kṛṣṇa has even expanded Himself as Kṣīrodakaśāyī Viṣṇu (Paramātmā) who resides in every atom and in the heart of every living being. The Lord comes personally to perform wonderful pastimes and make these stories worthwhile to speak for the benefit of all."

Śukadeva Gosvāmī stated that by following the laws of God, written by Lord Brahmā's sons the Manus, humans receive good guidance and free themselves from fruitive activities. Ultimately, they can provide shelter for all the other living entities.

"This world is created specifically as a place for conditioned souls to seek salvation and be free from fruitive activities simply by devotional service" Śukadeva Gosvāmī said, looking side to side, glancing at the King and sages. "What a blessing it is to have a human body, the facility to lead a regulated life, read transcendental scriptures like the *Śrīmad-*

Bhāgavatam, and chant the Lord's name!"

Śukadeva Gosvāmī revealed how the Lord produced the elements of matter, from which Lord Brahmā then produced everything else in the universe.

Mahārāja Parīkṣit looked puzzled, "Are you saying that the Supreme Lord as well as Lord Brahmā are both creators of this world?"

"Well, in a way, yes," said Śukadeva Gosvāmī. "The Lord created the original materials of the universe, and Lord Brahmā, who is empowered by the Lord, used the materials to engineer this material world." Śukadeva Gosvāmī paused. "In the material world, there is a system of power and responsibility based on the performance of pious work. In the spiritual world, everyone's desire is to serve and surrender to the Lord. Therefore, Kṛṣṇa is the only controller and has no competitors. However, Kṛṣṇa empowers and situates those who perform pious and devotional activities in positions of control to maintain and to guide others. These controllers such as Lord Brahmā – who is a demigod – are called adhidaivik, or the controlling deity. They controlled living entity is called the adhyātmic person, and the material body is the adhibautic puruṣaḥ."

"So the demigods can't control the adhyātmic living entity without his body (the *adhibhautika puruṣaḥ*)?" asked Mahārāja Parīkṣit.

"That's right. The body is the medium for the controller to control; therefore, the controller, the controlled, and the body are all interdependent on each other. However, the Supreme Controller, Lord Kṛṣṇa, can see this interdependence that He created, and therefore, is Himself the only independent!"

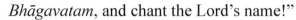

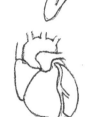

"As Kṛṣṇa resides in all atoms and in everyone's heart, surely there must be some independence in everyone?" asked the king.

"But it is Kṛṣṇa's independence, not the living entities'!" replied Śukadeva Gosvāmī. "By relying on Kṛṣṇa within the heart as Supersoul, the living entities can hear Kṛṣṇa, recognize they are one with Him, and learn how to follow Him."

"One with Him?!" Mahārāja Parīkṣit was disappointed. "How can you become one with Kṛṣṇa?"

"You can understand you have the quality of the Lord and can listen to Him," replied Śukadeva Gosvāmī. "The material body is actually a great boon and an opportunity to seek a personal relationship with Kṛṣṇa and connect to Him. He is within the heart as a person, as Lord Nārāyaṇa.

"Everything in creation exists because of His mercy and is created for His pleasure, including all activities, time, modes and the enjoying living entities."

Śukadeva Gosvāmī continued to explain material creation:

"Mahā-Viṣṇu was lying in the ocean
Sleeping and filled with desire
The sense energy, mental force, and bodily strength came first
And the fountainhead of total living force transpired

The totality of all entities became agitated,
So hunger and thirst were generated!
A desire to eat and drink came next
With the palate, tongue and tastes to supplement

A deity for each feature was there
To take the reins of activities
For the material world is a simple game
Of the controller, controlled, and bodies

Then manifested the Supreme's desire to speak
And speeches vibrated from His mouth
The deity of fire was created
To extinguish any and all doubts

The desire to smell odors
Was followed by nostrils and respiration.
Then came into existence
nasal instruments and odor, deity of air, and smell!

The Lord desired to see Himself
As well as His creation
So the sun, the eyes and vision were generated
With the object of sight and phenomenal creation

The ears, power of hearing and deity came
As the sages desired to know and hear
The topic of the Self was the most desired
As the aural reception became most dear

Then came physical characteristics of matter,
Softness, hardness, warmth, and cold
The skin, the pores, hairs on the body were created
And looked after by the trees who lord them all

To perform varieties of work
The two hands, controlling strength, and Indra became manifest
Sense organs and the desire to control movement were there
So legs and Viṣṇu came to represent

Then the genitals for sex pleasure
Came with the deity Prajāpati
To produce offspring and taste heavenly nectar
In health and honest prosperity

To evacuate the refuse of the body
The anus was then put in place
The sensory organs and deity Mitra
Could then work and navigate

The desire to move from one body to another
Was granted by the navel, air of departure, and death
Along with the coming of life through birth
For each soul and for each breath

The Lord then desired to have food and drink
And the intestines and arteries were created
The rivers and seas became their deities
Metabolism became strong and stimulated

To think of His activities and His own energies
The heart became manifested
The mind, determination and desire were there

With the moon, as deity, completely dedicated

Then the seven elements of the body!
A thin layer on the skin, skin, flesh, blood, fat,
Marrow and bone – all made of earth, water and fire
As life breath made of sky air and water was intact

At last the subtleties of material creation came into existence
The false ego and the material modes it creates
The best is to stay clear from such illusions
By using intelligence and seeking good association."

Śukadeva Gosvāmī confirmed that Kṛṣṇa is always transcendental and descends in His transcendental form out of affection for His parts and parcels. His forms and activities may appear to be same as those of a conditioned soul but He is unaffected by such activities.

All the living entities are created by the Supreme Lord according to their past deeds, from the highest forms of life such as the demigods like Indra, and great sages like Bhṛgu and Vyāsa, to the lowest forms of life such as the serpentines, ghosts and spirits. Different living creatures such as demigods, humans, and hellish beings, come into being depending on their different modes of material nature. But the highest man is the one who serves the devotees of the Lord and takes their association.

"Like Nārada Muni…" Parīkṣit Mahārāja thought silently.

Śukadeva Gosvāmī added, "The Supreme

Personality appears in different incarnations after creation just to guide the living entities back home. At the end of the millennium, the Lord Himself comes in the form of Rudra, the destroyer, and annihilates the whole creation. The living entities, called the marginal energies, merge into the body of Mahā-Viṣṇu during what is called the winding up period, either to be reborn into the material world or lifted back up to the spiritual sky."

"But, O King, for the devotees, the only wish is to serve the Lord by taking up pure devotional service. These activities in the *Bhāgavatam* really do not interest the devotees much at all because they know that by taking to the process of devotional service, they will become qualified to enter into the Kingdom of God, and serve the Lord personally in Goloka Vṛndāvana."

Key Messages

- Look them up in your *Śrīmad-Bhāgavatam.*
- Put them in your own words to help you memorize them.
- Discuss each one further.
- Apply them in your life.

Theme	References	Key Messages
What is liberation?	2.10.6	We have material bodies because we forgot our relationship with Kṛṣṇa and wanted to enjoy independent of Him. If we follow scriptural instructions, accept a spiritual master, and perform devotional service, we can permanently give up our material bodies and go back to our original spiritual form. This is called liberation. In fact, by reading or hearing from literatures such as the *Śrīmad-Bhāgavatam*, we can purify ourselves and achieve liberation even in the conditional state of material existence.
Living entities are fully dependent on Kṛṣṇa	2.10.20	Kṛṣṇa is absolutely independent and all living entities are absolutely dependent on Kṛṣṇa. We are able to see when Kṛṣṇa desires to see, we can smell when Kṛṣṇa smells, and so on. By His mercy, we can think of doing something independently, but we cannot act independently. Everything is first desired by the Supreme Lord and only then the living entity can act upon it.
Making the best use of our senses	2.10.24	Our sense organs (ears, eyes, nose, etc.) are created by Kṛṣṇa's will. Kṛṣṇa controls the demigods, the demigods control our sense organs, and our senses control us. Therefore, it is clear that Kṛṣṇa is the ultimate controller and our senses are never independent. The best course of action for us is to utilize our senses in the service of Kṛṣṇa, who is known as the Lord of the senses (Hṛṣīkeśa). Devotional service (bhakti) provides the pathway to utilize our senses in Kṛṣṇa's service.
Importance of devotee association	2.10.41	All of us are influenced by the mode of passion because of our tendency to control material nature according to our desires. Depending on our association, we can also become influenced either by the mode of goodness or by the mode of ignorance in varying degrees. The best association is that of the Lord's devotees by which one can counteract the influences of the modes of passion and ignorance, develop good habits, and make great progress in devotional service.

Understanding the Story

Now it's time for you to check how well you understood the story by answering these multiple-choice questions. (Answers at the end of the chapter.)

1. What is transcendental knowledge?
   a) Knowledge about the laws of the country we currently live in.
   b) Knowledge about the Lord, His devotees, other living entities, and the material creation.
   c) Knowledge about rules and regulations to be followed at school, on roads and in our place of work.
2. How should we acquire transcendental knowledge?
   a) It must be heard from proper authorities in disciplic succession.
   b) It can be learned by reading any spiritual books found in a book shop or library.
   c) We can try to understand this knowledge by speculating with our mind.
3. What was Śukadeva Gosvāmī's response to Parīkṣit Mahārāja's question as to why the material creation takes place?
   a) The material world was created so Nārada Muni could travel to different universes.
   b) It becomes home for the Supreme Lord after the spiritual world is destroyed by Rudra at the end of each millennium.
   c) Out of His causeless mercy, the Lord manifests the material creation to fulfil the desire of the rebellious living entities who wish to enjoy separately from Him.
4. Who provides the main elements needed to start the process of creation?
   a) Lord Brahmā.
   b) Lord Kṛṣṇa in the form of Mahā-Viṣṇu.
   c) Lord Śiva.
5. Once creation is performed, what is the role of the Lord?
   a) The Lord leaves all the living entities in the material world to suffer for eternity and goes back to His abode in the spiritual world to enjoy.
   b) Out of His love for us He appears in the universe in different incarnations to reclaim the conditioned living entities. Finally, the Lord Himself in the form of Rudra annihilates the complete creation.
   c) In order to sport with the living entities the Lord annihilates material creation soon after the creation is completed.
6. What facilities does the Lord give living entities for material enjoyment?

a) To allow the living entities to engage in material enjoyment, the Lord gives them forms with senses, intelligence, and body.
b) The Lord does not give them any facilities as He can be the only enjoyer.
c) The Lord gives them spiritual bodies that do not get diseased, grow old, or die so that living entities can enjoy in the material word forever.

7. Who controls the facilities living entities are given for enjoyment?
 a) The living entity because they are using these facilities.
 b) The demigods. For example, the sun-god controls the sense of sight as we cannot see anything without the sun.
 c) The Supreme Lord fully controls the ordinary living entities and demigods and they cannot do anything without His sanction.
8. What is the difference between material creation and the spiritual world?
 a) As they are both created by Kṛṣṇa, the material and spiritual worlds are the same, only separated by distance.
 b) The material manifestation of the Lord is temporary so it is created and annihilated again and again, whereas, the spiritual world is eternal and full of bliss.
 c) The material world is real as we live here, but the spiritual world does not exist as we have never seen it.
9. What happens to the Supreme Lord when He appears in the material creation for a short period of time, for example as Nṛsiṁha or Matsya?
 a) His body is affected by material conditions such as old age, death, disease, envy, anger etc.
 b) He is always transcendental and unaffected by material contamination.
 c) He gets trapped in the repeated cycle of birth and death and therefore keeps appearing in different bodies such as a fish, tortoise, etc.
10. How can we remain under Kṛṣṇa's protection while we are in the material world?
 a) If we obey the laws of the Lord as explained in the scriptures, we can achieve perfect peace of mind and always remain under His protection.
 b) We pray to demigods who are the real protectors and sanction Kṛṣṇa's protection of His devotees.
 c) By thoroughly enjoying the material world we can show our appreciation for Kṛṣṇa's creation and therefore earn His protection.
11. What can we do to go back to the transcendental realm?
 a) By dedicating all of our activities, our possessions, our senses, and even our family to the service of Viṣṇu we can get rid of all material contaminations in our heart and go back to the spiritual world.

b) Everyone goes to the transcendental realm after death so we can continue to live our life according to our circumstances.
c) It is impossible to go back to the transcendental realm as it is very far away.

Higher-Thinking Questions

Now it's time to deepen your understanding of Chapter 10 by delving into Śrīla Prabhupāda's purports for this chapter and reflecting upon the following questions.

1. What are the ten subject matters of the *Śrīmad-Bhāgavatam*? Give examples from the scriptures on three of the topics. (Examples: Creation and sub creation by Mahā-Viṣṇu and Brahmā respectively).
2. Explain how the Lord is both within and without everything and give some examples of how this is true.
3. "By following the laws of God, written by Lord Brahmā's sons the Manus, humans receive good guidance and free themselves from fruitive activities". Give examples of how humans can free themselves from the reactions of fruitive activities.
4. Kṛṣṇa is the only independent and all of us are dependent on the Lord and demigods. Think of some examples from your day to day life that illustrate the truth of this sentence.
5. What is the difference between "being one with God" and "knowing God in the heart"? Explain why meditating on the personal form of the Lord is better than merging into Him.
6. Why do devotees prefer Kṛṣṇa in His two-handed form? What are His qualities in the two-handed form that make him more attractive to His devotee?

ACTIVITIES

In this section you will find many exciting things to do! They will get you thinking, moving, drawing, acting, and most importantly, having loads of fun!

Critical Thinking Activities
. . . to bring out the spiritual investigator in you!

BHĀGAVATAM AT YOUR FINGERTIPS

Description: List the ten topics of the *Śrīmad-Bhāgavatam* on each of the fingers in the image provided in Resource 1. Write down a sentence about each in the space provided below. Consult the answers section of this chapter for examples of sentences you can write. You can cut out the hands and stick them on a pair of gloves, making your own '*Bhāgavatam* gloves'!

1.

2.

3.

4.

5.

6.

7.

8.

9.

10.

BHĀGAVATAM MIND MAP

Create a mind map to visually arrange information of the ten topics covered by the *Śrīmad Bhāgavatam*. You can find examples of mind maps on the internet. You can place a drawing of Kṛṣṇa or write *Śrīmad-Bhāgavatam* in the center bubble, and make ten branches/bubbles around the center bubble and fill them with the ten subjects. Add at least one more fact to each category after reading this chapter. As you continue to study *Bhāgavatam*, you will find more information on these ten categories.

SENTENCE STARTERS

Based on the chapter summary and verse translations, complete the following sentences:

1. Speeches were vibrated from the Lord's mouth because ______________________

   ____

2. The nostrils and respiration were generated because ______________________

   ____

3. The eyes and power of vision became manifested because ______________________

   ____

4. The ears, the power of hearing and the controlling deity of hearing became manifested because ____

5. The two hands and their controlling strength became manifested because ____________

   ____

6. His legs became manifested because ____________________________________

   ____

7. The abdomen, intestines, and the arteries became manifest because ___________

   ____

8. The heart, mind, moon and determination became manifest because ___________

   ____

9. The navel and air of departure was manifested because ____________________

____

10. The trees were generated because ____

____

Analogy Activities . . . to bring out the scholar in you!

MANIFEST AND UNMANIFEST

Verse 43: *Thereafter, at the end of the millennium, the Lord Himself in the form of Rudra, the destroyer, will annihilate the complete creation as the wind displaces the clouds.*

In this verse, the creation, maintenance and destruction of the universe is compared to clouds. In the water cycle, clouds are created, stay for some time in the sky, and are ultimately dispersed by the wind, or shower down as rain. We know that water particles remain in the air in the form of vapor before they condense to form clouds. These water particles, although the same as the cloud, are the "unmanifest" form of the cloud before condensing.

Creation is explained in a similar way in this verse. In the purport, Śrīla Prabhupāda explains the process by quoting verses 8.19-20 from the Bhagavad-gītā.

Read these verses and understand the manifest and unmanifest stage of creation. Then complete the following table with reference to the analogy. Answers can be found at the end of this chapter.

Reference object	Manifest stage	Unmanifest stage
Cloud		
Creation		

Next, draw a simple water cycle diagram in the space below and depict the manifest and unmanifest stage of the cloud. In the space below that, draw a similar cyclic diagram of the universe's creation, maintenance and destruction and label the manifest and unmanifest stages. Remember that the stages in the two cycles do NOT have to correspond exactly. See examples at the end of this chapter.

The water cycle

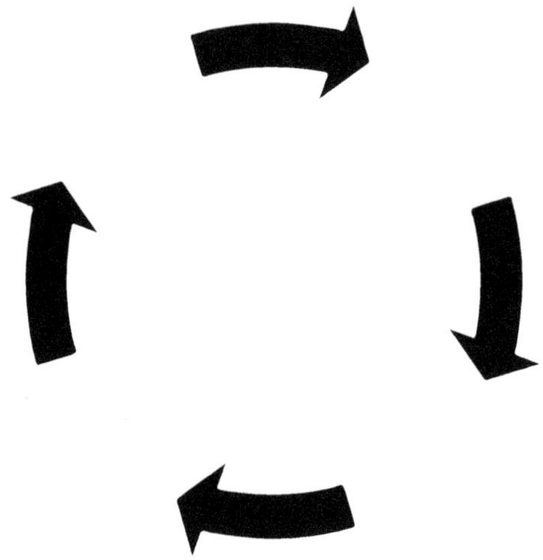

The cycle of creation

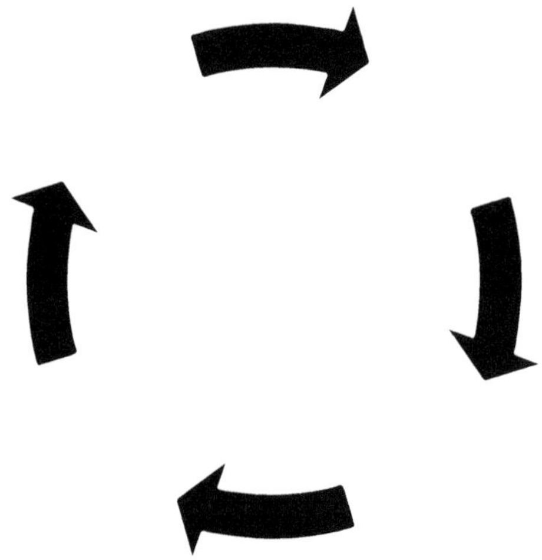

Introspective Activities
. . . to bring out the reflective devotee in you!

Description: In the purport to verse 5 of this chapter Śrīla Prabhupāda says: "the material creation is created for the salvation of the conditioned souls." The Lord comes to the external world to attract us by His pastimes.
Make a list of your favorite pastimes of Kṛṣṇa. Why do you like each pastime? What does it mean for you? Is there a person in the pastime that you can relate to? Why does Kṛṣṇa attract you in your favorite pastimes?

Artistic Activities
. . . to reveal your creativity!

NUTSHELL SCULPTURE

Description: Śukadeva Gosvāmī narrated the entire *Śrīmad-Bhāgavatam* in a nutshell, as spoken by the Supreme Lord himself to Brahmā. Discuss the meaning of this sentence and read the second paragraph of the story summary. Make a list of the ten subjects of *Śrīmad-Bhāgavatam* to create this piece of art. You can see an example in Resource 2.

You will need:
A nutshell, wire / thread, some fabric, pens, paints, collage pictures, glue.

Steps:
1. On your fabric, paint, draw or collage your list of ten things.
2. Hang your work on the wall at the top and gather it at the bottom and secure with wire or thread. Place your nutshell at the base of the material as if your collage is expanding from the nutshell.

ELEMENTS MEMORY GAME

Description: Try and remember the sixteen elements – fire, water, earth, air, and ether; sound, form, taste, smell, and touch; eyes, ears, nose, tongue, skin and mind.

You will need: Pen, pencil, paper, scissors,

Steps:

1. Draw each of the elements or design a text for each element and write out each word.
2. Cut out each element and study them carefully. Try to remember them all.
3. Test yourself and write down as any as you can remember. Play a game with a friend, so your friend takes away two or three elements, and you have to remember which ones are missing. You can increase the number of elements taken away each time you play.

Writing Activities . . . to bring out the writer in you!

GET THE WORDS RIGHT

Some of the words in the sentences and passages selected from the summary are scrambled up. Can you make the scrambled words right?

1. Śukadeva Gosvāmī was very pleased that the sages of Naimiṣāraṇya were so ivustinieqi ___________ about the transcendental spestima ___________ of the Lord.
2. Mahā-Viṣṇu, the first expanded puruṣa incarnation of the Lord, was lying in the Causal Ocean, giilhann ___________ and exhaling.
3. The Lord comes personally to perform wonderful pastimes and make these stories hheliwwrot ___________ to speak for the benefit of all.
4. This world is created specifically as a place for conditioned souls to seek salvation and be free from evrufiti ___________ activities simply by devotional service.
5. In the spiritual world, everyone's desire is to serve and redersnur ___________ to the Lord. Therefore, Kṛṣṇa is the only rentcoroll ___________ and has no competitors.
6. He is duffeenact ___________ by the material activities.
7. Different living creatures such as gimsedod ___________, humans, and shheill ___________ beings come into being depending on their different modes of material nature.
8. At the end of the mmunnellii ___________, the Lord Himself comes in the form of Rudra, the deerstory ___________, and annihilates the whole creation.

WORD JUMBLE MATCHING

The following words are all jumbled up! Unjumble them first and then draw a line from the organ to match the activity that organ performs.

Organ	
Jumbled	Unjumbled
nguoet	
uomth	
eons	
eeys	
aesr	
iksn	
Ndhas nda gles	

Action	
Jumbled	Unjumbled
ese	
uothc	
staet	
keasp	
lesml	
rkow	
ehra	

After reading the story summary, choose three of the above sets of organ/activities, then elaborate on what kind of hearing, what kind of seeing, etc., are these organs originally intended for.

1. ____

2. ____

3. ____

PUNCTUATION PRACTICE

Description: The following passage is from the Story Summary, but someone forgot to punctuate it! Edit it, using punctuation marks: periods, commas, apostrophes, and quotation marks. Add capital letters. Check your answer against the edited version in the answer section.

actually the lord is very clever and do you know why because he has so many incarnations he has his original two-handed form in goloka Vṛndāvana the *Śrīmad-Bhāgavatam* which is his sound incarnation is also non-different from him by his causeless mercy Kṛṣṇa has even expanded himself as Kṣīrodakaśāyī Viṣṇu (Paramātmā) who resides in every atom and in the heart of every living being the lord comes personally to perform wonderful pastimes and make these stories worthwhile to speak for the benefit of all.

Śukadeva Gosvāmī stated that by following the laws of god written by lord Brahmās sons the manus humans receive good guidance and free themselves from fruitive activities ultimately they can provide shelter for all the other living entities.

KEYWORDS

- Explain the meanings of the following keywords from the summary.
- Use each word in a sentence (either in oral or written form).
- Find at least one synonym and one antonym.
- Identify the word's part of speech (noun, verb, adjective, pronoun, or adverb).

Key Word *(part of speech)*	**Definition**	**Synonym & Antonym**
granted (________________)		**Syn.** **Ant.**
subtlety (________________)		**Syn.** **Ant.**
engineer (________________)		**Syn.** **Ant.**
marginal (________________)		**Syn.** **Ant.**
demigod (________________)		**Syn.** **Ant.**
exactly (________________)		**Syn.** **Ant.**

SEQUENCING

Given below are few of the events that have happened in Chapter 10, Bhāgavatam is the Answer to all Questions. They are all mixed up. Arrange them in the order mentioned in the summary of the chapter.

1. At last the subtleties of material creation came into existence / The false ego and the material modes that it creates / The best is to stay clear from such illusions / By using intelligence and seeking good association.
2. "What a blessing it is to have a human body, the facility to lead a regulated life, read transcendental scriptures like the *Śrīmad-Bhāgavatam*, and chant the Lord's name!"
3. "The Supreme Personality appears in different incarnations after creation just to guide the living entities back home.
4. "By relying on Kṛṣṇa within the heart as Supersoul, the living entities can hear Kṛṣṇa, recognize they are one with Him, and learn how to follow Him."
5. But, O King, for the devotees, the only wish is to serve the Lord by taking up pure devotional service.
6. He has His original two-handed form in Goloka Vṛndāvana. The *Śrīmad-Bhāgavatam*, which is His sound incarnation is also non-different from Him.
7. Śukadeva Gosvāmī explained to Mahārāja Parīkṣit how the *Śrīmad-Bhāgavatam* is divided into 10 subject matters
8. The totality of all entities became agitated, / So hunger and thirst were generated! / A desire to eat and drink came next / With the palate, tongue, and tastes to supplement.
9. Different living creatures such as demigods, humans, and hellish beings come into being depending on their different modes of material nature.

WHAT DO YOU THINK?

Set 1 - Tick the statements that you think are correct.

1. It is the duty of every living entity to use the senses to please and serve the demigod who is in charge of the respective senses.
2. The best way to acquire the habits and the influence of the mode of goodness is to associate with others who are in the mode of goodness.
3. The Supreme Lord is directly and personally involved with all aspects of the

creation, maintenance, and destruction of the material universe.

4. Without the help of the legs one cannot move from one place to another, and therefore Indra has special control over the legs of all human beings, which are meant for performing yajñas.
5. The desires for all kinds of sense perception and sense organs exist in the Supreme, so that is why they take place in the individual persons.
6. The power of hearing and the instruments for hearing are given to us for hearing about the Self, or about the Lord, and not to hear the vibrations of mundane affairs.
7. Kṛṣṇa creates the material universe primarily to give a chance to conditioned souls to revive their forgotten relationship with Him.

WORD SEARCH

I	H	W	R	R	Y	E	E	J	D	E	T	V	A	R
H	M	N	K	B	U	C	J	D	N	S	V	N	Y	M
C	R	P	L	D	N	H	P	H	G	F	E	N	E	R
Z	I	G	E	E	G	O	D	H	E	A	D	T	R	K
T	V	M	I	T	E	V	O	I	E	O	E	H	T	L
E	N	C	S	U	U	K	C	M	G	R	C	Z	I	E
N	S	E	G	O	V	S	Y	M	N	S	T	G	A	B
D	H	P	D	S	C	M	F	A	V	H	U	Z	M	Y
J	L	W	E	N	G	G	L	C	S	E	K	S	E	K
P	N	R	J	X	E	R	L	I	E	L	L	R	N	F
P	R	N	S	D	G	P	J	R	B	T	G	E	B	M
A	K	A	N	U	A	S	E	F	T	E	V	W	O	Q
T	Q	R	D	D	E	M	Y	D	G	R	O	I	S	I
F	U	E	R	J	D	D	A	U	S	C	F	A	T	Y
S	E	I	T	I	V	I	T	C	A	C	P	L	S	Q

ACTIVITIES	COSMIC	DEPENDENT	ETERNAL
GODHEAD	IMPETUS	MAITREYA	SAUNAKA
	SCIENCE	SHELTER	

CROSSWORD

Across

1. What does Mahā-Viṣṇu create after entering into each universe?
5. Who requested Sūta to narrate the conversation between Vidura and Maitreya?
7. Who narrated the conversation between Śukadeva Gosvāmī and Parīkṣit Mahārāja to the sages at Naimiṣāraṇya?

Down

2. Which form does Lord Kṛṣṇa come in to annihilate the material creation?
3. What are the sixteen elements created by Mahā-Viṣṇu called?
4. The Supreme Lord manifests this material creation simply to fulfill the desire of living entities to ____ separately from Him.
6. Who narrated *Śrīmad Bhāgavatam* for the first time?
8. How many subjects does the *Śrīmad Bhāgavatam* talk about?

RESOURCE 1: ***Bhāgavatam*** **at your fingertips**

RESOURCE 2: Nutshell Sculpture

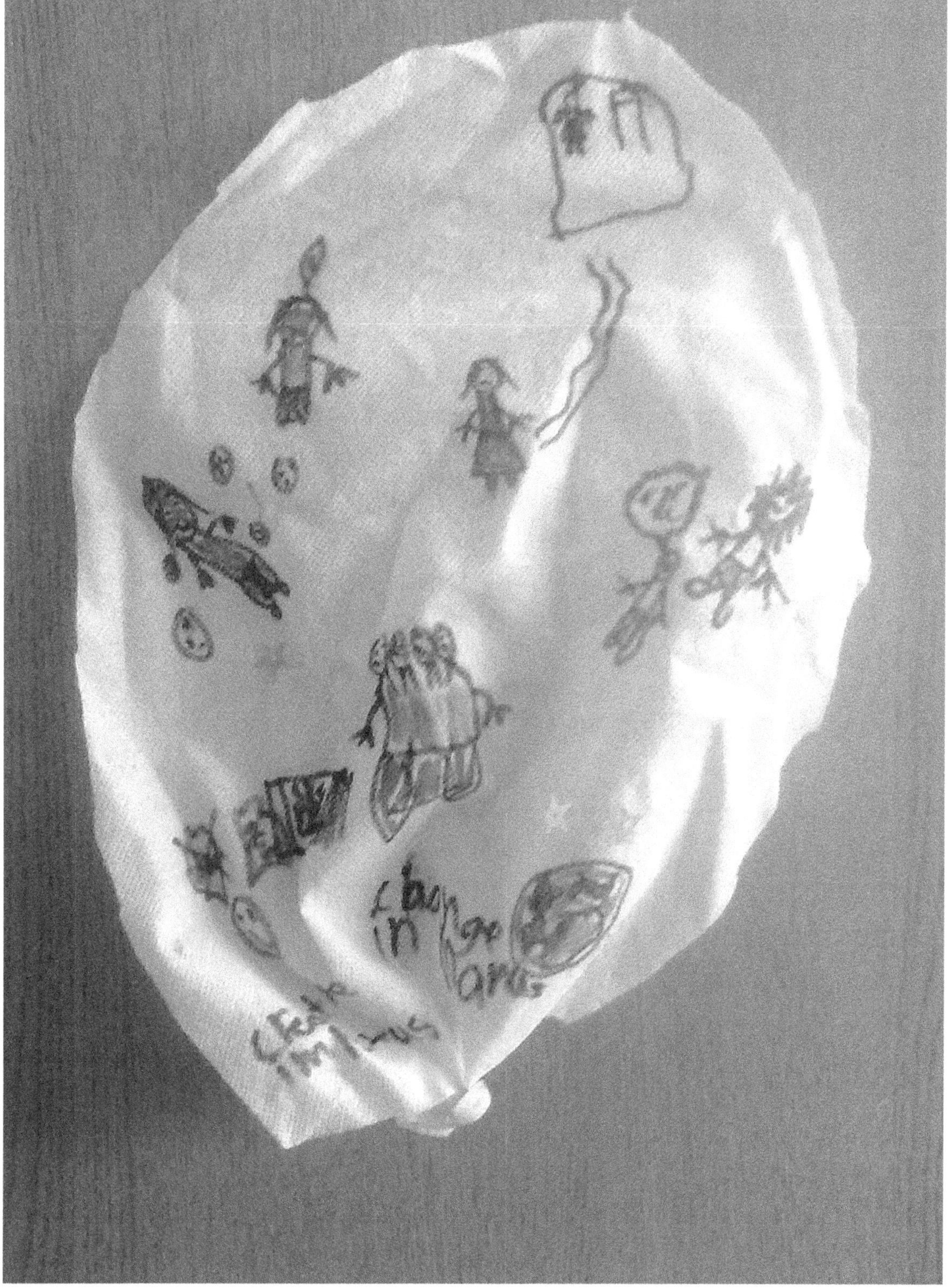

ANSWERS

Understanding the Story (pages 298-300)
1)b, 2)a, 3)c, 4)b, 5)b, 6)a, 7)c, 8)b, 9)b, 10)a, 11)a

Bhāgavatam at your fingertips (page 301)

1. *Sarga* (Primary Creation): The material world is created with sixteen elements.
2. *Visarga* (Secondary Creation): Lord Brahmā creates varieties in the universe with the sixteen elements on the order of Lord Viṣṇu.
3. *Sthānaṁ:* refers to the situation of the living entities who suffer or enjoy in this material world.
4. *Manvatara:* refers to the periods of the Manus, their laws and activities.
5. *Ūtayaḥ:* refers to the desire to do fruitive work in the material world.
6. *Poṣaṇam:* refers to the protection the Lord gives the devotees in this world.
7. *Īśa-anukathāḥ:* describes the activities of the Lord and His great devotees.
8. *Nirodhaḥ*, refers to the merging of all the living entities within the body of Mahā-Viṣṇu as He lies in mystic slumber after the world is wound up.
9. *Muktiḥ* (Liberation) refers to the living entity becoming free from the material body.
10. Kṛṣṇa, the Supreme Personality of Godhead, the original source of all energies, the summum bonum, is the last topic.

Manifest and Unmanifest (pages 303-304)

Reference object	Manifest stage	Unmanifest stage
Cloud	Cloud	Water vapor in the air
Creation	Material world in its full variety	Merged and dormant in Lord Mahā-Viṣṇu's body

Sentence starters (pages 302-303)

1. Speeches were vibrated from the Lord's mouth because the Lord desired to speak.
2. The nostrils and respiration were generated because the Lord desired to smell odors.
3. The eyes and power of vision became manifested because the Lord desired to see Himself.
4. The ears, the power of hearing and the controlling deity of hearing became manifested because the great sages wanted to know.
5. The two hands and their controlling strength became manifested because the Lord desire to perform varieties of work.
6. His legs became manifested because the Lord desired to control movement.
7. The abdomen, intestines, and the arteries became manifest because the Lord desired to have food and drink.
8. The heart, mind, moon and determination became manifest because the Lord desired to think about the activities of His own energy.
9. The navel and air of departure was manifested because the Lord desired to move from one body to another.
10. The trees were generated because there was a desire to perceive physical characteristics of matter, such as softness, hardness, warmth, cold, etc.

The water cycle (page 304)

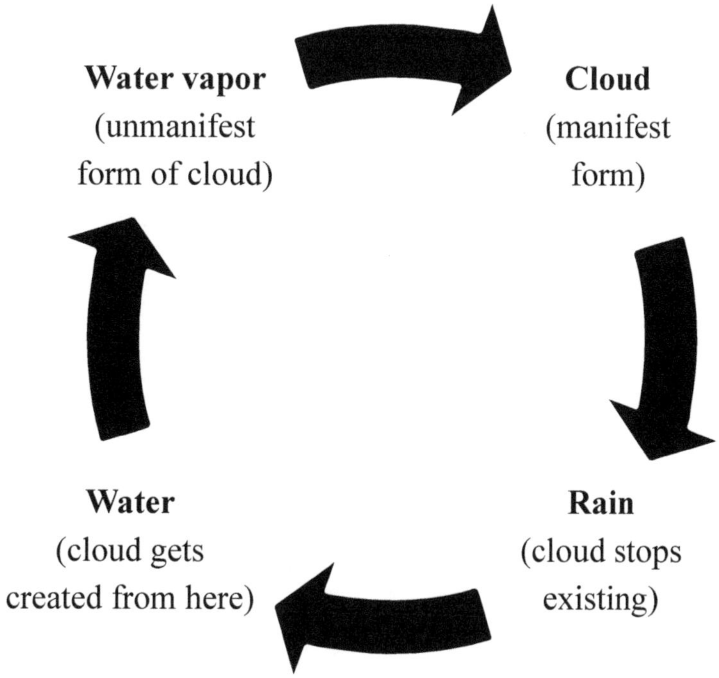

The cycle of creation (page 304)

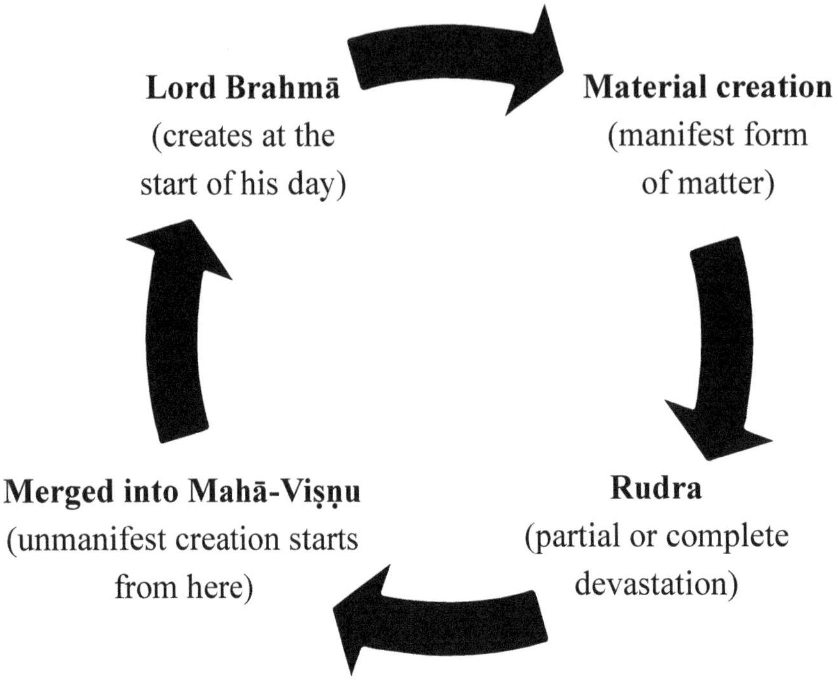

Get the Words Right (page 307)

1. inquisitive, pastimes
2. inhaling
3. worthwhile
4. fruitive
5. surrender, controller
6. unaffected
7. demigods, hellish
8. millennium, destroyer

Word Jumble Matching (pages 307-308)

Organ	
Jumbled	Unjumbled
nguoet	tongue
uomth	mouth
eons	nose
eeys	eyes
aesr	ears
iksn	skin
Ndhas nda gles	Hands and legs

Action	
Jumbled	Unjumbled
ese	see
uothc	touch
staet	taste
keasp	speak
lesml	smell
rkow	work
ehra	hear

Punctuation practice (pages 308-309)

"Actually, the Lord is very clever, and do you know why? Because He has so many incarnations! He has His original two-handed form in Goloka Vṛndāvana. The *Śrīmad-Bhāgavatam*, which is His sound incarnation is also non-different from Him. By His causeless mercy, Kṛṣṇa has even expanded Himself as Kṣīrodakaśāyī Viṣṇu (Paramātmā) who resides in every atom and in the heart of every living being. The Lord comes personally to perform wonderful pastimes and make these stories worthwhile to speak for the benefit of all."

Śukadeva Gosvāmī stated that by following the laws of God, written by Lord Brahmā's sons the Manus, humans receive good guidance and free themselves from fruitive activities. Ultimately, they can provide shelter for all the other living entities.

Keywords (page 309)

Key Word *(part of speech)*	**Definition**	**Synonym & Antonym**
granted (verb or adverb)	Verb: to give or accord; transfer. Adverb: admittedly; it is true (used in the beginning of the sentence).	**Syn.** Given, accepted **Ant.** Prohibited, denied

subtlety (noun)	a) a fineness. b) the quality or state of being subtle.	**Syn.** Acuteness, sensitivity **Ant.** vulgarity
engineer (noun or verb)	Noun: a person who designs builds or maintains engines or machines. Verb: To design or build.	**Syn.** Planner, builder. Form, put together. **Ant.** destroy
marginal (adjective)	a) relating to or at the edge or margin. b) Minor or not in important; not central.	**Syn.** Small, minimal **Ant.** Central, interior, mainstream
demigod (noun)	a) a being with partial or lesser divine status than God; a minor deity. b) a man who is greatly admired or respected.	**Syn.** Angel, hero, god **Ant.** demon
exactly (adverb)	a) to emphasize the accuracy of a figure or description. b) to confirm, or to agree	**Syn.** Entirely, certainly **Ant.** Roughly, somewhat

Sequencing (page 310)

1. Śukadeva Gosvāmī explained to Mahārāja Parīkṣit how the *Śrīmad-Bhāgavatam* is divided into 10 subject matters.
2. He has His original two-handed form in Goloka Vṛndāvana. The *Śrīmad-Bhāgavatam*, which is His sound incarnation is also non-different from Him.
3. "What a blessing it is to have a human body, the facility to lead a regulated life, read transcendental scriptures like the *Śrīmad-Bhāgavatam*, and chant the Lord's name!"

4. "By relying on Kṛṣṇa within the heart as Supersoul, the living entities can hear Kṛṣṇa, recognize they are one with Him, and learn how to follow Him."
5. The totality of all entities became agitated, / So hunger and thirst were generated! / A desire to eat and drink came next / With the palate, tongue and tastes to supplement.
6. At last the subtleties of material creation came into existence / The false ego and the material modes that it creates / The best is to stay clear from such illusions / By using intelligence and seeking good association.
7. Different living creatures such as demigods, humans, and hellish beings come into being depending on their different modes of material nature.
8. "The Supreme Personality appears in different incarnations after creation just to guide the living entities back home.
9. But, O King, for the devotees, the only wish is to serve the Lord by taking up pure devotional service.

What do you think? (pages 310-311)

1. Incorrect
2. Correct
3. Incorrect
4. Incorrect
5. Correct
6. Correct
7. Correct

Word Search (page 312)

I							E						A	
	M					C							Y	
C		P			N								E	
	I		E	E	G	O	D	H	E	A	D	T	R	
T		M	I	T							E		T	
	N	C	S		U					R			I	
	S	E		O		S			N	S			A	
			D		C			A		H			M	
				N			L			E				
					E					L				
						P				T				
A	K	A	N	U	A	S	E			E				
								D		R				
S	E	I	T	I	V	I	T	C	A					

Crossword (page 313)

Across

1. water
5. saunaka
7. suta

Down

2. rudra
3. sarga
4. enjoy
6. kṛṣṇa
8. ten

Lightning Source UK Ltd.
Milton Keynes UK
UKHW030507130220
358633UK00006B/146

9 781733 927222